The American Revolution

A History in Documents

FEDERAL HALL
The Seat of Congress

Printed & Sold by A Doolittle New-Haven 1793

The American
Revolution
A History in Documents

Steven C. Bullock

OXFORD
UNIVERSITY PRESS

For Christopher and for his cousins,
Conor and Kevin
Geoffrey and Scott
Calvin and Ian
Derrick, Zachary, Joel, and Aaron

General Editors

Sarah Deutsch
Professor of History
University of Arizona

Carol K. Karlsen
Professor of History
University of Michigan

Robert G. Moeller
Professor of History
University of California, Irvine

Jeffrey N. Wasserstrom
Associate Professor of History
Indiana University

Board of Advisors

Steven Goldberg
Social Studies Supervisor
New Rochelle, N.Y., Public Schools

John Pyne
Social Studies Supervisor
West Milford, N.J., Public Schools

OXFORD
UNIVERSITY PRESS

Oxford   New York
Auckland   Bangkok   Buenos Aires   Cape Town   Chennai
Dar es Salaam   Delhi   Hong Kong   Istanbul   Karachi   Kolkata
Kuala Lumpur   Madrid   Melbourne   Mexico City   Mumbai   Nairobi
São Paulo   Shanghai   Singapore   Taipei   Tokyo   Toronto

Copyright © 2003 by Steven C. Bullock

Design: Sandy Kaufman
Layout: Loraine Machlin

Published by Oxford University Press, Inc.
198 Madison Avenue, New York, New York 10016
www.oup-usa.com

Library of Congress Cataloging-in-Publication Data
Bullock, Steven C.
  The American Revolution : a history in documents / Steven C. Bullock.
    p. cm. -- (Pages from history)
Summary: Uses contemporary documents to explore the American
Revolution,
from the colonists' break with Great Britain through the struggle to
create a successful government for the new United States.
Includes bibliographical references (p.   ) and index.
  ISBN 978-0-19-513224-3

  1. United States--History--Revolution, 1775-1783--Sources--Juvenile
literature. [1. United States--History--Revolution,
1775-1783--Sources.] I. Title. II. Series.
  E203 .B95 2003
  973.3--dc21

                                              2003004206

Printed in the United States of America on acid-free paper

Cover: *As British troops march into the town of
Concord, Massachusetts, on April 19, 1776, their
commanders view the situation from a hillside cemetery.
Earlier that morning, the soldiers had already fired on
colonists in Lexington, starting the war that led to
American independence. This image was drawn only a
few days after the event by a Connecticut militiaman
whose company arrived too late to join the battle.*

Frontispiece: *In 1789, New York City's Federal
Hall served as the site of both the first meeting of
Congress under the new United States Constitution
and the inauguration of George Washington as the
nation's first President. In this 1790 engraving,
Washington is being sworn in on the second
floor balcony.*

Title page: *Thirteen hands hold on to a chain symbolizing the new nation. Despite this powerful
image of unity, the question of independence led to
intense controversy.*

Contents

120650

What Is a Document?

To the historian, a document is, quite simply, any sort of historical evidence. It is a primary source, the raw material of history. A document may be more than the expected government paperwork, such as a treaty or passport. It is also a letter, diary, will, grocery list, newspaper article, recipe, memoir, oral history, school yearbook, map, chart, architectural plan, poster, musical score, play script, novel, political cartoon, painting, photograph—even an object.

Using primary sources allows us not just to read *about* history, but to read history itself. It allows us to immerse ourselves in the look and feel of an era gone by, to understand its people and their language, whether verbal or visual. And it allows us to take an active, hands-on role in (re)constructing history.

Using primary sources requires us to use our powers of detection to ferret out the relevant facts and to draw conclusions from them; just as Agatha Christie uses the scores in a bridge game to determine the identity of a murderer, the historian uses facts from a variety of sources—some, perhaps, seemingly inconsequential—to build a historical case.

The poet W. H. Auden wrote that history was the study of questions. Primary sources force us to ask questions—and then, by answering them, to construct a narrative or an argument that makes sense to us. Moreover, as we draw on the many sources from "the dust-bin of history," we can endow that narrative with character, personality, and texture—all the elements that make history so endlessly intriguing.

Cartoon
This political cartoon addresses the issue of church and state. It illustrates the Supreme Court's role in balancing the demands of the 1st Amendment of the Constitution and the desires of the religious population.

Illustration
Illustrations from children's books, such as this alphabet from the New England Primer, tell us how children were educated, and also what the religious and moral values of the time were.

In *Adam's* Fall
We Sinned all.

Thy Life to Mend
This *Book* Attend.

The *Cat* doth play
And after slay.

A *Dog* will bite
A Thief at night.

An *Eagles* flight
Is out of sight.

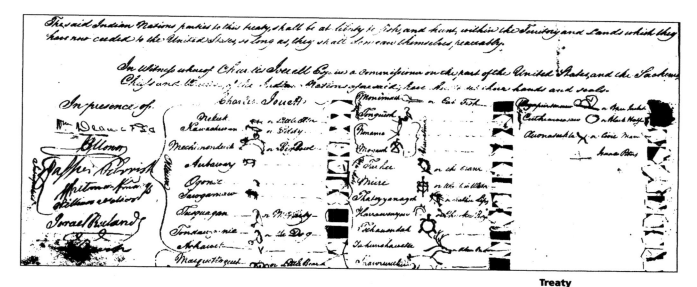

Treaty

A government document such as this 1805 treaty can reveal not only the details of government policy, but information about the people who signed it. Here, the Indians' names were written in English transliteration by U.S. officials; the Indians added pictographs to the right of their names.

Map

A 1788 British map of India shows the region prior to British colonization, an indication of the kingdoms and provinces whose ethnic divisions would resurface later in India's history.

Literature

The first written version of the Old English epic *Beowulf*, from the late 10th century, is physical evidence of the transition from oral to written history. Charred by fire, it is also a physical record of the wear and tear of history.

How to Read a Document

This book presents documents, or primary sources, about the American Revolution. Many of them describe people's experiences (often their own) or attempts to convince others of the moral rightness or the practical benefits of taking a particular action. In trying to make sense of these pieces, it is important to recognize that they were shaped, molded to fit different purposes. Think about describing an exciting day to a sympathetic friend. Now imagine explaining the same events to a suspicious police officer. Both descriptions could be true, but each would probably highlight different events, use different language, and describe feelings differently.

The writers, speakers, and even artists represented in this book also made a similar set of choices. Asking questions about the author's view of their intended audience is an important way of understanding a document's significance. We can ask questions like: How do the authors shape their ideas and stories? What do they emphasize? What do they leave out? What moral values do they take for granted? What do they expect their readers to agree or disagree with?

Even words themselves can mean different things. For example, "liberty" is a key idea during these years. It could suggest what many of us often mean today when we use the word, the freedom to do what we want. But it could also mean not having to pay a tax, being able to vote for leaders, and even being allowed to keep other people in slavery—or all of these things at once.

Asking these sorts of questions about the documents is only a start, of course. But paying attention to ways that people use words and shape their presentations can help us understand more fully why the American Revolution is one of the most exciting and important periods in American history.

Title
The title page of Revolutionary-era books such as Thomas Paine's 1776 *Common Sense* conveyed a good deal of information. Even the titles themselves tended to be longer and more descriptive than most titles today. The lengthy subtitle here notes the work's main sections. The author's name, however, often did not appear. A great deal of political writing in this period was anonymous.

Motto
Quotations from other authors played an important part in eighteenth-century political argument. Although the popular British poet James Thompson was not opposed to the British monarchy, Paine employs his lines here to underline the argument that hereditary monarchy was a foolish idea that Americans should reject. The letter "s" in the beginning or middle of a word was printed in a way that looks like present-day "f."

Imprint
The imprint indicates the location, printer, and date of a work. As the imprint here notes, *Common Sense* was originally published in Philadelphia. This edition was printed in New York shortly afterwards to meet the expected demand for the popular piece in that area. Although the publication date is not noted here, it was probably soon after the January 1776 appearance of the original edition.

Images
The images in this book are not simply illustrations. They are also primary source documents that can be as revealing as the written word. Paul Revere's popular print of the Boston Massacre appeared only a few days after it occurred in March 1770. The image and variations on it by Revere and others were the only pictures of the event that people saw.

Engravings
Although they could not be as large or as visually rich as a good painting, engravings were cheaper and could be reproduced easily. Made by printing from a metal plate from which an image had been scraped away, they were then printed as part of magazines, newspapers, or books. Or they could, as with this example, be sold separately. Copies of this print were colored by hand before they were sold.

Messages
Many of the images in this period sought to make a statement about a controversial issue. Paul Revere's print of the Boston Massacre appeared only a few days after the incident. It was titled "The Bloody Massacre Perpetrated in King Street Boston." The clothing, facial expressions, and gestures of the soldiers and civilians reinforce this interpretation. The testimonies of witnesses suggest a more chaotic scene in which the crowd was larger and much more aggressive than is shown here.

COMMON SENSE;

ADDRESSED TO THE

INHABITANTS

O F

A M E R I C A,

On the following interesting

S U B J E C T S.

I. Of the Origin and Design of Government in general, with concise Remarks on the English Constitution.

II. Of Monarchy and Hereditary Succession.

III. Thoughts on the present State of American Affairs.

IV. Of the present Ability of America, with some miscellaneous Reflections.

A NEW EDITION, with several Additions in the Body of the Work. To which is added an APPENDIX; together with an Address to the People called QUAKERS.

N. B. The New Addition here given increases the Work upwards of one Third.

Man knows no Master save creating HEAVEN,
Or those whom Choice and common Good ordain.
THOMSON.

PHILADELPHIA PRINTED.
And SOLD by W. and T. BRADFORD. [1776

Madness and the Revolution

Benjamin Rush, perhaps the most influential American physician of the late eighteenth-century, held an unusual view of the American Revolution. He thought that it caused mental illness. In an essay published in 1789, he argued that some supporters of the American side had become so obsessed with liberty during the war with Great Britain that they could not accept any form of government afterward. As a result, they developed a "species of insanity" that he called *Anarchia*, referring to "anarchy," a society without government. Loyalists, people who had opposed independence, often suffered from another type of mental sickness caused by defeat, what he called *Revolutiania*.

Rush, a signer of Declaration of Independence and a professor of chemistry, did not believe that Americans were unusually unbalanced. On the contrary, people who had supported the Revolution had been especially healthy. Inspired by "the love of liberty and their country," American soldiers had been able to endure "hunger, cold, and nakedness," with "patience" and "firmness." Patriotic civilians received similar benefits. They experienced "uncommon cheerfulness" and even increased fertility. Some formerly childless couples had even been able to conceive for the first time during the war. Rush believed that such unusual developments were not surprising, since the Revolution had naturally led to "effects . . . both upon the mind and body, which have seldom occurred."

Benjamin Rush was the first professor of chemistry in America and the new nation's most important physician. Rush's many articles and pamphlets helped encourage the adoption of the American Constitution, the expansion of education for women, and the end of slavery in Pennsylvania and the northern United States.

Rush's account of the medical effects of the Revolution was a part of his continuing attempt to make sense of the sweeping changes in which he had participated. The difficulties he had in doing so are perhaps not surprising. More than two centuries later, the events that led to the creation of the United States of America still seem extraordinary. The war for independence, which had ended only five years before Rush's 1789 essay, had been fought against the dominant superpower of the time, then at the height of its eighteenth-century influence. The conflict lasted longer than any later American war except the Vietnam War, and in proportion to the population it resulted in three times as many American deaths as World War II.

The effects of the Revolution lasted long beyond the war. Beside establishing the United States of America itself, the Revolution also created a system of government that still operates and the emphasis on equality and individual rights that still distinguishes American culture. The Revolution and its aftermath also changed American society, ending slavery in the North and encouraging new opportunities for women to gain formal education—reforms that Rush himself fought for.

Even allowing for the difficulties of interpreting such major developments at close range, Rush's ideas about insanity brought on by the Revolution seem more than a bit bizarre—although certainly less dangerous than his later belief that the proper remedy for almost any major illness was removing large quantities of the sick person's blood. But he based his somewhat suspect conclusions upon a series of perceptive observations in the essay that help to underline some of the key characteristics of the Revolution that he helped to create.

Rush believed that the Revolution's impact upon the human body was particularly great because the colonists had been so closely attached to their mother country. Family relations, legal customs, trade, and a common sense of pride in the British nation and its form of government—connected Great Britain with its colonies.

Rush noted that these bonds had been developing for almost two hundred years by the time the American colonies declared their independence. Britons had first settled permanently on the mainland in 1607; by 1776, the colonists numbered about 2.5 million. One-fifth of them were Africans, who had been brought to America against their will. Others came from Holland, Germany, Ireland, and France. Despite this diversity of origins,

Britain's influence was disproportionately significant. Trade, political engagement, and printed materials all helped to spread not only its goods but also political ideas that emphasized individual liberty and limited government.

Ironically, the strongest evidence of these close ties lay in the anger with which the colonists turned against Britain. After 1765 imperial leaders imposed a variety of new colonial taxes and regulations, primarily to raise money to pay the debts created by the French and Indian War and the new obligations that victory had created. Britain also wanted to enforce regulations that had been largely ignored in its colonies. The colonists, however, saw things differently. They believed that their liberties, a foundation of their national identity, were at stake. For most, at least until the Revolutionary War began, opposition to British measures was not opposition to Britain itself, but a defense of British ideals. As Rush noted in 1788, the colonists' "resentments" were magnified by "the number and force of these ancient bonds of affection and union."

The Revolution that resulted from the breaking of these ancient bonds with Britain, Rush observed, affected everyone, "every inhabitant of the country of both sexes." "An indifferent, or neutral spectator of the controversy," he observed, "was scarcely to be found in any of the states." Although many Americans (perhaps more than half) had attempted to remain neutral at the beginning of the war, continued fighting eventually forced colonists to choose sides.

The circumstance affecting these decisions varied by place, time, and even individual situation. New York City remained in British hands from 1776 to the end of the Revolution. New England saw much more fighting at the beginning of the war; the South at the end. But even for people who were never close to a battle (and there were not many in a war that touched all new thirteen states), the Revolution affected them in a variety of ways from inflation and taxation to new governments in the states as well as the nation. And everyone would have known someone who served in the armed forces. About 9 percent of the population served in the American military, and about one out of every eight of these men died.

Not everyone supported this substantial effort. Before, during, and after the Revolution, Americans disagreed, often violently. Perhaps twice as many Americans supported the British as fought for independence. Some one thousand African-American Loyalists, almost all former slaves, settled in Africa after the war, having decided that their own battle for liberty required taking the British side. In all, perhaps sixty to eighty thousand Americans left, rather than acknowledge the claims of the new nation.

Even against an opposition that included perhaps one-fifth of the American population and had the world's most powerful military forces on its side, the Patriots still failed to present a united front. As General Washington pleaded with Congress during the beginning of the war to supply his Continental Army adequately, Benjamin Rush and others engaged in a prolonged campaign to remove him. Rush's discussion of the Revolution's physical and mental effects similarly formed part of an important debate. His essay warning of the madness of rejecting good government was written in late 1788 as the Bill of Rights was being written and Pennsylvania's constitution was under bitter attack. The Constitution of the United States had been accepted earlier that year by only a narrow margin over the opposition of a majority of Americans.

A large part of the difficulties of unifying Americans lay in their recognition that a great deal was at stake. "It was generally believed by the friends of the Revolution," Rush recalled in 1788, "that the very existence of *freedom* upon our globe, was involved in the issue of the contest in favor of the United States." The problems involved in both defining what this freedom meant and how it should be put into practice provoked endless discussions, angry exchanges, and even outright rebellions. For Rush, these questions involved not only political but physical and mental health. The wrong choices could literally lead to insanity.

Rush, however, also warned that the results of people's actions could not be fully predicted. His autobiography even suggested that "human nature has derived more honor from [the decision for independence] than it deserves." "Not one man in a thousand," he wrote, had either thought about or "wished for the independence of our country in 1774" and very few in 1776 "foresaw the immense influence [the decision] would soon have upon the national and individual characters of Americans." He and others were mostly "blind actors in the business."

Rush did not consider the unexpected results of independence and other decisions a reason to stop fighting for greater freedom. He often insisted that the Revolution was not simply a single event, something that happened once. Instead, it was a continuing process. The end of the war, he cautioned in 1788, "did not terminate the American Revolution." Instead, as he had written the previous year, "nothing but the first act of the great drama is closed."

Such a view of the Revolution suggests some ways of approaching the documents collected here. These materials illuminate not only the great principles and figures that played a part in the Revolution, but also a variety of less well-known people—individuals and groups whose sacrifices were just as great and whose contributions were perhaps as essential to the outcome. The documents also illustrate the range of choices and possibilities open to people at the time. Such a vision of the Revolution sometimes lacks the heroism and moral certainty of an interpretation that stresses the far-reaching wisdom of patriotic leaders. But seeing the changes from Rush's perspective requires rejecting the common impulse to worship the founding fathers as god-like individuals. The documents included here suggest that paying attention to the participation of all Americans, noting the unexpected consequences of people's choices, and recognizing the continuing nature of the process, provides a clearer understanding of—and a greater appreciation for—what Rush rightly called a "great drama."

Chapter One

The Family Quarrel

The Coming of the Revolution

I n 1768, Benjamin Rush visited London. A physician and a professor of chemistry at the College of Philadelphia, Rush later became a leader in the Revolutionary movement and a signer of the Declaration of Independence. But in 1768, he wanted to sit on the king's throne. He was visiting the meeting place of the House of Lords, the upper house of the British legislature, when he noticed it. His guide resisted Rush's request to try out the throne, but finally gave him permission. The experience, Rush explained to a friend later, was so overwhelming that he could not even think straight: "Such a crowd of ideas poured in upon my mind that I can scarcely recollect one of them." The entire room made him feel "as if [he] walked on sacred ground."

As Rush's overwhelming reactions suggest, the connection between Americans and their mother country had continued to be strong past the middle of the eighteenth century. Indeed, in many ways, the relationship was growing closer. The dramatic growth of population, settlement, and economy within the colonies meant that they traded more with Great Britain, and these trade routes also served as pathways by which ideas, fashions, and visitors moved between the center and the edges of the British empire. The American Revolution has often been seen as merely the final step in a process of separation. The experience of Rush and others suggests that in many ways the colonies were becoming more like Great Britain and more closely tied to it. Even after more than a century of American settlement, colonists still spoke of going to Britain as going "home."

Despite Rush's deep emotional connection with Britain, however, his loyalty was not unconditional. When he entered the House of Commons, the other branch of the British legislature, he was at first

In this 1765 political cartoon, the American artist John Singleton Copley uses a complicated series of symbols to attack the Stamp Act. On the right, the symbol of Britain, Britannia, flies across the Atlantic. She brings "Pandora's Box," the mythical origin of evil in the world, representing the Stamp Act. Beneath the Tree of Liberty lies America, portrayed as an Indian. The protectors of Liberty, including Minerva (the helmeted goddess of wisdom), try to keep the tax from America, who is already near death.

considerably less impressed. It was, he noted, "the place where the infernal scheme for enslaving America" began. Rush looked around the "cursed" room until he found the spot where William Pitt, Britain's prime minister during its triumph in the Seven Years War (or French and Indian War), had spoken out against taxing the colonies. After sitting in Pitt's seat for a long time, Rush rose and recited Pitt's words aloud: "Americans are the sons, not the bastards of Englishmen." Remembering this powerful defense of the colonists' liberties and their place in the English national family inspired him almost as much as sitting on the throne. "I was ready," he wrote, "to kiss the very walls that had re-echoed to his voice upon that glorious occasion."

Rush's strong sense of the importance of British freedom (and the dangers of losing it) matched his awe at the majesty of the British government. In theory, freedom and government were closely allied. Both Britons and colonists regularly celebrated the British "constitution," meaning not a written document but its system of government. The later American Patriot, and President, John Adams argued in 1765 that this constitution represented "the most perfect combination of human powers in society which finite wisdom has yet contrived . . . for the preservation of liberty and the production of happiness." Three years later, Rush similarly was most moved not by the thought of being free from Britain but by being recognized as a full member of its family.

But loyalty and liberty were not so closely allied in practice. In the years after the Seven Years War ended in 1763, Americans' loyalty to the British government and their acceptance of British values often pulled them in different directions. Starting most notably with the 1765 Stamp Act that aroused Pitt's empassioned defense of the Americans, the British government attempted to change the terms of the colonists' place in the empire. The colonies would be a source of revenue; their trade would be regulated more carefully. Americans did not see these changes as simple adjustments to old policies. Instead

Paul Revere's 1770 engraving for the Boston Gazette celebrates Britain's role in protecting liberty. The female symbol of Britain holds a liberty cap (symbolic of deliverance from slavery) on a pole in one hand. With the other, she sets free a captive bird.

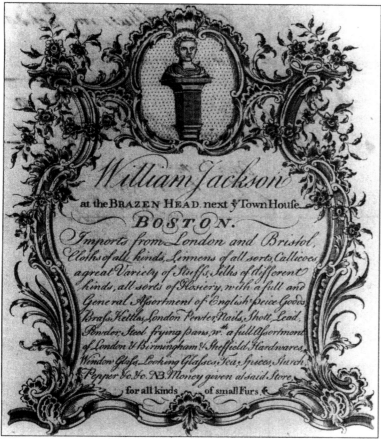

Growing Ties

The same year that Rush visited London, William Jackson left there to become a merchant in Boston. A year later, in 1769, he had Paul Revere engrave the trade card at left to advertise his business. The consumer goods that Jackson and other merchants brought into the colonies were an important part of the growing ties between Great Britain and her colonies—and an increasingly significant part of the British economy. By 1770 the mainland colonies took nearly 40 percent of the mother country's export trade, up from only 10 percent at the beginning of the century. The range of Jackson's merchandise suggests the wide variety of imported wares available to the colonists. Revere and others had already made such merchandise a target of the colonies' resistance to British policies, organizing boycotts of British goods to pressure the government as early as 1765. Jackson's later refusal to stop importing goods angered the opponents of British policies. When the war came, he was banished to Great Britain.

the new measures represented frightening threats to their liberty to have a say in their government that distinguished Britain from other nations. The colonists fought what Rush called the "infernal scheme" in formal meetings, in pamphlets, and on the streets. When the British government failed to back down fully, many colonists eventually decided, as Rush did later, that the only way to retain their rights was to break away from the king and Parliament. British liberties could be preserved only by resisting the British government and eventually repudiating Britain itself.

Growing Children

J. Hector St. John de Crèvecoeur was an enthusiastic promoter of America. After serving in the French army during the Seven Years War, he settled in New York among his former enemies. When he returned to France during the Revolutionary War, he celebrated American life in a book called *Letters*

In this portrait by John Singleton Copley, Nicholas Boylston rests his arm on his account books. The casual elegance of his pose and the richness of his clothing reveal his wealth and status as one of Boston's most successful merchants.

from an American Farmer, published in 1782. This letter, titled "What Is an American?" notes the differences a newcomer from England would notice upon first arriving in America, particularly the opportunities that America offered for individual success and the diversity of Europeans in the colonies. Although his descriptions stress both the relative unimportance of social standing and America's economic advantages, they ignore the difficulties faced by African Americans and Native Americans.

Here he beholds fair cities, substantial villages, extensive fields, an immense country filled with decent houses, good roads, orchards, meadows, and bridges, where an hundred years ago all was wild, woody and uncultivated! What a train of pleasing ideas this fair spectacle must suggest; it is a prospect which must inspire a good citizen with the most heartfelt pleasure. The difficulty consists in the manner of viewing so extensive a scene. He is arrived on a new continent; a modern society offers itself to his contemplation, different from what he had hitherto seen. It is not composed, as in Europe, of great lords who possess every thing, and of a herd of people who have nothing. Here are no aristocratical families, no courts, no kings, no bishops, no ecclesiastical dominion, no invisible power giving to a few a very visible one; no great manufacturers employing thousands, no great refinements of luxury. The rich and the poor are not so far removed from each other as they are in Europe. Some few towns excepted, we are all tillers of the earth, from Nova Scotia to West Florida. We are a people of cultivators, scattered over an immense territory, communicating with each other by means of good roads and navigable rivers, united by the silken bands of mild government, all respecting the laws, without dreading their power, because they are equitable. We are all animated with the spirit of an industry which is unfettered and unrestrained, because each persons works for himself. If he travels through our rural districts he views not the hostile castle, and the haughty mansion, contrasted with the clay-built hut and miserable cabbin, where cattle and men help to keep each other warm, and dwell in meanness, smoke, and indigence. A pleasing uniformity of decent competence appears throughout our habitations. The meanest of our log-houses is a dry and comfortable habitation. Lawyer or merchant are the fairest titles our towns afford; that of farmer is the only appellation of the rural inhabitants of our country. It must take some time ere he can reconcile himself to our dictionary, which is but short in words of dignity, and names of honour. . . .

The next wish of this traveller will be to know whence came all these people? they are a mixture of English, Scotch, Irish, French, Dutch, Germans, and Swedes. From this promiscuous breed, the race now called Americans have arisen.

Raising Money and Rising Anger

In early 1765 the British government proposed a major tax for Americans. It required the use of specially marked ("stamped") paper for all printed and official uses. As Connecticut's agent, a lobbyist who represented that colony's interests in London, Jared Ingersoll watched the Parliamentary debates about what came to be called the Stamp Act. He reported his observations to the colony's governor, Thomas Fitch, in this February 1765 letter. Like nearly all Americans, both men objected to the Stamp Act as a violation of their rights to be taxed only by the consent of their own representatives. But, as Ingersoll notes in his report, British politicians did not share this view. Even leaders sympathetic to American interests accepted the supremacy of Parliament and the idea of virtual representation, which suggested that all parts of Britain, including the colonies, were represented in Parliament whether or not they were actually able to cast votes. Although Ingersoll opposed the Stamp Act, he attempted to profit from it once it was passed and became a stamp distributor in Connecticut, which promised to bring in a great deal of money. In the end, however, Ingersoll and the other "stampmen" earned only the scorn of their fellow colonists as men who betrayed their country for the promise of "a little ungodly Gain."

The Stamp Act passed by Parliament in 1765 signified the first time the British government had taxed the colonies directly. It required Britain and its colonies to use paper that had been marked with revenue stamps. These are examples of revenue stamps that were marked on the paper.

The principal attention has been to the stamp bill that has been preparing to lay before Parliament for taxing America. The point of the authority of Parliament to impose such tax I found on my arrival here was so fully and universally yielded that there was not the least hopes of making any impressions that way. Indeed it has appeared since that The House would not suffer to be brought in, nor would any one member undertake to offer to the House any petition from the colonies that held forth the contrary of that doctrine. . . . I beg leave to give you a summary of the arguments which are made use of in favor of such authority.

The House of Commons, say they, is a branch of the supreme legislature of the nation, and which in its nature is supposed to represent, or rather to stand in the place of, the Commons; that is, of the great body of the people who are below the dignity of peers; that this House of Commons consists of a certain number of men chosen by certain people of certain places, which electors, by the way, they insist are not a tenth part of the people, . . . and that this House of Commons therefore is now fixed and ascertained and is a part of the supreme unlimited power of the nation, as in every state there must be some unlimited power and authority; and that when it is said that they represent the commons of England it cannot mean that they do so because those commons choose them, for in fact by far the greater part do not.

As Ingersoll notes, the argument among British politicians concentrated on the advantages or disadvantages of the proposal, not on whether the act violated American liberty.

They further urge that the only reason why America has not been heretofore taxed in the fullest manner has been merely on account of their infancy and inability; that there have been, however, not wanting instances of the exercise of this power in the various regulations of the American trade, the establishment of the post office, etc., and they deny any distinction between what is called an internal and external tax as to the point of the authority imposing such taxes. And as to the charters in the few provinces where there are any, they say in the first place the king cannot grant any that shall exempt them from the authority of one of the branches of the great body of legislation, and in the second place say the king has not done or attempted to do it. . . . In short, they say a power to tax is a necessary part of every supreme legislative authority, and that if they have not that power over America, they have none, and then America is at once a kingdom of itself.

On the other hand, those who oppose the bill say it is true the Parliament have a supreme unlimited authority over every part and branch of the king's dominions, and as well over Ireland as any other place, yet we believe a British Parliament will never think it prudent to tax Ireland. 'Tis true they say that the commons of England and of the British Empire are all represented in and by the

House of Commons, but this representation is confessedly on all hands by construction and virtually only as to those who have no hand in choosing the representatives, and that the effects of this implied representation here and in America must be infinitely different in the article of taxation. Here in England the member of Parliament is equally known to the neighbor who elects and to him who does not; the friendships, the connections, the influences are spread through the whole. If by any mistake an Act of Parliament is made that prove injurious and hard, the member of Parliament here sees with his own eyes and is moreover very accessible to the people; not only so, but the taxes are laid equally by one rule and fall as well on the member himself as on the people. But as to America, from the great distance in point of situation, from the almost total unacquaintedness, especially in the more northern colonies, with the members of Parliament, and they with them, or with the particular ability and circumstances of one another, from the nature of this very tax laid upon others not equally and in common with ourselves, but with express purpose to ease ourselves, we think, say they, that it will be only to lay a foundation of great jealousy and continual uneasiness, and that to no purpose, as we already by the regulations upon their trade draw from the Americans all that they can spare. At least they say this step should not take place until or unless the Americans are allowed to send members to Parliament; for *who of you,* said Col. [Issac] Barré nobly in his speech in the House upon this occasion; *who of you reasoning upon this subject feels warmly from the heart* (putting his hand to his own breast) *for the Americans as they would for themselves or as you would for the people of your own native country?*

An American owner of this tea pot, which proclaims opposition to the Stamp Act, would soon have to decide whether to participate in boycotts of British goods. After 1767, these non-importation agreements would include the tea that might be served in this pot.

The Virginia Resolves, passed by the Virginia House of Burgesses on May 30, 1765, outlined the colonists' arguments against the Stamp Act. They were sponsored mainly by Patrick Henry, a new legislator who was already well known for his oratory (according to a later biographer, Henry proclaimed the phrase "Give me liberty or give me death" in 1775). The intercolonial Stamp Act Congress that met the following October made similar points.

Resolved, That the first Adventurers and Settlers of this his Majesty's Colony and Dominion of *Virginia* brought with them, and transmitted to their Posterity, and all other his Majesty's Subjects since inhabiting in this his Majesty's said Colony, all the Liberties,

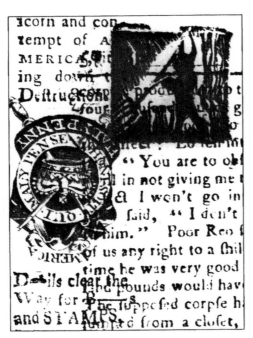

When the Stamp Act went into effect, the Boston-born Isaiah Thomas was a sixteen-year-old printer in British Canada. Thomas found a unique way to dramatize his opposition. In printing The Nova-Scotia and Halifax Gazette, *he bordered the revenue stamp with an image of the devil "clear[ing] the Way for . . . STAMPS."*

Awake! Awake, my Countrymen, and, by a regular & legal Opposition, defeat the Designs of those who enslave us and our Posterity. Nothing is wanting but your own Resolution.

—*Boston Gazette,*
October 7, 1765

Privileges, Franchises, and Immunities, that have at any Time been held, enjoyed, and possessed, by the people of *Great Britain.*

Resolved, That by two royal Charters, granted by King *James* the First, the Colonists aforesaid are declared entitled to all Liberties, Privileges, and Immunities of Denizens and natural Subjects, to all Intents and Purposes, as if they had been abiding and born within the Realm of *England.*

Resolved, That the Taxation of the People by themselves, or by Persons chosen by themselves to represent them, who can only know what Taxes the People are able to bear, or the easiest Method of raising them, and must themselves be affected by every Tax laid on the People, is the only Security against a burthensome Taxation, and the distinguishing Characteristic of *British* Freedom, without which the ancient Constitution cannot exist.

Resolved, That his Majesty's liege People of this his most ancient and loyal Colony have without Interruption enjoyed the inestimable Right of being governed by such Laws, respecting their internal Polity and Taxation, as are derived from their own Consent, with the Approbation of their Sovereign, or his Substitute; and that the same hath never been forfeited or yielded up, but hath been constantly recognized by the Kings and People of *Great Britain.*

The protests against the Stamp Act went beyond petitions and arguments that called for public action. In American cities, mobs pressured the stamp tax collectors to resign. In Boston, the opposition to the Stamp Act turned particularly violent. Less than two weeks after the forced resignation of a stamp distributor, a crowd attacked the houses of two other people who had seemingly supported the Stamp Act— and then went on to destroy the mansion of the colony's lieutenant governor, Thomas Hutchinson. The mob suspected (wrongly) that the unpopular Hutchinson had helped to prepare the Stamp Act. The wealthy young Josiah Quincy, Jr., recorded this incident in his diary on August 27, 1765. Like many colonial leaders, Quincy opposed the Stamp Act and feared violent protests against it.

The destructions, demolitions, and ruins caused by the rage of the Colonies in general—perhaps too justly inflamed—at that singular and ever-memorable statute called the Stamp Act, will make the present year one of the most remarkable eras in the annals of North America. And that peculiar inflammation, which fired the breasts of the people of New England in particular, will always distinguish them as the warmest lovers of liberty; though undoubtedly, in the fury of revenge . . . they committed acts totally unjustifiable.

The populace of Boston, about a week since, had given a very notable instance of their detestation of the above unconstitutional Act, and had sufficiently shown in what light they viewed the man who would undertake to be the stamp distributor. But, not content with this, the last night they again assembled in King's Street; where, after having kindled a fire, they proceeded, in two separate bodies, to attack the houses of two gentlemen of distinction, who, it had been suggested, were accessories to the present burthens; and did great damage in destroying their houses, furniture, &c., and irreparable damage in destroying their papers.

Both parties, who before had acted separately, then unitedly proceeded to the Chief-Justice's house. . . . This rage-intoxicated rabble . . . beset the house on all sides, and soon destroyed every thing of value. . . . The destruction was really amazing; for it was equal to the fury of the onset. . . .

The distress a man must feel on such an occasion can only be conceived by those who the next day saw his Honor the Chief-Justice come into court, with a look big with the greatest anxiety, clothed in a manner which would have excited compassion from the hardest heart. . . . What must an audience have felt, whose

The violence in King's Street was against two customs officials, Benjamin Hallowell, comptroller, and William Storey, deputy registrar of the Admiralty.

A crowd protests the Stamp Act by attacking an effigy, or an image, of New Hampshire's stamp distributor. In the foreground, a man picks up a stone to throw at the figure.

Glorious News.

BOSTON, Friday 11 o'Clock, 16th *May* 1766.
THIS Inftant arrived here the Brig Harrifon, belonging
to *John Hancock*, Efq; Captain *Shubael Coffin*, in 6
Weeks and 2 Days from LONDON, with important
News, as follows.

From the LONDON GAZETTE.

Weftminfter, *March* 18th, 1766.

THIS day his Majefty came to the Houfe of Peers, and being in his royal
robes feated on the throne with the ufual folemnity, Sir Francis Moli-
neux, Gentleman Ufher of the Black Rod, was fent with a Meffage
from his Majefty to the Houfe of Commons, commanding their attendance in the Houfe of Peers. The Commons being come thither accordingly,
his Majefty was pleafed to give his royal affent to

An ACT to REPEAL an Act made in the laft Seffion of Parliament, in-
tituled, an Act for granting and applying certain Stamp-Duties and other Duties
in the Britifh Colonies and Plantations in America, towards further defraying
the expences of defending, protecting and fecuring the fame, and for amending
fuch parts of the feveral Acts of Parliament relating to the trade and revenues
of the faid Colonies and Plantations, as direct the manner of determining and
recovering the penalties and forfeitures therein mentioned.

Alfo ten public bills, and feventeen private ones.

Yefterday there was a meeting of the principal Merchants concerned in the
American trade, at the King's Arms tavern in Cornhill, to confider of an Ad-
drefs to his Majefty on the beneficial Repeal of the late Stamp-Act.

Yefterday morning about eleven o'clock a great number of North American
Merchants went in their coaches from the King's Arms tavern in Cornhill to the
Houfe of Peers, to pay their duty to his Majefty, and to exprefs their fatisfac-
tion at his figning the Bill for Repealing the American Stamp-Act, there was
upwards of fifty coaches in the proceffion.

Laft night the faid gentleman difpatched an exprefs for Falmouth, with fifteen copies of the Act for repealing the Stamp-Act, to be forwarded immediately for New York.

Orders are given for feveral merchantmen in the river to proceed to fea immediately on their refpective voyages to North America, fome of whom have
been cleared out fince the firft of November laft.

Yefterday meffengers were difpatched to Birmingham, Sheffield, Manchefter,
and all the great manufacturing towns in England, with an account of the final
decifion of an auguft affembly relating to the Stamp-Act.

*Bostonians first heard of the repeal of
the Stamp Act through a newspaper
brought by a ship from London. A
local printer published the account as a
single sheet called a broadside. It helped
give Bostonians the mistaken impression
that colonial taxation was as unpopular in Britain as it was in America.*

compassion had before been moved by what
they knew he had suffered, when they heard
him pronounce the following words in a manner which the agitations of his mind dictated?

GENTLEMEN,—There not being a quorum
of the court without me, I am obliged to
appear. Some apology is necessary for my
dress: indeed, I had no other. Destitute of
every thing,—no other shirt; no other gar-
ment but what I have on; and not one in my
whole family in a better situation than
myself. The distress of a whole family around
me, young and tender infants hanging about
me, are infinitely more insupportable than
what I feel for myself, though I am obliged to
borrow part of *this* clothing

Sensible that I am innocent, that all the
charges against me are false, I can't help feeling: and though I am not obliged to give an
answer to all the questions that may be put
me by every lawless person, yet I call God to
witness,—and I would not, for a thousand
worlds, call my Maker to witness to falsehood,—I say, I call my Maker to witness, that
I never, in New England or Old, in Great
Britain or America, neither directly nor indi-
rectly, was aiding, assisting, or supporting—
in the least promoting or encouraging—what
is commonly called the Stamp Act; but, on
the contrary, did all in my power, and strove
as much as in my lay, to prevent it. This is not
declared through timidity; for I have nothing
to fear. They can only take away my life,
which is of but little value when deprived of
all its comforts, all that was dear to me, and nothing sur-
rounding me but the most piercing distress.

I hope the eyes of the people will be opened, that they
will see how easy it is for some designing, wicked men to
spread false reports, to raise suspicions and jealousies in the
minds of the populace, and enrage them against the innocent: but, if guilty, this is not the way to proceed. The laws
of our country are open to punish those who have offended.
This destroying all peace and order of the community,—all
will feel its effects; and I hope all will see how easily the

people may be deluded, inflamed, and carried away with madness against an innocent man.

I pray God give us better hearts!

"We Are Therefore—SLAVES"

Protest against British policy involved not only action in the streets but also political discussions in newspapers and pamphlets. The most widely read and reprinted of all statements of the emerging Patriot position was John Dickinson's *Letters from a Farmer in Pennsylvania*. Dickinson wrote them to oppose the 1767 Townshend Acts, laws that imposed duties, or taxes, on a number of common imports such as paper, glass, paint, and tea. His twelve essays were originally published in a Philadelphia newspaper in late 1767. They were reprinted in almost every American city the following year. Identifying himself as a farmer, an occupation often viewed as morally virtuous, Dickinson—who was actually a lawyer—refined and popularized the arguments against British actions that had been developed during the Stamp Act crisis and from a long tradition of British and American political argument. The new British measures, Dickinson argues, means that Americans are in danger of falling into slavery.

There is an another late act of parliament, which appears to me to be unconstitutional, and as destructive to the liberty of these colonies, as that mentioned in my last letter; that is, the act for granting the duties on paper, glass, etc.

The parliament unquestionably possesses a legal authority to *regulate* the trade of *Great-Britain*, and all her colonies. Such an authority is essential to the relation between a mother country and her colonies; and necessary for the common good of all. He, who considers these provinces as states distinct from the *British Empire*, has very slender notions of *justice*, or of their *interests*. We are but parts of a *whole*; and therefore there must exist a power somewhere to preside, and preserve the connection in due order. This power is lodged in the parliament; and we are as much dependent on *Great-Britain*, as a perfectly free people can be on another.

I have looked over *every statute* relating to these colonies, from their first settlement to this time; and I find every one of them founded on this principle, till the *Stamp-Act* administration. *All before*, are calculated to regulate trade, and preserve or promote a mutually beneficial intercourse between the several constituent

After the Wilmington, North Carolina, stamp collector agreed to resign, "a large Bonfire was made, and no Person appeared in the Streets without having LIBERTY, in large Capital Letters, in his Hat."

—*Pennsylvania Gazette*, January 2, 1766

THE PATRIOTIC AMERICAN FARMER.

J—N D·K-NS—N, Esq; Barrister at Law.

Who with Attic Eloquence, and Roman Spirit, hath asserted the Liberties of the British Colonies in America.

'Tis nobly done to Stem Taxations Rage,
And raise the Thoughts of a degenerate Age,
For Happiness and Joy, from Freedom spring;
But Life in Bondage is a worthless Thing.

John Dickinson gained fame as the author of Letters from a Farmer in Pennsylvania. *But his role in the Revolution went much further than as an author. Although he opposed independence in 1776, he fought on the American side during the war, held the highest government office in both Delaware and Pennsylvania, and served in the Constitutional Convention, where he was a strong supporter of the small states. This image, which first appeared in a 1772 Boston almanac, may have been engraved by Paul Revere.*

parts of the empire; and though many of them imposed duties on trade, yet those duties were always imposed *with design* to restrain the commerce of one part, that was injurious to another, and thus to promote the general welfare. The raising a revenue thereby was never intended.

Dickinson continues, arguing that the 1764 Sugar Act, which included a revised tax on foreign molasses, is the first British legislation that speaks of using customs duties not to regulate trade but to raise money ("raising a revenue").

A few months after came the *Stamp-Act*, which reciting this, proceeds in the same strange mode of expression, thus—"And whereas it is just and necessary, that provision be made FOR RAISING A FURTHER REVENUE WITHIN YOUR MAJESTY'S DOMINIONS IN AMERICA, *towards defraying the said expences,* we your Majesty's most dutiful and loyal subjects, the COMMONS OF GREAT-BRITAIN &c. GIVE and GRANT, &c." as before.

The last act, granting duties upon paper, &c. [the Townshend Acts] carefully pursue these modern precedents. The preamble is, "Whereas it is expedient THAT A REVENUE SHOULD BE RAISED IN YOUR MAJESTY'S DOMINIONS IN AMERICA, *for making a more certain and adequate provision for defraying the charge of the administration of justice, and the support of civil government in such provinces. . . ."*

Here we may observe an authority *expressly* claimed and exerted to impose duties on these colonies; not for the regulation of trade; not for the preservation or promotion of a mutually beneficial intercourse between the several constituent parts of the empire, heretofore the *sole objects* of parliamentary institutions; but *for the single purpose of levying money upon us.*

This I call an innovation; and a most dangerous innovation.

Dickinson went on in later letters to argue that, as Americans could not do without the British paper and glass that were taxed by the Townshend duties, they had no choice but to pay the taxes. His seventh letter picks up his discussion on this point.

Some persons may think this act of no consequence, because the duties are so *small*. A fatal error. *That* is the very circumstance most alarming to me. For I am convinced, that the authors of this law would never have obtained an act to raise so trifling a sum as it must do, had they not intended by *it* to establish a *precedent* for future use. . . .

The late act is founded on the destruction of this constitutional security. If the parliament have a right to lay a duty of Four Shillings and Eight-pence on a hundred weight of glass, or a ream of paper, they have a right to lay a duty of any other sum on either. They may raise the duty, as the author before quoted says has been done in some countries, till it "exceeds seventeen or eighteen times the value of the commodity." In short, if they have a right *to* levy a tax of *one penny* upon us, they have a right to levy a *million* upon us: For where does their right stop? At any given number of Pence, Shillings or Pounds? To attempt to limit their right, after granting it to exist at all, is as contrary to reason—as granting it to exist at all, is contrary to justice. If *they* have any right to tax *us*—then, whether *our own money* shall continue in *our own pockets* or not, depends no longer on *us*, but on *them*. "There is nothing which" we can call our own; or, to use the words of Mr. *Locke*—"WHAT PROPERTY HAVE WE IN THAT, WHICH ANOTHER MAY, BY RIGHT, TAKE, WHEN HE PLEASES, TO HIMSELF?"

These duties, which will inevitably be levied upon us—which are now levying upon us—are *expressly* laid FOR THE SOLE PURPOSES OF TAKING MONEY. This is the true definition of *"taxes."* They are therefore *taxes.* This money is to be taken from *us.* We are therefore *taxed. Those* who are *taxed* without their own consent, expressed by themselves or their representatives, are *slaves. We are taxed* without our own consent, expressed by ourselves or our representatives. *We* are therefore—SLAVES.

Miserable vulgus
A miserable tribe.

John Locke

John Locke was a seventeenth-century English writer whose writings on philosophy, education, and government were highly influential in America as well as in England. This quotation refers to Locke's argument that governments were created by people to defend "life, liberty, and property." Thomas Jefferson would use a form of that phrase in the Declaration of Independence.

Violence in the Streets

William Shepard experienced the opposition to British policies at first hand. As a customs official in Philadelphia, Shepard had to enforce regulations that growing numbers of Americans saw as unfair. In this April 1769 letter to his superiors, the customs commissioners in Boston, he explains the difficulties he had endured.

On Saturday 1st instant, about ten o'clock in the morning, a seizure was made by the collector in consequence of an order from the inspector general, of near fifty pipes [casks] of Madeira wine, which was lodged in a store belonging to Mr. Andrew

Hodge. . . . Between 11 and 12 o'clock I waited upon the inspector general and acquainted him that I had great reason to suspect that it was the intention of some of the inhabitants to rescue the wines from the officers. He told me that he would take care to prevent it. . . . They [a mob at the store that afternoon] likewise prevented the collector's executing his duty, obliging him to go away, swearing they would shoot him if he attempted it. They pelted him with stones, glass bottles, etc., one of which struck him in the lip and hurt it considerably. It was by this time near dusk. . . . This procured an order for [a] captain and 50 men to assist the king's officers, but they did not get to the custom house till ten o'clock that night, near an hour before which the lock which the collector put on the store was broke off by the mob, and the door forced open and all the wines therein taken out and put on board three lighters or shallops and carried up the river. All the time they were transacting this matter they swore revenge and destruction against me, taking it for granted that I was the cause of making the seizure. . . .

lighters, shallops

Lighters and shallops were types of boats.

On Sunday 2d instant, I found in the necessary house [outhouse] belonging to my lodgings the following abusive letter directed "To the infamous Scoundrel Sheppard—altho I sign no name yet I sware by God Almighty that I will be revenged on you for this day's affair and put it out of your Power ever to hurt any body else for the future, believe what I say." I gave the inspector general, Mr. Williams, the above letter, who told me he would show it to the governor. The affair of the seizure was matter of conversation all Sunday. Everybody inveterate against me, saying they were sure it would not have happened if I had not informed the collector thereof. Some particular persons told me they thought it would be dangerous for me to venture out. . . .

Upon my return home about a quarter past ten o'clock, two men of a sudden came up to me, one of them without saying a word to me, struck me as hard as he could in the pit of my stomach, which immediately deprived me of breath and I fell down. He took the advantage with some weapon, I apprehend a knife, and slit my nose. . . . I received several blows upon my face which bruised it greatly, caused a large swelling. While this piece of cruelty was transacted I recovered strength enough to endeavour to defend myself. I got my right hand into my pocket and cocked the pistol that was in it, intending to discharge the same at him through my pocket, but as soon as he heard the guard of the pistol spring back he run from me. I, upon his retreat, fired it at him but am uncertain whether I hit him or not, am apt to think I did. . . .

I could not think of tarrying among a set of people, under my present circumstances, whose greatest pleasure would be to have an opportunity of burying me. The few acquaintance that I had at Philadelphia were afraid of being seen to keep company with me that so [that] I was in a manner alone in the city without a friend to assist me in any trouble. I was obliged to confine myself at home a nights, as I did not know what murderous intentions the people had determined to execute against me. As I passed through the streets I was the object that everybody stared and gazed at. I at present think myself unable to persevere any longer at Philadelphia, for the trouble and abuse I meet with there appears to be impossible for me to encounter with, and yet my desires are so great to be continued and fixed in it, that notwithstanding their opposition, I can't think of quitting the field.

Tarring and feathering was not often used to punish opponents of the American cause, but it did occur. This French engraving shows the preparation for one such event. John Malcolm, a Boston customs worker, mockingly told a crowd that his earlier experience being tarred and feathered in Maine had not been "done in a proper manner." Bostonians accepted his challenge to try again. The tar (despite what is pictured here) was applied on a wharf, the feathers came from two pillows. Malcolm was carried around the city in a cart for four hours.

In Boston, hostility toward customs officers became so strong that the British government stationed troops there in 1768. Growing tensions between the soldiers and Bostonians came to a head on March 5, 1770, when a hostile crowd harassed a sentry in front of the city's custom house. A party of eight British soldiers sent out to relieve him faced similar mistreatment. Finally, some of the soldiers fired on the crowd, wounding six and killing five Bostonians. The incident quickly became known as the Boston Massacre. Captain Thomas Preston, the unit's commander, was jailed that night with his men and charged with murder. A week later, Preston prepared the single best eyewitness account of the event. Although he expected to be hanged for the killings, Preston's trial ended in an acquittal.

About 9 [o'clock] some of the guard came to and informed me the town inhabitants were assembling to attack the troops. . . . This, as I was captain of the day, occasioned my repairing immediately to the main guard. In my way there I saw the people in great commotion, and heard them use the most cruel and horrid threats

Harassing Customs Officials

John Rowe recorded this account in his diary of a May 1773 attack—apparently verbal—upon British customs officials.

Two of the [Customs] Commissioners were very much abused yesterday when they came out from the Publick Dinner at Concert Hall, Mr. Hulton & Mr. Hallowell. Wm. Mollineaux, W'm Dennie, Paul Revere & several others were the Principal Actors.

against the troops. In a few minutes after I reached the guard, about 100 people passed it and went towards the custom house where the king's money is lodged. They immediately surrounded the sentry posted there, and with clubs and other weapons threatened to execute their vengeance on him. I was soon informed by a townsman their intention was to carry off the soldier from his post and probably murder him. . . . This I feared might be a prelude to their plundering the king's chest [the money stored in the custom's house]. I immediately sent a non-commissioned officer and 12 men to protect both the sentry and the king's money, and very soon followed myself to prevent, if possible, all disorder, fearing lest the officer and soldiers, by the insults and provocations of the rioters, should be thrown off their guard and commit some rash act. They soon rushed through the people, and by charging their bayonets in half-circles, kept them at a little distance. Nay, so far was I from intending the death of any person that I suffered the troops to go to the spot where the unhappy affair took place without any loading in their pieces; nor did I ever give orders for loading them. This remiss conduct in me perhaps merits censure; yet it is evidence, resulting from the nature of things, which is the best and surest that can be offered, that my intention was not to act offensively, but the contrary part, and that not without compulsion.

The mob still increased and [was] more outrageous, striking their clubs or bludgeons one against another, and calling out, come on you rascals, you bloody backs, you lobster scoundrels, fire if you dare, G-d damn you, fire and be damned, we know you dare not, and much more such language was used. . . . While I was thus speaking, one of the soldiers having received a severe blow with a stick, stepped a little on one side and instantly fired, on which turning to and asking him why he fired without orders, I was struck with a club on my arm, which for some time deprived me of the use of it, which blow had it been placed on my head, most probably would have destroyed me. On this a general attack was made on the men by a great number of heavy clubs and snowballs being thrown at them, by which all our lives were in imminent danger, some persons at the same time from behind calling out, damn your bloods—why don't you fire. Instantly three or four of the soldiers fired, one after another, and directly after three more in the same confusion and hurry. The mob then ran away, except three unhappy men who instantly expired. . . . One more is since dead, three others are dangerously, and four slightly wounded. The whole of this melancholy affair was transacted in

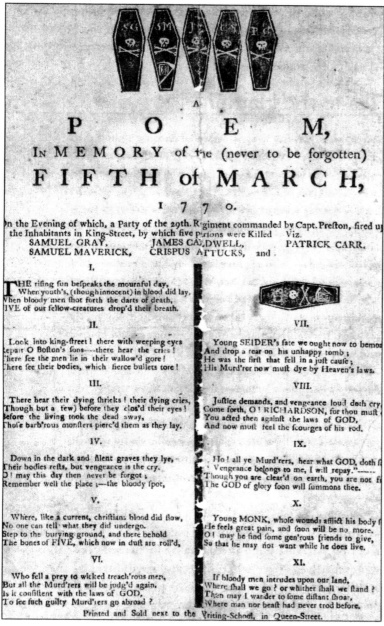

A

POEM,

In MEMORY of the (never to be forgotten)

FIFTH of MARCH,

1 7 7 0.

On the Evening of which, a Party of the 29th. Regiment commanded by Capt. Preston, fired upon the Inhabitants in King-Street, by which five persons were Killed   Viz.
SAMUEL GRAY.   JAMES CALDWELL,   PATRICK CARR.
SAMUEL MAVERICK,   CRISPUS ATTUCKS, and

I.

THE rising sun bespeaks the mournful day,
When youth's, (though innocent) in blood did lay,
When bloody men shot forth the darts of death,
FIVE of our fellow-creatures drop'd their breath.

II.

Look into king-street! there with weeping eyes
Repair O Boston's sons——there hear the cries!
There see the men lie in their wallow'd gore!
There see their bodies, which fierce bullets tore!

III.

There hear their dying shrieks! their dying cries,
Though but a few) before they clos'd their eyes!
Before the living took the dead away,
Those barb'rous monsters pierc'd them as they lay.

IV.

Down in the dark and silent graves they lye,
Their bodies rests, but vengeance is the cry.
O! may this day then never be forgot;
Remember well the place;—the bloody spot,

V.

Where, like a current, christians blood did flow,
No one can tell what they did undergo.
Step to the burying-ground, and there behold
The bones of FIVE, which now in dust are roll'd,

VI.

Who fell a prey to wicked treach'rous men,
But all the Murd'rers will be judg'd again.
Is it consistent with the laws of GOD,
To see such guilty Murd'rers go abroad?

VII.

Young SEIDER's fate we ought now to bemoan
And drop a tear on his unhappy tomb;
He was the first that fell in a just cause;
His Murd'rer now must dye by Heaven's laws.

VIII.

Justice demands, and vengeance loud doth cry,
Come forth, O! RICHARDSON, for thou must
You acted then against the laws of GOD,
And now must feel the scourges of his rod.

IX.

Ho! all ye Murd'rers, hear what GOD, doth
"Vengeance belongs to me, I will repay."——
Though you are clear'd on earth, you are not
The GOD of glory soon will summons thee.

X.

Young MONK, whose wounds afflict his body
He feels great pain, and soon will be no more.
O! may he find some gen'rous friends to give,
So that he may not want while he does live.

XI.

If bloody men intrudes upon our land,
Where shall we go? or whither shall we stand?
Then may I wander to some distant shoar,
Where man nor beast had never trod before.

Printed and Sold next to the Writing-School, in Queen-Street.

American radicals who opposed British measures found the Boston Massacre a powerful means of gaining support. This broadside calls for "vengeance" upon the "Murd'rers" who killed Bostonians, such as Christopher Seider (noted by the coffin in the text). He was actually killed by British sympathizer Ebenezer Richardson in a riot against a customs official.

almost 20 minutes. On my asking the soldiers why they fired without orders, they said they heard the word fire and supposed it came form me. This might be the case as many of the mob called out fire, fire, but I assured the men that I gave no such order; that my words were, don't fire, stop your firing. In short, it was scarcely possible for the solders to know who said fire, or don't fire, or stop your firing. . . .

Remembering the Massacre

On the first anniversary of the Boston Massacre, Dr. Joseph Warren, dressed in a toga to recall Roman ideals, addressed a meeting commemorating the event.

THE FATAL FIFTH OF MARCH, 1770, CAN NEVER BE FORGOTTEN—The horrors of THAT DREADFUL NIGHT are but too deeply impressed on our hearts—Language is too feeble to paint the emotions of our souls, when our streets were stained with the BLOOD OF OUR BRETHREN,—when our ears were wounded by the groans of the *dying*, and our eyes were tormented with the sight of the mangled bodies of the *dead*.—When our alarmed imagination presented to our view our houses wrapt in flames,—our children subjected to the barbarous caprice of the raging soldiery,—our beauteous virgins exposed to all the insolence of unbridled passion,—our virtuous wives, endeared to us by every tender tie, falling a sacrifice to worse than brutal violence.

I am, though perfectly innocent, under most unhappy circumstances, having nothing in reason to expect but the loss of life in a very ignominious manner, without the interposition of his Majesty's royal goodness.

Tea in the Harbor

The Sons of Liberty was a series of loosely linked local groups that directed opposition to British measures. These resolutions to boycott tea were passed by the New York City organization on December 15, 1773. They begin by presenting the Patriot view of British actions from the 1767 Townshend Acts to 1773. The resolutions discuss the success of the Americans' agreements not to import or consume British goods—and the measures they recommended to strengthen resistance to the new Tea Act, which kept the Townshend Act's tax on tea and granted England's East India Company a monopoly on shipping it to, and distributing it within, the colonies. If colonists bought the tea (which would become less expensive), then the Sons' attempts to resist taxes would be severely damaged. A New York newspaper introduced the document by noting that it had been "signed by a great number of the principal gentlemen of the city, merchants, lawyers, and other inhabitants of all ranks, and it is still carried about the city, to give an opportunity to those who have not yet signed to unite with their fellow-citizens, to testify their abhorrence to the diabolical project of enslaving America."

It is essential to the freedom and security of a free people, that no taxes be imposed upon them but by their own consent, or their representatives. For "what property have they in that which another may, by right, take when he pleases to himself?" The former is the undoubted right of Englishmen, to secure what they expended millions and sacrificed the lives of thousands. And yet, to the astonishment of all the world, and the grief of America, the commons of Great Britain, after the repeal of the memorable and detestable stamp-act, reassumed the power of imposing taxes on the American colonies. . . . And thus they who, from time immemorial, have exercised the right of giving to, or withholding from the crown, their aids and subsidies, according to their own free will and pleasure, signified by their representatives in parliament, do, by the act in question, deny us, their brethren in

America, the enjoyment of the same right. As this denial, and the execution of that act, involves our slavery, and would sap the foundation of our freedom, whereby we should become slaves to our brethren and fellow subjects, born to no greater stock of freedom than the Americans—the merchants and inhabitants of this city, in conjunction with the merchants and inhabitants of the ancient American colonies, entered into an agreement to decline a part of their commerce with Great Britain, until the above mentioned act should be totally repealed.

This agreement operated so powerfully to the disadvantage of the manufacturers of England that many of them were unemployed. To appease their clamors, and to provide the subsistence for them, which the non-importation had deprived them of, the parliament, in 1770, repealed so much of the revenue act as imposed a duty on glass, painters' colors, and paper, and left the duty on tea, as a test of the parliamentary right to tax us. The merchants of the cities of New York and Philadelphia, having strictly adhered to the agreement, so far as it is related to the importation of articles subject to an American duty, have convinced the ministry, that some other measures must be adopted to execute parliamentary supremacy over this country, and to remove the distress brought on the East Indian company, by the ill-policy of that act. Accordingly, to increase the temptation to the shippers of tea from England, an act of parliament passed the last session, which gives the whole duty on tea, the company were subject to pay, upon the importation of it into England, to the purchasers and exporters. . . . They have chartered ships to bring the tea to this country, which may be hourly expected, to make an important trial of our virtue. If they succeed in the sale of that tea, we shall have no property that we can call our own, and then we may bid adieu to American liberty.

The resolutions declare that opponents of the measures were endangering "the liberties of America" and risking "slavery" (that is, loss of all freedom).

A LIST of the Names of those who AUDACIOUSLY continue to counteract the UNITED SENTIMENTS of the BODY of Merchants thro'out NORTH-AMERICA; by importing British Goods contrary to the Agreement.

John Bernard,
(In King-Street, almost opposite Vernon's Head.
James McMasters,
(On Treat's Wharf.
Patrick McMasters,
(Opposite the Sign of the Lamb.
John Mein,
(Opposite the White-Horse, and in King-Street.
Ame & Elizabeth Cummings,
(Opposite the Old Brick Meeting House, all of Boston.
And, Henry Barnes,
(Trader in the Town of Marlboro'.
HAVE, and do still continue to import Goods from London, contrary to the Agreement of the Merchants.—They have been requested to Store their Goods upon the same Terms as the rest of the Importers have done, but absolutely refuse, by conducting in this Manner.
IT must evidently appear that they have prefered their own little private Advantage to the Welfare of America : It is therefore highly proper that the Public should

The Sons of Liberty enforced the boycotts on British goods partly by publicizing the names of people who violated the agreements. This Boston newspaper advertisement names six merchants who continued to import despite the agreement, suggesting that they were to be considered "Enemies to their Country."

I think the Parliament of Great Britain hath no more right to put their hands into my pocket, without my consent, than I have to put my hands into yours for money.

—From a letter by George Washington to Bryan Fairfax, July, 1774

Therefore, to prevent a calamity which, . . . is the most to be dreaded—slavery, and its terrible concomitants—we, the subscribers . . . agree to associate together, under the name and style of the sons of New York, and engage our honor to, and with each other faithfully to observe and perform the following resolutions, viz.

1st, *Resolved,* That whoever shall aid, or abet, or in any manner assist, in the introduction of tea, from any place whatsoever, into this colony, while it is subject, by a British act of parliament, to the payment of a duty, for the purpose of raising a revenue in America, he shall be deemed an enemy to the liberties of America.

2nd, *Resolved,* That whoever shall be aiding, or assisting, in the landing, or carting of such tea, from any ship, or vessel, or shall hire any house, storehouse, or cellar or any place whatsoever, to deposit the tea, subject to a duty as aforesaid, he shall be deemed an enemy to the liberties of America.

3rd, *Resolved,* That whoever shall sell, or buy, or any manner contribute to the sale, or purchase of tea, subject to a duty as aforesaid, or shall aid, or abet, in transporting such tea by land or water, from this city, until the 7th George III chap. 46, commonly called the revenue act, shall be totally and clearly repealed, he shall be deemed an enemy to the liberties of America.

4th, *Resolved,* That whether the duties on tea, imposed by this act, be paid in Great Britain, or in America, our liberties are equally affected.

5th, *Resolved,* That whoever shall transgress any of these resolutions, we will not deal with, or employ, or have any connections with him.

The arrival of the tea which was regulated by the Tea Act in American ports during the fall of 1773 posed a direct challenge to American Patriots. Once again, Boston witnessed the most violent reactions to British measures. When Lieutenant Governor Thomas Hutchinson refused to allow the tea ships to leave without unloading their cargo, the Patriots finally decided to destroy it. One of the participants in the carefully organized action that came to be called the Boston Tea Party recalled his experiences to a journalist some sixty years later. George Robert Twelves Hewes, one of the last survivors of the disguised "Indians" who threw the tea overboard into Boston Harbor, was a young shoemaker at the time.

It was now evening, and I immediately dressed myself in the costume of an Indian, equipped with a small hatchet, which I and my

associates denominated the toma-
hawk, with which, and a club, after
having painted my face and hands
with coal dust in the shop of a black-
smith, I repaired to Griffin's wharf,
where the ships lay that contained the
tea. When I first appeared in the
street, after being thus disguised, I fell
in with many who were dressed,
equipped and painted as I was, and
who fell in with me, and marched in
order to the place of our destination.
When we arrived at the wharf, there
were three of our number who
assumed an authority to direct our

operations, to which we readily submitted. They divided us into
three parties, for the purpose of boarding the three ships which
contained the tea at the same time. The name of him who commanded the division to which I was assigned, was Leonard Pitt. . . .
We were immediately ordered by the respective commanders to
board all the ships at the same time, which we promptly obeyed.
The commander of the division to which I belonged, as soon as
we were on board the ship, appointed me boatswain, and ordered
me to go to the captain and demand of him the keys to the hatches and a dozen candles. I made the demand accordingly, and the
captain promptly replied, and delivered the articles; but requested
me at the same time to do no damage to the ship or rigging. We
then were ordered by our commander to open the hatches, and
take out all the chests of tea and throw them overboard, and we
immediately proceeded to execute his orders; first cutting and
splitting the chests with our tomahawks, so as thoroughly to
expose them to the effects of the water. In about three hours from
the time we went on board, we had thus broken and thrown overboard every tea chest to be found in the ship; while those in the
other ships were disposing of the tea in the same way, at the same
time. We were surrounded by British armed ships, but no attempt
was made to resist us. We then quietly retired to our places of residence, without having any conversation with each other, or taking any measures to discover who were our associates; nor do I
recollect of our having had the knowledge of the name of a single
individual concerned in the affair, except that of Leonard Pitt, the
commander of my division, who I have mentioned. There
appeared to be an understanding that each individual should

Perhaps expressing disdain for the American action, this 1789 British engraving of the Boston Tea Party shows colonists rowing away with boxes of tea for personal use. Attempts to take tea were harshly punished.

*The People should never rise,
without doing something to be
remembered—something notable.
And striking. This Destruction
of the Tea is so bold, so daring,
so firm, intrepid and inflexible,
and it must have so important
Consequences, and so lasting,
that I can[']t but consider it
as an Epocha of History.*
—A diary entry by John
Adams, December 17, 1773

Colonial Support

The Coercive Acts by which the British attempted to isolate Boston after the Tea Party helped build sympathy for that city—and for the resistance movement. A group of people in Essex County, Virginia, sent a cargo of grain to Boston's poor in September 1774. In the letter that accompanied the shipment, they sent this message.

We can venture to assure you, that the Virginians are warmly disposed to assist them, and hope for their steady and prudent perseverance in the common cause of our country, from whence only we can hope for a happy termination of our distresses. We pray God for an happy issue to our virtuous struggles, and we beg leave to assure you that we have the most sincere regard for our northward brethren.

volunteer his services, keep his own secret, and risk the consequences for himself. No disorder took place during that transaction, and it was observed at that time, that the stillest night ensued that Boston had enjoyed for many months.

Hewes's account notes the punishments meted out to people who tried to use the Boston Tea Party not as an expression of public outrage but as an opportunity for private gain.

During the time we were throwing the tea overboard, there were several attempts made by some of the citizens of Boston and its vicinity, to carry off small quantities of it for their family use. To effect that object, they would watch their opportunity to snatch up a handful from the deck, where it became plentifully scattered, and put it into their pockets. One Captain O'Connor, whom I well knew, came on board for that purpose, and when he supposed he was not noticed, filled his pockets, and also the lining of his coat. . . . He had . . . to run a gauntlet through the crowd upon the wharf; each one, as he passed, giving him a kick or a stroke.

The next day we nailed the skirt of his coat, which I had pulled off, to the whipping post in Charlestown, the place of his residence, with a label upon it, commemorative of the occasion which had thus subjected the proprietor to the popular indignation.

Another attempt was made to save a little tea from the ruins of the cargo, by a tall aged man, who wore a large cocked hat and white wig, which was fashionable at that time. He had slightly slipped a little into his pocket, but being detected, they seized him, and taking his hat and wig from his head, threw them, together with the tea, of which they had emptied his pockets, into the water. In consideration of his advanced age, he was permitted to escape, with now and then a slight kick.

The next morning, after we had cleared the ships of the tea, it was discovered that very considerable quantities of it was floating upon the surface of the water; and to prevent the possibility of any of its being saved for use, a number of small boats were manned by sailors and citizens, who rowed them into those parts of the harbour wherever the tea was visible, and by beating it with oars and paddles, so thoroughly drenched it, as to render its entire destruction inevitable.

By 1773, the Sons of Liberty realized the need to expand their bases of resistance. They increasingly sought to reach out to other groups, including some that had previously been only

marginally involved with political life. A powerful example of this broadening participation came in Edenton, North Carolina, where, in October 1774, fifty-one women signed this agreement to follow the recommendations of the Continental Congress about British goods.

As we cannot be indifferent on any occasion that appears to affect the peace and happiness of our country; and as it has been thought necessary for the publick good to enter into several particular Resolves by a meeting of Members of Deputies from the whole Province, it is a duty that we owe not only to our near and dear relations and connexions, but to ourselves, who are essentially interested in their welfare, to do every thing as far as lies in our power to testify our sincere adherence to the same; and we do therefore accordingly subscribe this paper as a witness of our fixed intention and solemn determination to do so.

Some patriots celebrated the actions of women they called the "Daughters of Liberty." But women's involvement in political activity was new and troubling to many people in both America and Britain. A British artist mocked "Society of Patriotic Ladies" in Edenton, North Carolina, in a cartoon that portrays the 1774 signing as a scene of extensive disorder (the dog, the child, and the slave are symbols of low status). Such confusion, the engraving suggests, resulted from women moving into activities for which they were unsuited.

Chapter Two

Breaking the Bonds

War and Independence

I n April 1775, fighting broke out between American Patriots and Great Britain at Lexington and Concord, Massachusetts. Amos Doolittle was one of the thousands of volunteer soldiers, members of the part-time local military organizations known as militias, who hurried to support the Americans. His Connecticut company arrived outside of Boston by April 29, ten days after the battles of Lexington and Concord. Doolittle, an engraver, remained with his company in Cambridge for some three or four weeks, expecting the hostilities to continue. He took advantage of the time to visit the battle sites. Soon afterward he issued a series of four engravings based on his visits.

Doolittle's first print depicts the encounter on Lexington's green, where the first shots of the Revolution were fired. Warned by Paul Revere that the British troops were on their way to confiscate Patriot military supplies, the American militia had assembled there after mid-night. The British finally arrived around dawn and things quickly got out of hand. A shot or shots were fired—each side later blamed the other. The British soldiers began to attack. After the officers regained control, the British troops left for Concord after three cheers and a victory volley from their guns. Eight Americans were wounded; nine were dead. Doolittle's engraving exaggerates the orderliness of the attack, suggesting that the British were solely to blame for the deaths and starting the war.

By April 1775, many Americans believed the British were attacking American liberties. A smaller number, like Doolittle, also believed that they needed to resist these actions—with violence if necessary. Far fewer desired full independence from Great Britain. A year after the

Amos Doolittle's depiction of the first shots of the Revolution portrays the Patriot view of the event. Doolittle shows a British officer commanding his troops to fire on the militiamen. But it is more likely that a stray shot began the attack.

confrontations at Lexington and Concord, the goal of the fighting remained unclear. But the options gradually narrowed as the war continued and British attitudes toward the colonies hardened. In July 1776, Congress finally voted that the colonies should be free and independent. Although this declaration resolved the purpose of fighting, it raised new concerns: How would this independence be won? And, even if enough Americans could be convinced of the need to fight, could they defeat the world's most powerful and successful military power?

The Road from Lexington and Concord

Besides Paul Revere, a network of other Patriots spread the word across New England about the British movement toward Concord. Most militia companies, like Doolittle's, arrived too late for the battles. One of these soldiers, John Jones, sent a letter to his wife three days after the first shots were fired. He had marched from his home in Princeton, Massachusetts, to Concord, some thirty miles away, expecting to participate in the battle he describes. Instead he found the British back in their Boston barracks and a number of Patriot troops housed at Harvard College. In this April 1775 letter he informs his wife of the casualties and asks her to send clothing for a relative. As the postscript about flaxseed, which was grown to make thread for linen, suggests, women during the Revolution often had to take up the responsibility of running the family farm while their husbands and sons served in the military.

Cambridge Apr 22, 1775

Loving Wife—

There was a hot Battle fought Between the Regulars that march'd to Concord and our People, on Wednesday the 19 of this Instant in which many on both sides were slain/but most of the Enemies/as we heard before we march'd. As we marched to Concord we were often Inform'd that the Enemy had marched from Boston a second time [and] had got as far as Lincoln—we hurried on as fast as Possible Expecting to meet them in Concord but when we arrived there we were Inform'd that they had Return[ed] from their first Engagement to Charleston—from which they are gone to Boston—we are now stationed in one of y^e

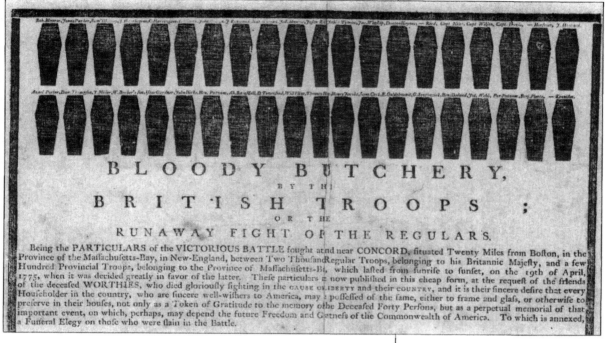

BLOODY BUTCHERY,

BY THE

BRITISH TROOPS ;

OR THE

RUNAWAY FIGHT OF THE REGULARS.

Being the PARTICULARS of the VICTORIOUS BATTLE fought at and near CONCORD, situated Twenty Miles from Boston, in the Province of the Massachusetts-Bay, in New-England, between Two Thousand Regular Troops, belonging to his Britannic Majesty, and a few Hundred Provincial Troops, belonging to the Province of Massachusetts-Bay, which lasted from sunrise to sunset, on the 19th of April, 1775, when it was decided greatly in favor of the latter. These particulars are now published in this cheap form, at the request of the friends of the deceased WORTHIES, who died gloriously fighting in the CAUSE of LIBERTY and their COUNTRY, and it is their sincere desire that every Householder in the country, who are sincere well-wishers to America, may be possessed of the same, either to frame and glass, or otherwise to preserve in their houses, not only as a Token of Gratitude to the memory of the Deceased Forty Persons, but as a perpetual memorial of that important event, on which, perhaps, may depend the future Freedom and Greatness of the Commonwealth of America. To which is annexed, a Funeral Elegy on those who were slain in the Battle.

Colleges as are many more of ye Army—all in good health Through the Divine goodness and hope for ye Blessing of Heaven.

In ye first Combat among those that were slain were Lieut John Bacon of Newham two mills, Nat Chamb^n and 2 others from Needham—Elias Haven from Springfield—

If you have an Opportunity you may find Brother Hapgoods a Shirt and pair of Stockings—Tis uncertain when we shall Return may we all be Enabled to Repent & turn to our God that he may save us from Ruin.

I am with the Greatest Respect your Affectionate & Loving Husband till Death.

John Jones

N.B. my Best Love to Brother Jones & Children—Let us all be Patient & Remember that it is ye hand of God

Capt Moore has sold his flaxseed but if you apply in season you may get some of Mr. Woods—

News about the battles at Lexington and Concord quickly spread beyond New England. In New Jersey, emboldened Patriots expanded their activities. The colony's royal governor, William Franklin, found this deeply troubling. This letter from Franklin in May 1775 explains the situation to Lord Dartmouth, secretary of state for the colonies. Franklin was

On this 1775 broadside the two rows of coffins represent the colonials killed by the British during the battles of Lexington and Concord. Below the description of the fight, a poem (not shown here) commemorates the slain.

Goodbye to the King

In the wake of the battles at Lexington and Concord in 1775, an anonymous radical bade farewell to the king in a Salem, Massachusetts, newspaper article.

King George the third adieu! No more shall we bleed in defense of your person, your breach of covenant, your violation of faith, your turning a dear ear to our cries for justice, for covenanted protection and salvation from the oppressive, tyrannical, and bloody measures of the British Parliament and [your] putting a sanction upon all their measures to enslave and butcher us, have DISSOLVED OUR ALLEGIANCE to your crown and government! Your sword that ought in justice to protect us, is now drawn with a witness to destroy us. O George see thou to thy own house.

the son (born outside of marriage) of the leading Patriot, Benjamin Franklin. Unlike his father, William remained loyal to the king and hoped that the two sides could be reconciled. The battles in Massachusetts, which he clearly found inexplicable, dashed his hopes.

To the Right Honble the Earl of Dartmouth
Perth Amboy, May 6th 1775
The Accounts we have from Massachusetts Bay respecting the Proceedings of the King's Troops, and the late Engagement between them and the Inhabitants of that Province, have occasioned such an Alarm and excited so much Uneasiness among the People throughout this and the other Colonies, that there is Danger of their committing some outrageous Violences before the present Heats can subside. They are arming themselves, forming into Companies, and taking uncommon Pains to perfect themselves in Military Discipline. Every Day new Alarms are spread, which have a Tendency to keep the Minds of the People in a continual Ferment, make them suspicious, and prevent their paying any Attention to the Dictates of sober Reason and common Sense. . . .

All legal Authority and Government seems to be drawing to an End here, and that of Congresses, Conventions, and Committees establishing in their Place. The People are everywhere entering into Associations similar to that of New York, whereby they engage to "adopt and endeavour carry into Execution *whatever Measures* may be recommended by the *Continental Congress,* or resolved upon by the *Provincial Convention,* and that they will *in all Things follow* the Advice of their *General Committees,*" &c. . . .

[I]t is greatly to be regretted that the late Skirmish happened at the Time it did, as it has, in its Consequences, proved one of the most unlucky Incidents that could have occurred in the present Situation of Affairs. It will not only be a Means of retarding, if not entirely defeating the Wishes & Measures of His Majesty for a happy Reconciliation; but will endanger the Lives & properties of every Officer of Government in the King's Colonies to the Southward of New England who may refuse to acquiesce in their Proceedings. It has, indeed, been repeatedly declared that they were determined to make Reprisals, and that in case Gen.l Gage should seize upon or punish any of the people of that Country, they would seize upon the King's Officers & Friends of Government, throughout the Colonies, and treat them in the same Manner.

Causes and Necessities

When the Second Continental Congress met in May 1775, the delegates faced new problems. British actions had seemed threatening when the First Continental Congress had adjourned the previous fall, but now war had actually begun. The new Congress issued a "Declaration of the Causes and Necessities of Taking Up Arms" on July 6, 1775, explaining and justifying the creation of an army to fight a government to which they still claimed allegiance. Even less than a year earlier, most delegates, like most Americans, still sought reconciliation. Thomas Jefferson, who wrote the first draft of the document, later complained that the extensive revisions made by the more moderate John Dickinson stressed too strongly for the need for compromise. Both versions, however, ultimately made the same point: although oppressive British actions had driven the American colonies into military action, reconciliation was still possible.

If it was possible for men, who exercise their reason, to believe, that the Divine Author of our existence intended a part of the human race to hold an absolute property in, and an unbounded power over others, marked out by his infinite goodness and wisdom, as the objects of a legal domination never rightfully resistible, however severe and oppressive, the Inhabitants of these Colonies might at least require from the Parliament of Great Britain some evidence, that this dreadful authority over them, has been granted to that body. But a reverence for our great Creator, principles of humanity, and the dictates of common sense, must convince all those who reflect upon the subject, that government was instituted to promote the welfare of mankind, and ought to be administered for the attainment of that end. . . .

Our cause is just. Our union is perfect. Our internal resources are great, and, if necessary, foreign assistance is undoubtedly attainable.—We gratefully acknowledge, as signal instances of the Divine favour towards us, that his Providence would not permit us to be called into this severe controversy, until we were grown up to our present strength, had been previously exercised in warlike operation, and possessed of the means of defending ourselves—With hearts fortified with these animating reflections, we most solemnly, before God and the world, declare, that, exerting the utmost energy of those powers, which our beneficent Creator hath graciously bestowed upon us, the arms we have been compelled by our enemies to assume, we will, in defiance of every hazard, with unabating firmness and perseverence, employ for the preservation of our liberties; being with our [one] mind resolved to die Free men rather than live Slaves.

Lest this declaration should disquiet the minds of our friends and fellow-subjects in any part of the empire, we assure them that we mean not to dissolve that Union which has so long and so happily subsisted between us, and which we sincerely wish to see restored.—Necessity has not yet driven us into that desperate measure, or induced us to excite any other nation to war against them.—We have not raised armies with ambitious designs of separating from Great Britain, and establishing independent states. We fight not for glory or for conquest. We exhibit to mankind the remarkable spectacle of a people attacked by unprovoked enemies, without any imputation or even suspicion of offence. They boast of their privileges and civilization, and yet proffer no milder conditions than servitude or death.

Events after mid-1775 rapidly pushed Congress and many colonists toward independence. King George III believed that a group of scheming Americans had already made that decision. In this speech to Parliament on October 26, 1775, he claimed that the colonists' protestations of continued loyalty were only attempts to hide their desire to revolt. Britain had acted gently before, he argued. But now such "moderation" had outlived its usefulness. Less than two months later, Parliament passed the Prohibitory Act extending the state of hostilities against the colonies. Now American ships and their cargoes would be treated as "the ships and effects of open enemies."

Those who have long too successfully laboured to inflame my people in America by gross misrepresentations and to infuse into their minds a system of opinions repugnant to the true constitution of the colonies, and to their subordinate relation to Great Britain, now openly avow their revolt, hostility, and rebellion. They have raised troops, and are collecting a naval force; they have seized the public revenue, and assumed to themselves legislative, executive, and judicial powers, which they already exercise in the most arbitrary manner over the persons and properties of their fellow subjects; and although many of these unhappy

America must be a colony of England or treated as an enemy. Distant possessions standing upon an equality with the superior state is more ruinous than being deprived of such connections.

—George III, letter to the Earl of Dartmouth, June 10, 1775

people may still retain their loyalty and may be too wise not to see the fatal consequence of this usurpation, and wish to resist it; yet the torrent of violence has been strong enough to compel their acquiescence till a sufficient force shall appear to support them.

The authors and promoters of this desperate conspiracy have in the conduct of it derived great advantage from the difference of our intentions and theirs. They meant only to amuse by vague expressions of attachment to the parent state and the strongest protestations of loyalty to me, whilst they were preparing for a general revolt. On our part, though it was declared in your last session that a rebellion existed within the province of the Massachusetts Bay, yet even that province we wished rather to reclaim than to subdue. The resolutions of Parliament breathed a spirit of moderation and forbearance; conciliatory propositions accompanied the measures taken to enforce authority, and the coercive acts were adapted to cases of criminal combinations amongst subjects not then in arms. I have acted with the same temper; anxious to prevent, if it had been possible, the effusion of

"The Political Cartoon for the Year 1775" was published in a British magazine. It shows George III and Chief Justice Lord Mansfield foolishly driving the country (represented by the carriage) off a cliff. Pulled by horses labeled "Obstinacy" and "Pride," the vehicle tramples on the protections of the Magna Carta and the Constitution. Above, the devil flies away with Britain's credit while America (in the left background) burns.

the blood of my subjects and the calamities which are inseparable from a state of war; still hoping that my people in American would have discerned the traitorous views of their leaders and have been convinced that to be a subject of Great Britain, with all its consequences, is to be the freest member of any civil society in the known world.

The rebellious war now levied is become more general and is manifestly carried on for the purpose of establishing an independent empire. I need not dwell upon the fatal effects of the success of such a plan. The object is too important, the spirit of the British nation too high, the resources with which God hath blessed her too numerous, to give up so many colonies which she has planted with great industry, nursed with great tenderness, encouraged with many commercial advantages, and protected and defended at much expense of blood and treasure.

News of the king's speech arrived in the colonies in January 1776. That same month, Thomas Paine's pamphlet *Common Sense* was published. It gained immediate and widespread popularity and was reprinted twenty-four times in that year alone. It would (according to Paine himself) eventually sell an extraordinary 150,000 copies. Paine attacks the colonies' continuing connection with Britain, using ordinary language with extraordinary vigor. Independence would not be a dangerous experiment, he argues, but a remarkable opportunity. Paine particularly ridicules monarchy and hereditary succession, arguing instead that Americans should create a simple form of government that would be fully responsive to the people's will. The new country could "begin the world over again."

Paine begins his piece by distinguishing between society, which is good, and government, which is a necessary evil.

Thomas Paine, who began life in England, played an important role in the American Revolution and also participated in the French Revolution. "A share in two revolutions," he wrote, "is living to some purpose."

Society in every state is a blessing, but government even in its best state is but a necessary evil; in its worst state an intolerable one; for when we suffer, or are exposed to the same miseries *by a government*, which we might expect in a country *without government*, our calamities are heightened by reflecting that we furnish the means by which we suffer. Government, like dress, is the badge of lost innocence; the palaces of kings are built on the ruins of the bowers of paradise. For were the impulses of conscience clear, uniform, and irresistibly obeyed, man would need no other lawgiver; but that not being the case, he finds it necessary to surrender up a part of his property to furnish means for the protection of the rest; and this he is induced to do by the same prudence which in every other case advises him out of two evils to choose the least. *Wherefore*, security being the true design and end of government, it unanswerably follows that whatever *form* thereof appears most likely to ensure it to us, with the least expence and greatest benefit, is preferable to all others.

Another of Paine's key themes is the foolishness of monarchy. A hereditary king, he argues, is as absurd as a hereditary mathematician.

As the exalting one man so greatly above the rest cannot be justified on the equal rights of nature, so neither can it be defended on the authority of scripture; for the will of the Almighty, as declared by Gideon and the prophet Samuel, expressly disapproves of government by kings. All anti-monarchial parts of scripture have been very smoothly glossed over in monarchial governments, but they undoubtedly merit the attention of countries which have their governments yet to form. . . .

To the evil of monarchy we have added that of hereditary succession; and as the first is a degradation and lessening of ourselves, so the second, claimed as a matter of right, is an insult and an imposition on posterity. For all men being originally equals, no *one* by *birth* could have a right to set up his own family in perpetual preference to all others for ever, and though himself might deserve *some* decent degree of honors of his contemporaries, yet his descendants might be far too unworthy to inherit them. One of the strongest *natural* proofs of the folly of hereditary right in kings, is, that nature disapproves it, otherwise she would not so frequently turn it into ridicule by giving mankind an *ass for a lion*. . . .

England, since the conquest, hath known some few good monarchs, but groaned beneath a much larger number of bad ones; yet no man in his senses can say that their claim under William the

COMMON SENSE;

ADDRESSED TO THE

INHABITANTS

OF

AMERICA,

On the following interesting

SUBJECTS.

I. Of the Origin and Design of Government in general, with concise Remarks on the English Constitution.

II. Of Monarchy and Hereditary Succession.

III. Thoughts on the present State of American Affairs.

IV. Of the present Ability of America, with some miscellaneous Reflections.

A NEW EDITION, with several Additions in the Body of the Work. To which is added an APPENDIX; together with an Address to the People called QUAKERS.

N. B. The New Addition here given increases the Work upwards of one Third.

Man knows no Master save creating HEAVEN,
Or those whom Choice and common Good ordain.
THOMSON.

PHILADELPHIA PRINTED,
And sold by W. and T. BRADFORD. C1776.

Twenty-five editions of Thomas Paine's Common Sense *appeared in 1776. This cover page is from the New York edition printed by John Anderson. When the British moved to take over the city later that year, Anderson fled, losing his household goods and printing equipment in the process.*

banditti

William the Conqueror, the illigitimate son of the Duke of Normandy (in northern France), invaded England in 1066 with what Paine calls a group of gangsters ("banditti"). William's victory established the English monarchy.

Paine sometimes used blanks in referring to the king in order to avoid prosecution by British authorities for his critism.

Conqueror is a very honorable one. A French bastard landing with an armed banditti, and establishing himself king of England against the consent of the natives, is in plain terms a very paltry rascally original.—It certainly hath no divinity in it. However, it is needless to spend much time in exposing the folly of hereditary right, if there are any so weak as to believe it, let them promiscuously worship the ass and lion, and welcome. I shall neither copy their humility, nor disturb their devotion. . . .

But Britain is the parent country, say some. Then the more shame upon her conduct. Even brutes do not devour their young, nor savages make war upon their families; wherefore the assertion, if true, turns to her reproach; but it happens not to be true, or only partly so, and the phrase *parent* or *mother country* hath been Jesuitically adopted by the *___ and his parasites, with a low papistical design of gaining an unfair bias on the credulous weakness of our minds. Europe, and not England, is the parent country of America. This new world hath been the asylum for the persecuted lovers of civil and religious liberty from *every part* of Europe. Hither have they fled, not from the tender embraces of the mother, but from the cruelty of the monster; and it is so far true of England, that the same tyranny which drove the first emigrants from home, pursues their descendants still.

Paine was particularly concerned to attack the idea of reconciliation with the British. Here he explains that Americans have the opportunity to establish a new nation ruled by laws rather than a king.

Europe is too thickly planted with kingdoms to be long at peace, and whenever a war breaks out between England and any foreign power, the trade of America goes to ruin, *because of her connection with Britain.* The next war may not turn out like the last, and should it not, the advocates for reconciliation now will be wishing for separation then, because, neutrality in that case, would be a safer convoy than a man of war. Every thing that is right or natural pleads for separation. The blood of the slain, the weeping voice of nature cries, 'TIS TIME TO PART. Even the distance at which the Almighty hath placed England and America, is a strong and natural proof, that the authority of the one, over the other, was never the design of Heaven. . . .

Men of passive tempers look somewhat lightly over the offences of Britain, and, still hoping for the best, are apt to call out, *'Come we shall be friends again for all this.'* But examine the passions and feelings of mankind. Bring the doctrine of reconciliation to the touchstone of nature, and then tell me, whether you can hereafter love, honour, and faithfully serve the power that hath carried fire and sword into your land? . . . Hath your house been burnt? Hath your property been destroyed before your face? Are your wife and children destitute of a bed to lie on, or bread to live on? Have you lost a parent or a child by their hands, and yourself the ruined and wretched survivor? If you have not, then are you not a judge of those who have. But if you have, and still can shake hands with the murderers, then are you unworthy the name of husband, father, friend, or lover, and whatever may be your rank or title in life, you have the heart of a coward, and the spirit of a sycophant. . . .

No man was a warmer wisher for reconciliation than myself, before the fatal nineteenth of April 1775, but the moment the event of that day was made known, I rejected the hardened, sullen tempered Pharaoh of *___ for ever; and disdain the wretch, that with the pretended title of FATHER OF HIS PEOPLE can unfeelingly hear of their slaughter, and composedly sleep with their blood upon his soul. . . .

But where says some is the King of America? I'll tell you Friend, he reigns above, and doth not make havoc of mankind like the Royal ___ of Britain. Yet that we may not appear to be defective even in earthly honours, let a day be solemnly set apart for proclaiming the charter; let it be brought forth placed on the divine law, the word of God; let a crown be placed thereon, by which the world may know, that so far as we approve of monarchy, that in America THE LAW IS KING. For as in absolute governments the King is law, so in free countries the law *ought* to be King; and there ought to be no other. But lest any ill use should afterwards arise, let the crown at the conclusion of the ceremony be demolished, and scattered among the people whose right it is.

The difficulties of fighting a war without seeking independence can be seen in this resolution passed by Congress on May 10, 1776. It was given a fuller and more radical preamble five days later. This act "recommends" that the governments set up by the British be rejected. If necessary, it states, new governments should be created. Massachusetts radical John Adams, the moving force behind this resolution, later claimed that it was the key move toward independence. But even as it calls for new governments, the resolution still refers to "these colonies," which suggests continued British control.

Common Sense—Yes and No

Americans were divided in their reaction to Thomas Paine's Common Sense.

Writing from Connecticut in March 1776, James Cogswell, in a letter to Joseph Ward, declared that *"Common Sense* has made many proselytes, and I believe will open the eyes of the common people." In Virginia, the wealthy Colonel Landon Carter similarly found many people who admired it. He, however, did not. He told one supporter in February that Paine's piece was "as rascally and nonsensical as possible." "It is quite scandalous," he had written earlier in his diary, "and disgraces the American cause much."

John Adams probably wrote this list of things that the Continental Congress needed to do while he was on his way to Philadelphia in early 1776. The last point is a "Declaration of Independency."

Whereas his Britannic Majesty, in conjunction with the lords and commons of Great Britain, has, by a late act of Parliament, excluded the inhabitants of these United Colonies from the protection of his crown; And whereas, no answer, whatever, to the humble petitions of the colonies for redress of grievances and reconciliation with Great Britain, has been or is likely to be given; but, the whole force of that kingdom, aided by foreign mercenaries, is to be exerted for the destruction of the good people of these colonies; And whereas, it appears absolutely irreconcileable to reason and good Conscience, for the people of these colonies now to take the oaths and affirmations necessary for the support of any government under the crown of Great Britain, and it is necessary that the exercise of every kind of authority under the said crown should be totally suppressed, and all the powers of government exerted, under the authority of the people of the colonies, for the preservation of internal peace, virtue, and good order, as well as for the defence of their lives, liberties, and properties, against the hostile invasions and cruel depredations of their enemies; therefore

Resolved, That it be recommended to the respective assemblies and conventions of the United Colonies, where no government sufficient to the exigencies of their affairs have been hitherto established, to adopt such government as shall, in the opinion of the representatives of the people, best conduce to the happiness and safety of their constituents in particular, and America in general.

For Governor William Franklin of New Jersey, the move toward political independence encouraged by his father Benjamin threatened his personal freedom. Governor Franklin's last-ditch attempt to reassert his authority over the colony by summoning the colony's legislature in mid-1776 led the provincial congress, a group that rejected British control, to pass these resolutions on June 14. The congress branded Franklin "an enemy to the liberties of this country." Three days later, the Patriot leaders posted guards outside his house; soon afterward they took him prisoner. William Franklin did not regain his liberty until late 1778.

Resolved, That in the opinion of this congress, the proclamation of William Franklin, esq. late governor of New Jersey, bearing date the thirtieth day of May last, in the name of the king of Great Britain, appointing a meeting of the general assembly, to be held on the twentieth of this instant, June, ought not to be obeyed.

Resolved, That, in the opinion of this congress, all payments of money on account of salary or otherwise, to the said William Franklin, esq. as governor, ought from henceforth, to cease; and that the treasurer or treasurers of this province, shall account for the monies in their hands to this congress, or to the future legislature of this colony.

By order of the congress,
SAMUEL TUCKER, President

After fighting as a soldier in the war, the painter Jonathan Trumbull decided that he would portray the scenes of the Revolution. His painting, which shows the committee that drafted the Declaration of Independence (which included Thomas Jefferson) submitting the document to Congress, was composed with the advice of Jefferson himself.

Free and Independent

As order crumbled in the colonies, the members of the Continental Congress believed independence was necessary. By the beginning of July 1776, delegates were ready to vote on whether the colonies should be "free and independent States." On the second day of July, Congress passed the vote. The next day, John Adams, who had seconded the motion for independence, wrote to his wife Abigail about the vote. His letter reveals the mixture of fear and excitement felt by supporters of independence. Adams believed that the decision to reject British control would be celebrated for years to come on July 2, when the actual vote for independence had taken place—not on the fourth of July (when it is commemorated today to celebrate Congress's approval of the Declaration of Independence).

Unanimous Resolution of the People of Ashby, Massachusetts, July 1, 1776

That should the honourable Congress, for the safety of the Colonies, declare them independent of *Great Britain*, the inhabitants of *Ashby* will solemnly engage with their lives and fortunes to support them in the measure.

Yesterday, the greatest question was decided, which ever was debated in America, and a greater, perhaps, never was nor will be decided among men. A resolution was passed without one dissenting colony, "that these United Colonies are, and of right ought to be, free and independent States, and as such they have, and of right ought to have, full power to make war, conclude peace, establish commerce, and to do all other acts and things which other States may rightfully do." You will see in a few days a Declaration setting forth the causes which have impelled us to this mighty revolution, and the reasons which justify it in the sight of God and man. A plan of confederation will be taken up in a few days. . . .

[T]he delay of this declaration to this time has many great advantages attending it. The hopes of reconciliation, which were fondly entertained by multitudes of honest and well-meaning, though weak and mistaken people, have been gradually and, at last, totally extinguished. Time has been given for the whole people maturely to consider the great question of independence, and to ripen their judgment, dissipate their fears, and allure their hopes, by discussing it in newspapers and pamphlets, by debating it in assemblies, conventions, committees of safety and inspection, in town and county meetings, as well as in private conversations, so that the whole people, in every colony of the thirteen, have now adopted it as their own act. This will cement the union, and avoid those heats, and perhaps convulsions, which might have been occasioned by such a declaration six months ago.

But the day is past. The second day of July, 1776, will be the most memorable epocha in the history of America. I am apt to believe that it will be celebrated by succeeding generations as the great anniversary festival. It ought to be commemorated, as the day of deliverance, by solemn acts of devotion to God Almighty. It ought to be solemnized with pomp and parade, with shows, games, sports, guns, bells, bonfires, and illuminations, from one end of this continent to the other, from this time forward, forevermore.

You will think me transported with enthusiasm, but I am not. I am well aware of the toil, and blood, and treasure, that it will cost us to maintain this declaration, and support and defended these States. Yet, through all the gloom, I can see the rays of ravishing light and glory. I can see that the end is more than worth all the means, and that posterity will triumph in that day's transaction, even although we should rue it, which I trust in God we shall not.

Although the vote of July 2, 1776, marked the actual break between Britain and the colonies, Congress believed it needed

to justify itself fully to both foreigners and the American people. This declaration of independence was so important that Congress appointed a committee to prepare it even before they formally debated the issue. The first draft of the document was written by Thomas Jefferson, who probably took only a day or two to complete the task. Then the committee and the entire Congress prepared the final version, which was passed on the fourth of July.

The Declaration of Independence is made up of three sections. The first section introduces independence by discussing the function of government and the right of revolution. Jefferson links general propositions about government (arguments that were widely accepted at the time) into a chain of arguments and applies them to America. This section of the Declaration, perhaps the least significant at the time, has since become the most important. Its assertion that "all men are created equal" originally referred to humans in the original state of nature before government, but since then it has become a powerful argument of attacking all sorts of inequalities.

A Declaration by the Representatives of the UNITED STATES OF AMERICA in General Congress assembled.

When in the course of human events it becomes necessary for one people to dissolve the political bands which have connected them with another, and to assume among the powers of the earth, the separate and equal station to which the laws of nature and of nature's god entitle them, a decent respect to the opinions of mankind requires that they should declare the causes which impel them to the separation.

We hold these truths to be self-evident; that all men are created equal; that they are endowed by their Creator with certain inalienable rights; that among these are life, liberty, and the pursuit of happiness; that to secure these rights, governments are instituted among men, deriving their just powers from the consent of the governed; that whenever any form of government becomes destructive of these ends, it is the right of the people to alter or to abolish it, and to institute new government, laying it's foundation on such principles, and organizing it's powers in such form as to them shall seem most likely to effect their safety and happiness. prudence indeed will dictate that governments long established should not be changed for light & transient causes, and accordingly all experience hath shewn, that mankind are more disposed

Revising the Declaration of Independence

In his handwritten copy of the Declaration of Independence, Thomas Jefferson recorded the changes made in the process of editing. The Declaration was considered first by the committee appointed for the purpose (some of the changes here may be in the handwriting of John Adams and Benjamin Franklin) and then by the entire Continental Congress. Jefferson continued to believe the committee's version was superior to the final document.

to suffer, while evils are sufferable, than to right themselves by abolishing the forms to which they are accustomed. but when a long train of abuses and usurpations, pursuing invariably the same object, evinces a design to reduce them under absolute despotism, it is their right, it is their duty, to throw off such government, & to provide new Guards for their future security. such has been the patient sufferance of these colonies; & such is now the necessity which constrains them to alter their former systems of government. the history of the present king of Great Britain is a history of repeated injuries and usurpations, all having in direct object the establishment of an absolute tyranny over these states. to prove this, let facts be submitted to a candid world.

Having laid a philosophical foundation, the Declaration then indicts the king for undermining American liberties. Jefferson notes a variety of grievances, some more clear and compelling than others. In this, he follows the example of a number of Patriot pronouncements that themselves were modeled on English predecessors.

He has refused his assent to laws, the most wholesome and necessary for the public good.

he has forbidden his governors to pass laws of immediate & pressing importance, unless suspended in their operation till his assent should be obtained; and when so suspended, he has utterly neglected to attend to them.

he has refused to pass other laws for the accommodation of large districts of people, unless those people would relinquish the right of representation in the legislature, a right inestimable to them, & formidable to tyrants only.

he has called together legislative bodies at places unusual, uncomfortable, & distant from the depository of their public records, for the sole purpose of fatiguing them into compliance with his measures.

he has dissolved Representative houses repeatedly, for opposing with manly firmness his invasions on the rights of the people.

he has refused for a long time, after such dissolutions, to cause others to be elected, whereby the legislative powers, incapable of annihilation, have returned to the people at large for their exercise, the state remaining in the meantime exposed to all the dangers of invasion from without, and convulsions within.

he has endeavored to prevent the population of these states; for that purpose obstructing the laws for naturalization of foreigners; refusing to pass others to encourage their migrations hither; & raising the conditions of new appropriations of lands.

he has obstructed the administration of justice by refusing his assent to laws for establishing judiciary powers.

he has made judges dependent on his will alone, for the tenure of their offices, and the amount & payment of their salaries.

he has erected a multitude of new offices, & sent hither swarms of officers to harrass our people, and eat out their substance.

he has kept among us, in time of peace, standing armies without the consent of our legislatures.

he has affected to render the military independent of, superior to, the civil power.

he has combined with others to subject us to a jurisdiction foreign to our constitution, and unacknowledged by our laws; giving his assent to their acts of pretended legislation

for quartering large bodies of armed troops among us;

for protecting them by a mock trial from punishment for any murders which they should commit on the inhabitants of these States;

for cutting off our trade with all parts of the world;

for imposing taxes on us without our consent;

for depriving us in many cases of the benefits of trial by jury;

for transporting us beyond seas to be tried for pretended offences;

for abolishing the free system of English laws in a neighbouring province, establishing therein an arbitrary government and enlarging its boundaries so as to render it at once an example & fit instrument for introducing the same absolute rule into these states.

for taking away our charters abolishing our most valuable laws, and altering fundamentally the forms of our governments;

for suspending our own legislatures, & declaring themselves invested with power to legislate for us in all cases whatsoever.

he has abdicated government here by declaring us out of his protection and waging war against us.

he has plundered our seas, ravaged our coasts, burnt our towns, and destroyed the lives of our people.

he is at this time transporting large armies of foreign mercenaries, to compleat the works of death, desolation & tyranny, already begun with circumstances of cruelty & perfidy scarcely paralleled in the most barbarous ages and totally unworthy the head of a civilized nation.

he has excited domestic insurrections amongst us, and has endeavoured to bring on the inhabitants of our frontiers, the merciless Indian savages, whose known rule of warfare is an undistinguished destruction of all ages, sexes and conditions.

he has constrained our fellow citizens taken captives on the high seas to bear arms against their country, to become the executioners of their friends & Brethren, or to fall themselves by their hands.

In every stage of these oppressions, we have petitioned for redress in the most humble terms; our repeated petitions have been answered only by repeated injury. a prince whose character is thus marked by every act which may define a tyrant, is unfit to be the ruler of a free people.

Nor have we been wanting in attentions to our Brittish brethren. We have warned them from time to time of attempts by their legislature to extend an unwarrantable jurisdiction over us. we have reminded them of the circumstances of our emigration and settlement here, we have appealed to their native justice & magnanimity, and we have conjured them by the tyes of our common kindred, to disavow these usurpations, which would inevitably interrupt our connections & correspondence. they too have been deaf to the voice of justice and of consanguinity; we must therefore acquiesce in the necessity which denounces our separation, and hold them, as we hold the rest of mankind, enemies in war, in peace friends.

The Declaration concludes with the Congressional resolution of independence that Congress had voted on two days earlier. It brings together the philosophic abstractions of the first part with the concrete grievances of the second to argue the necessity for independence.

We therefore the representatives of the United states of America, in General Congress assembled, appealing to the supreme judge of the world for the rectitude of our intentions, do, in the name, and by authority of the good people of these colonies, solemnly publish and declare, that these united colonies are and of right ought to be free and independent states; that they are absolved from all allegiance to the British Crown, and that all political connection between them and the state of Great Britain is & ought to be totally dissolved; & that as free and independent states, they have full power to levy war, conclude peace, contract alliances, establish commerce, & to do all other acts and things which independent states may of right do. And for the support of this declaration, with a firm reliance on the protection of divine providence, we mutually pledge to each other our lives, our fortunes and our sacred honor.

Charles Willson Peale painted a portrait of George Washington at the battle of Princeton in 1779. A year later, he made this engraving from a part of the painting. Keenly aware of his role as the symbol of the Revolution, Washington spent many hours posing for portraits, even during the war.

I beg it may be remembered, by every gentleman in this room, that I, this day, declare with the utmost sincerity, I do not think myself equal to the command I am honored with.

—George Washington's speech to the Continental Congress, June 16, 1775

Was Washington Good Enough?

Simply declaring independence was not enough. Americans had to win the war with Great Britain, which was determined to bring the colonies back into the empire. The primary means of American's resistance to the British was the Continental Army headed by George Washington. Washington was appointed commander in chief of the new army by Congress in June 1775. He remained in office until the war was won, more than eight years later. Among Washington's gifts was an imposing physical presence. Benjamin Rush was one of the many who found him impressive, going so far as to suggest in this October 1775 letter that other European leaders resembled personal servants by comparison.

General Washington has astonished his most intimate friends with a display of the most wonderful talents for the government of an army. His zeal, his disinterestedness, his activity, his politeness, and his manly behavior to General Gage in their late correspondence have captivated the hearts of the public and his friends. He seems to be one of those illustrious heroes whom providence raises up once in three or four hundred years to save a nation from ruin. If you do not know his person, perhaps you will be pleased to hear that he has so much martial dignity in his deportment that you would distinguish him to be a general and a soldier from among ten thousand people. There is not a king in Europe that would not look like a valet de chambre by his side.

Even George Washington's undeniable charm, however, could not convince Americans to support the army adequately. This September 1776 letter from Washington to the president of Congress John Hancock explains the problems of getting and keeping soldiers in the Continental Army. Writing from the Heights of Harlem (now a part of New York City, but then north of the city's boundaries), the general also reveals his lack of confidence in the local militias that often provided the army with backup support. Although recent historians have begun to recognize the militia's political and military contributions more fully, the lack of discipline and reliability among these volunteers seemed at the time to undermine Washington's goal of creating an effective fighting force that could survive a long war against the more experienced and better-supplied British army.

When Men are irritated [excited], and the Passions inflamed, they fly hastely and chearfully to Arms; but after the first emotions are over, to expect, among such People, as compose the bulk of an Army, that they are influenced by any other principles than those of Interest, is to look for what never did, and I fear never will happen; the Congress will deceive themselves therefore if they expect it.

A Soldier reasoned with upon the goodness of the cause he is engaged in, and the inestimable rights he is contending for, hears you with patience, and acknowledges the truth of your observations, but adds, that it is of no more Importance to him than others. The Officer makes you the same reply, with this further remark, that his pay will not support him, and he cannot ruin himself and Family to serve his Country, when every Member of the community is equally Interested and benefitted by his Labours. The few therefore, who act upon Principles of disinterestedness, are, comparatively speaking, no more than a drop in the Ocean. It becomes evidently clear then, that as this Contest is not likely to

In a letter to Congress on September 24, 1776, Washington begins by noting that the term of service for almost the entire army would soon expire. If Congress did not offer solders more money, he warned, few would re-enlist.

The Spoils of War

Plundering—taking food, supplies, and other valuables— from enemies, and even friends, had long been an important fringe benefit for soldiers. During the Revolution, military leaders on both sides worked hard to stop the practice. On January 1, 1777, Washington issued this order (and encouraged its reprinting in newspapers).

His Excellency General WASHINGTON strictly forbids all the officers and soldiers of the Continental army, of the militia, and all recruiting parties, plundering any person whatsoever, whether Tories or others. The effects of such persons will be applied to public uses in a regular manner, and it is expected that humanity and tenderness to women and children will distinguish brave Americans, contending for liberty, from infamous mercenary ravagers, whether British or Hessians.

British and German troops were even more notorious for such thefts. British General James Robertson told a Parliamentary hearing about rumors that the Hessians (mercenary German troops hired by the British Crown) had been promised "great plunder" by their leaders. Robertson also testified about the plundering that occurred after his arrival in Long Island and New York City.

I found in all the farms, the poultry, cows, and farm stocked; when I passed sometime afterwards, I found nothing alive.

be the Work of a day; as the War must be carried on systematically, and to do it, you must have good Officers, there are, in my Judgment, no other possible means to obtain them but by establishing your Army upon a permanent footing; and giving your Officers good pay. . . .

With respect to the Men, nothing but a good bounty can obtain them upon a permanent establishment; and for no shorter time than the continuance of the War, ought they to be engaged; as Facts incontestibly prove, that the difficulty, and cost of Inlistments, increase with time. . . . I shall therefore take the freedom of giving it as my opinion, that a good Bounty be immediately offered, aided by the proffer of at least 100, or 150 Acres of Land and a suit of Cloaths and Blankt, to each non-Comd. Officer and Soldier; as I have good authority for saying, that however high the Men's pay may appear, it is barely sufficient in the present scarcity and dearness of all kinds of goods, to keep them in Cloaths, much less afford support to their Families. . . .

To place any dependance upon Militia, is, assuredly, resting upon a broken staff. Men just dragged from the tender Scenes of domestick life; unaccustomed to the din of Arms; totally unacquainted with every kind of Military skill, which being followed by a want of confidence in themselves, when opposed to Troops regularly train'd, disciplined, and appointed, superior in knowledge, and superior in Arms, makes them timid, and ready to fly from their own shadows. Besides, the sudden change in their manner of living, (particularly in the lodging) brings on sickness in many; impatience in all, and such an unconquerable desire of returning to their respective homes that it not only produces shameful, and scandalous Desertions among themselves, but infuses the like spirit in others. Again, Men accustomed to unbounded freedom, and no controul, cannot brook the Restraint which is indispensably necessary to the good order and Government of an Army; without which, licentiousness, and every kind of disorder triumphantly reign. To bring Men to a proper degree of Subordination, is not the work of a day, a Month or even a year; and unhappily for us, and the cause we are Engaged in, the little discipline I have been labouring to establish in the Army under my immediate Command, is in a manner done away by having such a mixture of Troops as have been called together within these few Months.

Not only enlisting Continental soldiers, but supplying them with food, clothing, and equipment proved to be difficult.

Washington spent a good deal of his time encouraging members of Congress and state governments to provide for the army adequately. The difficulties he faced can be seen in this December 1779 letter to the governor of Delaware.

SIR—The situation of the army with respect to supplies, is beyond description alarming. It has been five or six weeks past on half allowance, and we have not more than three days bread, at a third allowance, on hand, nor any where within reach. When this is exhausted, we must depend on the precarious gleanings of the neighboring country. Our magazines are absolutely empty everywhere, and our commissaries entirely destitute of money or credit to replenish them. We have never experienced a like extremity at any period of the war. We have often felt temporary want from an accidental delay in forwarding supplies, but we always had something in our magazines and the means of procuring more. Neither one nor the other is at present the case.

This representation is the result of a minute examination of our resources. Unless some extraordinary and immediate exertions be made by the states from which we draw our supplies, there is every appearance that the army will infallibly disband in a fortnight.

As early as the end of 1776, a number of American leaders questioned Washington's military leadership (including those such as Benjamin Rush, who previously had been an enthusiastic supporter). The Americans had succeeded in driving the British troops from Boston, but as the war moved to New York, New Jersey, and Pennsylvania, Washington was much less effective. In this November 1776 letter from Adjutant General Joseph Reed to General Charles Lee, Reed complains about Washington's indecisiveness and suggests, without saying so openly, that Lee, a gifted British-born officer, could lead the army better than Washington.

Lee responded by agreeing with Reed, which created difficulties for the two. Washington had been waiting for a message from Lee, whose troops Washington needed to halt the American retreat. When the letter from Lee to Reed arrived, an anxious Washington opened it and discovered the plot. Although the angered Washington at first demanded Reed's resignation, Washington eventually asked him to stay on. The attacks on Washington's leadership, however, continued for another two years.

British plundering of American possessions remained in the popular imagination long after the war. This illustration appeared in a 1795 book.

The letter you will receive with this contains my Sentiments with Respect to your present Station: But besides this I have some additional Reasons for most earnestly wishing to have you where the principal Scene of Action is laid. I do not mean to flatter, nor praise you at the Expence of any other, but I confess I do think that it is entirely owing to you that this Army & the liberties of America so far as they are dependant on it are not totally cut off. You have Decision, a Quality often wanting in Minds otherwise valuable & I ascribe to this our Escape from York Island—from Kingsbridge & the Plains—& I have no Doubt had you been here the Garrison at Mount Washington would now have composed a Part of this Army. Under all these Circumstances I confess I ardently wish to see you removed from a Place where I think there will be little Call for your Judgment and Experience to the Place where they are like to be so necessary. Nor am I singular in my Opinion—every Gentleman of the Family the Officers & soldiers generally have a confidence in you—the enemy constantly inquire where you are, & seem to me to be less confident when you are present. . . .

General Washington's own Judgment [about the battle at Mount Washington], seconded by Representations from us, would I believe have saved the Men & their Arms but unluckily, General Greene's Judg[ment] was contrary this kept the General's Mind in a State of Suspence till the Stroke was struck—Oh! General—an indecisive Mind is one of the greatest Misfortunes that can befall an Army—how often have I lamented it this Campaign.

All Circumstances considered we are in a very awful & alarming state one that requires the utmost Wisdom and Firmness of Mind—as soon as the Season will admit I think yourself & some others should go to Congress & form the Plan of the new Army—point out their Defects to them and if possible prevail on them to bind their whole Attention to this great Object—even to the Exclusion of every other—If they will not or cannot do this, I fear all our Exertions will be in vain in this Part of the World."

Little Successes—and Big Ones

Although Washington continued to lose battles, he succeeded in winning the war. Ironically, this ultimate success was largely due to the cautiousness many complained about. As Washington argued to Congress, "We should on all Occasions avoid a general Action, or put anything to the Risque, unless compelled by a necessity." This strategy perhaps led to some

missed opportunities, but it also avoided many major losses and allowed the Continental Army to continue fighting. This astute assessment of the commander's strategy was written in late 1777 by Albigence Waldo, a Connecticut surgeon, during the middle of the roughest winter of the war, when the army was encamped at Valley Forge, Pennsylvania.

December 26[, 1777]

Many Country Gentlemen in the interior parts of the States who get wrong information of the Affairs & state of our Camp, are very much Surprized at G^l Washington's delay to drive off the Enemy, being falsely inform'd that his Army consists of double the Number of the Enemy's. . . . Impartial Truth in future History will clear up these points, and reflect lasting honour on the Wisdom & prudence of G^{enl} Washington. The greatest Number of Continental Troops that have been with his Excell^y this Campaign, never consisted of more than Eleven thousand; and the great Number of Militia in the field at Once were not more than 2000. Yet these accounts are exaggerated to 50 or 60,000. Howe, by the best, and most authentic Accounts has never had less than 10,000. If then, Genl Washington, by Opposing little more than an equal Number of young Troops, to Old Veterans has kept his Ground in general, Cooped them up in the City, prevented their making any considerable inroads upon him, Killed and wounded any considerable number of them in different Skirmishes, and made many proselytes to the Shrine of Liberty by these little successes, and by the prudence, calmness, sedateness & wisdom with which he facilitates all his Opperations. This being the case, and his not having wantonly thrown away the lives of his Soldiers, but reserved them for another Campaign (if another should Open in the Spring) which is of the utmost consequence This then cannot be called an Inglorious Campaign. If he had risk'd a General Battle, and should have proved unsuccessfull, what in the name of Heaven would have been our case this Day.

Right from the start of the war, France, a long-time opponent of Britain, provided secret aid to the American cause. This alliance became formal and public, however, only after the decisive American victory in the October 1777 Battle of Sara-toga. On February 6, 1778, the French government signed two treaties with the new United States. The Treaty of Amity and Commerce assured favorable treatment of American commerce. The accompanying Treaty of Alliance

By ORDER of His Excellency
Sir William Howe, K. B.
General and Commander in Chief, &c. &c. &c.

PROCLAMATION.

I DO hereby give Notice to the Inhabitants of the City of Philadelphia and its Environs, it is the Order of His Excellency, that " No Perfon whatever, living " within the faid City and its Environs, fhall appear in " the Streets between the Beating of the Tattoo, at Half " an Hour after Eight o'Clock in the Evening, and the " Revellie in the Morning, without Lanthorns: And all " who fhall be found abroad, within the Time aforefaid, " will be liable to be examined by the Patroles, and con- " fined, unlefs they fhall give a fatisfactory Account of " themfelves." And I do hereby enjoin and require the Inhabitants, and all others refiding in the faid City and its Environs, to pay ftrict Obedience to the faid Order, and govern themfelves accordingly.

Given under my Hand at Philadelphia, this 9th Day of January, in the Eighteenth Year of His Majefty's Reign.   JOS. GALLOWAY,
                                        Superintendent-General.

In this proclamation, the British imposed a curfew on occupied Philadelphia. Only people with lanterns (and thus visible to the guards) could travel at night.

sealed the military partnership. As the articles included here show, the Treaty of Alliance promised French support for the war until American independence was won and made careful provision for territories gained during the conflict. The favorable terms offered to the Americans (including France renouncing its claim to Canada) suggest that France's primary goal was to weaken Great Britain, a common enemy, rather than gain economic or territorial advantage.

The most Christian King and the United States of North America, to wit, New Hampshire, Massachusetts Bay, Rhode Island, Connecticut, New York, New Jersey, Pennsylvania, Delaware, Maryland, Virginia, North Carolina, South Carolina & Georgia, having this day concluded a Treaty of Amity & Commerce for the reciprocal advantage of their Subjects and Citizens, have thought it necessary to take into consideration the means of strengthening those engagements and of rendering them useful to the safety and tranquility of the two parties. . . .

Article 1   If war should break out between France & Great Britain during the continuance of the present war between the United States and England, his Majesty and the said United States shall make it a common cause and aid each other mutually with their good Offices, their counsels and their forces according to the exigence of conjunctures, as becomes good and faithful Allies.

Art 2d   The essential and direct end of the present defensive Alliance is to maintain effectually the liberty, sovereignty and independence absolute and unlimited of the said United States as well in matters of government as of Commerce. . . .

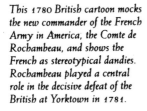

This 1780 British cartoon mocks the new commander of the French Army in America, the Comte de Rochambeau, and shows the French as stereotypical dandies. Rochambeau played a central role in the decisive defeat of the British at Yorktown in 1781.

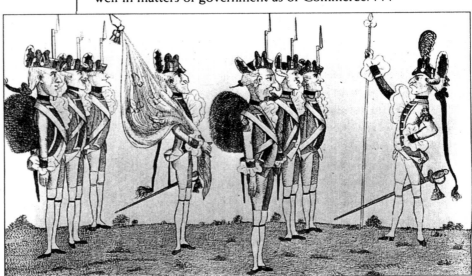

Art 5th If the United States should think fit to attempt the reduction of the British power remaining in the northern parts of America or the islands of Bermudas, those Countries or islands in case of success shall be confederated with or dependent upon the said United States.

Art 6th The most Christian King renounces forever the possession of the Islands of Bermudas as well as of any part of the Continent of North America which before the Treaty of Paris in 1763 or in virtue of that Treaty were acknowledged to belong to the Crown of Great Britain or to the United States heretofore called British Colonies or which are at this time or have lately been under the power of the King and Crown of Great Britain.

Art 7th If his Most Christian Majesty shall think proper to attack any of the islands situated in the Gulph of Mexico or near the Gulph, which are at present under the power of Great Britain, all the said isles in case of success shall appertain to the Crown of France.

Art 8th Neither of the two parties shall conclude either truce or peace with Great Britain without the formal consent of the other first obtained, and they mutually engage not to lay down their arms until the independence of the United States shall have been formally or tacitly assured by the Treaty or Treaties that shall terminate the War.

Although the French military forces in America seldom helped American troops directly, the two forces worked together to win the battle of Yorktown, Virginia, in October 1781. The victory convinced British leaders that they could not win back the colonies. Within six months, Prime Minister Lord North, a central supporter of the war, resigned and his successor began peace negotiations with the French and the Americans. The memoirs of Sir Nathaniel W. Wraxall, describe the impact the defeat at Yorktown had on the highest levels of the British government. Wraxall, a member of Parliament, notes the reception of the news by Prime Minister Lord North and Secretary of State for the Colonies Lord George Germain. This account begins after Germain learned the news on November 25 and informs other members of the government, including the prime (or "first") minister.

The First Minister's firmness, and even his presence of mind which had withstood the [Gordon] riots of 1780, gave way for a short time, under this awful disaster. I asked lord George afterwards,

On October 19, 1781, General Cornwallis and his 7,157 men officially surrendered to General Washington. This engraving is based on a painting by Jonathan Trumbull. At the center, a British officer delivers his commander's sword to General Benjamin Lincoln. Washington had refused to accept it because it was not given by his counterpart, General Cornwallis.

how he took the communication, when made to him. "As he would have taken a ball in the breast," replied lord George. "For he opened his arms, exclaiming wildly, as he paced up and down the apartment during a few minutes, "Oh God! it is all over!" Words he repeated many times, under emotions of the deepest agitation and distress. . . .

I dined on that day at Lord George's, and though the information which had reached London in the course of the morning from two different quarters was of a nature not to admit of long concealment, yet it had not been communicated either to me or to any individual of the company . . . .

[After dinner] Lord George having acquainted us that from Paris information had just arrived of the old Count de Maurepas, first minister, lying at the point of death, "It would grieve me," said I, "to finish my career, however far advanced in years, were I first minister of France, before I had witnessed the termination of this great contest between England and America."

"He has survived to see that event," replied lord George, with some agitation. . . .

"My meaning," said I, "is that if I were the Count de Maurepas, I should wish to live long enough to behold the final issue of the war in Virginia."

"He has survived to witness it completely," answered Lord George. "The army has surrendered, and you may peruse the particulars of the capitulation in that paper," taking at the same time one from his pocket, which he delivered into my hand not without visible emotion.

Published in 1781, before the end of the war, this poem by the poet and newspaper editor Philip Freneau humorously pretends to recite "an ancient Prophecy." The figures mentioned include King George III (of the House of Hanover) and General Gage (rhyming with cage). The initials B and C refer to generals Burgoyne and Cornwallis; "The Stars and the Lily" represent America and France respectively; and the lion symbolizes Britain.

When a certain great king, whose initial is G.
Shall force stamps upon paper, and folks to drink tea;
When these folks burn his tea and stampt paper, like stubble,
You may guess that this king is then coming to trouble.
But when a petition he treads under his feet,
And sends over the ocean an army and fleet;
When that army, half starv[e]d, and frantic with rage,
Shall be cooped up with a leader whose name rhymes to cage;
When that leader goes home dejected and sad,
You may then be assured the king's prospects are bad.
But when B. and C. with their armies are taken,
This king will do well if he saves his own bacon.
In the year seventeen hundred and eighty and two,
A stroke he shall get that will make him look blue;
In the years eighty-three, eighty-four, eighty-five,
You hardly shall know that the king is alive;
In the year eighty-six the affair will be over,
And he shall eat turnips that grow in Hanover.
The face of the lion shall then become pale,
He shall yield fifteen teeth, and be sheared of his tail.
O king, my dear king, you shall be very sore;
The Stars and the Lily shall run you on shore,
And your Lion shall growl—but never bite more.

Chapter Three

Taking Sides
The Experience of War

On July 4, 1776, the day Congress approved the Declaration of Independence, Cadwallader Colden, Jr., also made a declaration—against independence. Colden, the eldest son of New York's former acting governor and a devout member of the Church of England, had spent a troubled night praying and meditating about his situation. In the morning, he appeared before the Patriot's county committee and spoke boldly against what he considered an illegal rebellion. The committee's actions, he argued, led toward "independency, which he should ever oppose with all his might, and wished to the Lord that his name might be entered as opposed to the matter, and be handed down to the latest posterity, to show them his disapprobation of it." But, despite these strong convictions, Colden also promised not to act on them while the war continued. His careful distinction between words and deeds did not convince the committee. When Colden refused to sign an oath obliging him to take arms against the British, the committee sentenced him to jail. Colden spent the next two years in and out of custody before being banished to British-held territory.

As Colden's experiences suggest, taking a stand on the Revolution could have dangerous consequences. These potentially fatal decisions involved a variety of considerations: political philosophy, religious conviction, family loyalty, and even outright force. For Native Americans and some African-American slaves, these issues could be particularly problematic. Their interests usually lay fully with neither side, yet their support (or at least their acquiescence) was sought by both.

But as Colden tried to tell the committee in 1776, deeply held convictions did not necessarily lead to actions, and as leaders of both sides recognized, actions would decide the fate of "independency." Just as troubling, choices about the Revolution did not always work out as people intended. Chance, as well as choice, also shaped people's fate.

Americans in the Revolution fought not only with Britain but with themselves. This illustration of a contentious town meeting was prepared in the 1790s for a Revolutionary-era poem, "M'Fingal," which mocked the Tories.

Soldiers and civilians were often caught up in the Revolution whether they wanted to be or not. Their experiences reveal that the impact of the war went far beyond changes in government.

Problems of Loyalty

Even during the Revolution, Benjamin Rush, the Philadelphia physician who signed the Declaration of Independence, recognized that people could not be categorized as simply being for or against the Revolution. Within each side, a range of motivations and enthusiasms inspired various positions and attitudes. Although Rush's analysis, originally prepared during the Revolution and revised afterward, clearly favors independence, he also criticizes both sides. Like other revolutionaries, Rush called the American Loyalists Tories and the Patriots Whigs. These terms used the names of eighteenth-century Britain's two political parties. Tories had traditionally been more supportive of Crown power; Whigs had generally spoken more about liberty. Rush also notes that many people supported neither side.

I had frequent occasion to observe that Tories and Whigs were actuated by very different motives in their conduct, or by the same motives acting in different degrees of force. The following classes of each of them was published by me in the early stages of the war, in Dunlap's paper. There were Tories (1) from the attachment to power and office. (2) From an attachment to the British commerce which the war had interrupted or annihilated. (3) From an attachment to kingly government. (4) From an attachment to the hierarchy of the Church of England, which is was supposed would be abolished in America by her seperation [sic] from Great Britain. This motive acted chiefly upon the Episcopal clergy, more especially in the Eastern states. (5) From a dread of the power of the country being transferred into the hands of the Presbyterians. This motive acted upon many of the Quakers in Pennsylvania and New Jersey, and upon the Episcopalians in several of those states where they had been in possession of power, or of a religious establishment.

It cannot be denied, but that private and personal consideration actuated some of those men who took a part in favor of the American Revolution. There were Whigs (1) from a desire of possessing, or at least sharing, in the power of our country. It was said

[M]any of the children of Tory parents were Whigs.
—Benjamin Rush, an essay written in 1777

there were Whigs (2) from an expectation that a war with Great Britain would cancel all British debts. There certainly are Whigs (3) from the facility with which the tender laws enabled debtors to pay their creditors in depreciated paper money. (4) A few men were Whigs from ancient or hereditary hostility to persons, or families who were Tories. But the great majority of the people who took part with their country were Whigs (5) from a sincere and disinterested love of liberty and justice.

Both parties differed as much from their conduct as they did in the motives which actuated them. There were (1) furious Tories who had recourse to violence, and even to arms, to oppose the measures of the Whigs. (2) Writing and talking Tories. (3) Silent but busy Tories in disseminating Tory pamphlets and news papers and in circulating intelligence. (4) Peaceable and conscientious Tories who patiently submitted to the measures of the governing powers, and who shewed nearly equal kindness to the distressed of both parties during the war.

The Whigs were divided by their conduct into (1) Furious Whigs, who considered the tarring and feathering of a Tory as a greater duty and exploit than the extermination of a British army. These men were generally cowards, and shrunk from danger when called into the field by pretending sickness or some family disaster. (2) Speculating Whigs. These men infested our public councils, as well as the army, and did the country great mischief. A colonel of a regiment informed a friend of mine that he had made a great deal of money by buying poor horses for his waggon, and selling them again for a large profit after he had fattened them at the public expense. (3) Timid Whigs. The hopes of these people rose and fell with every victory and defeat of our armies. (4) Staunch Whigs. These were moderate in their tempers, but firm, inflexible, and persevering in their conduct. There was, besides these two classes of people, a great number of persons who were neither Whigs nor Tories. They had no fixed principles and accommodated their conduct to their interest, to events, and to their company. They were not without their uses. They protected both parties in many instances from the rage of each other, and each party always found hospitable treatment from them.

Perhaps the inhabitants of the United States might have divided nearly into three classes, viz. Tories, Whigs, and persons who were neither Whigs nor Tories. The Whigs constituted the largest class. The 3rd class were a powerful reinforcement to them after the affairs of America assumed a uniformly prosperous appearance.

I fear I Shall not Retreve the time and other losses Occas'd by that—I allmost Said Cursed Rebellion, Now Calld Glorious Revolution, as I sincerely now wish it may Ever prove to be, tho' I can't yet help thinking that we might have been happie at th[i]s Day, had we remained as we were.

—Cadwallader Colden, Jr.,
a letter to Henry Von Schaack,
June 13, 1790

Cadwallader Colden, Jr., had been an important target of New York Whigs, even before facing the county committee in July 1776. Although he neither supported Royal troops nor organized opposition to the Revolution, he posed a clear threat to the American cause as the son of an acting royal governor and a loud advocate of the British side. A little more than a year after the July meeting, he wrote this complaint about the Revolution and how it had treated him. During that time he had been jailed, allowed to return to his home (although not to visit his dying father in British-held New York City), and sentenced to be detained in Boston, a decision that was reversed. He was later jailed again aboard a prison ship, where he wrote this statement on August 7, 1777. The harassment continued. Within the next year, he would be freed, then placed under house arrest in a remote part of New York, and finally, almost a year after this statement, banished to New York City. His experiences reveal both the Patriots' desire to restrict loyalism to Britain and the difficulties of creating a consistent and clear means of doing so.

I have ever been opposed to any such measures as I thought were brought about with no other View but to advance this Grand Scheem of Independency or Republick Govern^t which (if Confirm'd), however it may gratify the Ambitions and Malignant Views of Some men, will never Leave the Country at Large so happy a People as they were and might for Ages have Remain'd, . . .

For professing these Sentements I have been abused, Insulted, threatened with distruction of Body & Estate, Imprisoned and Condemned to Banishment unless I would take the oath of Alegence to Imaginary State. This I have Refused to do in as Modest, but as positive Terms as I could, at the same time willing to give any Security for my Remaining Nuture [neutral] during the present Disputes. Yet still the Oath is now urged upon me Tho' I have Declared that, should I be vile enough to take it, I should not think myself bound by it.—And nothwithstanding this Declaration I am Yet now Promised that if I will but take the Oath I shall Remain with my Family Quiet and Undisturbed. Temptations great indeed. (But that I may not be Led into *Temptations* is my Daily Prayer.) Shall I now to Avoid a Little temperary Uneasyness and Inconveniency, Give the Lye to all my former Conduct and even appeal to the Majesty of Heaven to confirm this Lye?—God forbid!—Sho[ck]ing thought that one

Christian Can Expect this from another!—No, the Idea of being torn from my family, Distressing as it was to me, never suggested such a thought. And now that the Temptation is Less and that it has Pleased God to put it into their Hearts to Let me Remove with my Family, Resolved In the Name of God Let Me Go.

By the end of the war, the large majority of Americans supported the Revolution. Only about one-fifth had remained loyal to the king and some sixty to eighty thousand Americans had left the country. Things had been different earlier. At the beginning of the war, most Americans had hoped to stay neutral, refraining from taking any position at all. Among them was the Bostonian John Rowe. He was a wealthy merchant, owner of one of the ships involved in the Boston Tea Party, and a respected community leader. Yet in the earliest part of the war, he had been unwilling to support either side fully.

These entries from his diary trace his attitudes and actions from the beginning of the war in April 1775 to the end of British occupation of Boston the following year. During that time, Rowe socialized with British officers, sought to defend his goods from British soldiers after failing to get them and himself out of Boston, and then welcomed the arrival of the American Army. The selections end with Rowe's experience at the funeral of Joseph Warren, one of the first Patriot heroes of the Revolution. Warren had been killed at the Battle of Bunker Hill. When his body was found in an unmarked grave after the British occupation, it received a large, public burial. As a leader among Boston's Freemasons—an organization that included many leading members of the community—John Rowe was invited to march in the procession for Warren, a fellow member. The crowd reaction suggests that Rowe's attempt to remain on good terms with both sides had not gone unnoticed.

April 19. [1775] Last night the Grenadiers & Light Companies belonging to the several Regiments in this Town were ferry'd over Charles River & landed on Phipps Farm in Cambridge from whence they Proceeded on their way to Concord, where they arrived early this day. . . . A General Battle ensued which from what I can learn was Supported with Great Spirit on both Sides & continued untill the Kings Troops got back to Charlestown which was near Sunset.

In this 1790s engraving, an unruly crowd attacks a Loyalist. Rowdy, violent, and even cruel actions in the streets were as much a part of the Revolution as high-minded political discussions in print.

BOSTON

CHARLES TOWN

In this engraving from a 1780s English history book, the British burns Charlestown during their attack on Bunker Hill in 1775. British insensitivity to civilians during the war helped encourage support for the Americans.

Numbers were killed & wounded on Both Sides. . . . This Unhappy affair is a Shocking Introduction to all the Miseries of a Civil War.

April 27. [1775] The General has given Leave for All People to leave the Town that Choose with their Effects.

April 28. This day I apply'd to get a Pass to go out with my Effects but could not prevail.

Dec. 31. Thus endeth the Year 1775, a most fatal year for this Part of America.

12 Jan'y. [1776] I paid [British] Adm^l Shouldham a Visit this morning who is a Genteel man & Received me Politely.

Mar. 11. This morning I Rose very early & very luckily went to my warehouse—when I came there I found Mr Crian Brush with an Order & party from the Genl who were just going to Break Open the Warehouse which I prevented by sending for the Keys & Opening of the Doors. They took from me to the Value of Twenty Two hundred & Sixty Pounds Sterling according to the best Calculations I could make, in Linens, Checks, Cloths & Woolens. This Party behaved very Insolently & with Great Rapacity & I am very well Convinced, exceeding their orders to a Great Degree. They stole many things & plundered my Store. Words cannot Describe it.

Mar. 12. A Continual Fire from Both sides this night. They are hurrying off all their Provisions & destroying & mangling all Navigation, also Large Quantitys of Salt & other things they heave into the Sea & scuttle the stores. The Inhabitants are greatly terrified & alarmed for Fear of Greater Evils when the Troops leave this distressed Place.

Mar. 13. "The Confusion still continues & Plundering of Houses &c Increasing. Genl Robinson paid me a visit & eat a morsel of Provisions. . . . The Sailors from the Ships have Broke open my stores on my wharff & plundered them.

Mar. 17. This morning the [British] Troops evacuated the Town . . . . About Noon [American] Genl Putnam & some Troops came into Town to the Great Joy of the Inhabitants that Remained behind.

Mar. 19. Genl Washington & his Retinue were in Town yesterday, I did not hear of it otherwise should have paid my Respects & waited on him.

Mar. 26. After dinner I went with Mr. Parker & paid My Respects to Generall Washington who Received us very Politely.

Mar. 31. I gave Genl Washington an Invitation to dine who Returned with me a very Polite Answer.

April 8. Afternoon I went by invitation of Brother Webb to attend the Funeral of the Remains of Dr. Warren & went accordingly to the Council Chamber with a Design to Attend & Walk in Procession with the Lodges under my Jurisdiction with our Proper Jewells & Cloathing but to my great mortification was very much Insulted by some furious & hot Persons with^o the Least Provocation one of Brethren thought it most Prudent for me to Retire. I accordingly did so—this has caused some Uneasy Reflections in my mind as I am not Conscious to myself of doing anything Prejudicial to the Cause of America either by will or deed.

Friends, Families, and Fighting

The Revolution divided families as well as communities. Although Benjamin Franklin became a key leader in the Revolution, his son William, governor of New Jersey, remained loyal to the crown. As a result, William was imprisoned from June 1776 to October 1778. During this time, his father made no effort to help or even contact him. Benjamin Franklin left Pennsylvania to represent the American cause in France near

the end of 1776, taking William's son with him. When the former New Jersey governor was finally released from custody, he became a leader among American Loyalists. He moved to England before the war ended. In 1784, he wrote to his father. He explained he could not admit to having been wrong because he had "*always* acted from a Strong Sense of what I conceived my Duty to my King and Regard to my Country." Still he hoped to renew their formerly close relationship. The father's reply, written from Passy, outside Paris, in August of the same year was ambiguous. The father and son saw each other only once more in England during 1785. It was a short and unpleasant meeting.

Passy, Aug. 16, 1784

Dear Son,

I received your Letter of the 22d past, and am glad to find that you desire to revive the affectionate Intercourse, that formerly existed between us. It will be very agreeable to me; indeed nothing has ever hurt me so much and affected me with such keen Sensations, as to find myself deserted in my old Age by my only Son; and not only deserted, but to find him taking up Arms against me, in a Cause, wherein my good Fame, Fortune and Life were all at Stake. You conceived, you say, that your Duty to your King and Regard for your Country requir'd this. I ought not to blame you for differing in Sentiment with me in Public Affairs. We are Men, all subject to Errors. Our Opinions are not in our own Power; they are form'd and govern'd much by Circumstances, that are often as inexplicable as they are irresistible. Your Situation was such that few would have censured your remaining Neuter, *tho' there are Natural Duties which precede political ones, and cannot be extinguish'd by them.*

This is a disagreable Subject. I drop it. And we will endeavour, as you propose mutually to forget what has happened relating to it, as well as we can. I send your Son over to pay his Duty to you. You will find him much improv'd. He is greatly esteem'd and belov'd in this Country, and will make his Way anywhere. . . .

I shall be glad to see you when convenient, but would not have you come here at present. You may confide to your son the Family Affairs you wished to confer upon with me, for he is discre[e]t. And I trust, that you will prudently avoid introducing him to Company, that it may be improper for him to be seen with. I shall hear from you by him and any letters to me afterwards, will come safe under

Patriot *vs.* Loyalist

Patriot John Jay wrote to his Loyalist friend Peter Van Schaack on September 17, 1782.

Your judgment and consequently your conscience differed from mine on a very important question; but though, as an independent American, I considered all who were not for us, and you among the rest, as against us, yet be assured that John Jay did not cease to be a friend to Peter Van Schaack. . . . [I]t became our duty to take one side or the other, and no man is to be blamed for preferring the one which his reason recommended as the most just and virtuous.

MAGNA *Britannia: her Colonies* REDUC'D

This cartoon, created by Benjamin Franklin during the Stamp Act crisis, suggests that forcing the colonies to obey the new British measures would only injure Britain itself (in Latin Magna Britannia). The severed arm in the foreground holds an olive branch, symbolizing the colonies' desire for peace.

Cover directed to Mr. Ferdinand Grand, Banker at Paris. Wishing you Health, and more Happiness than it seems you have lately experienced, I remain your affectionate father,

B. Franklin.

The Loyalist Jonathan Boucher's account of his attempt to preach a sermon reveals the passions engaged on both sides of the Revolution. Boucher had come to America as a tutor for a rich Virginia family in 1759. He later became a minister of the Church of England, which became the American Episcopal Church after the Revolution. The dramatic incident described here took place in Maryland during 1775, where he had moved five years earlier. The colony's Whig governor had proclaimed a fast, calling on people to refrain from eating in order to concentrate public's attention on religion— and on British oppression. Mr. Harrison, Boucher's Whig assistant, planned to preach on the occasion. But Boucher decided to give the sermon himself. Soon after these events, he fled to England without giving another sermon. Boucher wrote his memoirs there after the war.

Mr. Harrison was in the desk, and was expected also, as I was soon told, to preach. This was not agreeable: but of how little significance was this compared to what I next saw, viz. my church filled with not less than 200 armed men, under the command of Mr.

CHESTER. LM.

And Slav'ry clank her galling chains.   New-england's God for ever reigns.

Let tyrants shake their iron rod.   We fear them not we trust in God.

2
Howe and Burgoyne and Clinton too.
With Prescot and Cornwallis join'd.
Together plot our Overthrow.
In one Infernal league combin'd.

3
When God inspir'd us for the fight.
Their ranks were broke, their lines were forc'd.
Their Ships were Shatter'd in our sight.
Or swiftly driven from our Coast.

4
The Foe comes on with haughty Stride.
Our troops advance with martial noise,
Their Vet'rans flee before our Youth.
And Gen'rals yield to beardless Boys.

5
What grateful Off'ring shall we bring.
What shall we render to the Lord?
Loud Halleluiahs let us Sing.
And praise his name on ev'ry Chord.

Just as Loyalist Jonathan Boucher held that proclaiming loyalty to the Crown was a religious duty, so Patriots argued that God supported their side. This song was written by William Billings, a pioneering Boston musician who published the first collection of music written solely by an American. In the first verse of this engraved copy from 1781, the first and third line of the words are below the third line of music; the second and fourth above it.

Osborne Sprigg, who soon let me know I was not to preach. I returned for answer that the pulpit was my own, and as such I would use it; and that there was but one way by which they could keep me out of it, and that was by taking away my life. . . . And so at the proper time, with my sermon in one hand and a loaded pistol in the other, like Nehemiah, I prepared to ascend the steps of the pulpit, when behold, one of my friends (Mr. David Crawford of Upper Marlborough) having got behind me, threw his arms around mine and held me fast. He assured me on his honor he had both seen and heard the most positive orders given to twenty men picked out for the purpose to fire on me the moment I got into the pulpit, which therefore he never would permit me to do, unless I was stronger than he and two or three others who stood close to him. I entreated him and them to go with me into the pulpit, as my life seemed to myself to depend on my not suffering these outrageous people to carry their point. . . . My well-wishers however prevailed—by force rather than by persuasion; and when I was down it is horrid to recollect what a scene of confusion ensued. A large party insisted I was right in claiming and using my own pulpit; but Sprigg and his company were now grown more violent, and soon managed so as to surround me . . . there was but one way to save my life. This was by seizing Sprigg, as I immediately did, by the collar, and with my cocked pistol in the other hand, assuring him that if any violence was offered to me I would instantly blow his brains out, as I most certainly would have done. I then told them that if he pleased he might conduct me to my horse, and I would leave them. This he did, and we marched together upwards of a hundred yards, I with one hand fastened in his collar and a pistol in the other, guarded by his whole company, whom he had the meanness to order to play on their drums the Rogues' March all the way we went, which they did. All farther that I could then do was to declare, as loud as I could speak, that he had now proved himself to be a complete coward and scoundrel.

Thus ended this dreadful day.

After the extraordinary success of *Common Sense* in early 1776, Thomas Paine continued to support the American side in a series of papers called *The American Crisis*. This now-famous passage is from the first essay, published in December 1776 at a time when the Americans had been forced to give up control of New York City and then retreat to New Jersey. The piece was so inspirational that Washington had it read to his troops on the eve of the battle of Trenton in 1776.

These are the times that try men's souls. The summer soldier and the sunshine patriot will, in this crisis, shrink from the service of their country; but he that stands it *now*, deserves the love and thanks of man and woman. Tyranny, like hell, is not easily conquered; yet we have this consolation with us, that the harder the conflict, the more glorious the triumph. What we obtain too cheap, we esteem too lightly: it is dearness only that gives every thing its value. Heaven knows how to put a proper price upon its goods; and it would be strange indeed if so celestial an article as FREEDOM should not be highly rated. Britain, with an army to enforce her tyranny, has declared that she has a right (*not only to* TAX) but 'TO BIND *us in* ALL CASES WHATSOEVER', and if being *bound in that manner*, is not slavery, then is there not such a thing as slavery upon earth. Even the expression is impious; for so unlimited a power can belong only to God.

Divided Loyalties

For most white Americans, the Whig's use of the words "slavery" and "galling chains" referred to the liberties of free

I cannot see on what grounds the king of Britain can look up to heaven for help against us: a common murderer, a highwayman, or a house-breaker, has as good a pretence as he.

—Thomas Paine, *The American Crisis*, no. 1, December 1776

Since Lord Dunmore's proclamation made its appearance here, it is said he has recruited his army . . . the amount of about 2000 men, including his black regiment, which is thought to be a considerable part, with this inscription on their breasts: "Liberty to slaves."

—*Maryland Gazette, December 14, 1775*

Lord Dunmore, British governor of Virginia at the start of the Revolution, was born in England, but he inherited the Scottish title of his family. In this portrait he wears the kilt and plaids of the Highland Scots. After serving as governor of New York and Virginia, he returned to England at the start of the Revolution. After the war, he became governor of the Bahamas.

whites, not to African Americans. But many enslaved people also found that the Revolution allowed them to be more than simply passive victims of their master's will. Some slaves were able to gain freedom by acting for one group or the other—or by simply running away during the confusion caused by wartime. Only a limited number of African Americans served in the Continental Army, and their service was never fully accepted. The most dramatic bid for black loyalties came from the British side. In November 1775, Lord Dunmore, the royal governor of Virginia, offered to free any slave or servant who joined the British troops. Although this proclamation shocked many whites (and helped turn them against the British), many blacks saw it as a chance to gain independence. Some three hundred slaves escaped to freedom in the first week. About eight hundred joined Lord Dunmore.

A PROCLAMATION

As I have ever entertained hopes that an accomodation might have taken place between Great Britain and this colony, without being compelled by my duty to do this most disagreeable, but now absolutely necessary duty, rendered so by a body of men, unlawfully assembled, firing on his majesty's tenders, and the formation of an army, and an army now of its march to attack his majesty's troops, and destroy the well disposed subjects of this colony. To defeat such treasonable purposes, and that all such traitors, and their abettors may be brought to justice, and that the peace and good order of this colony may be again restored, which the ordinary course of the civil law is unable to effect, I have thought fit to issue this my proclamation, hereby declaring that, until the aforesaid good purposes can be obtained, I do . . . determine to execute martial law . . . I do require every person capable of bearing arms to resort to his majesty's standard, or be looked upon as traitors to his majesty's crown and government, and thereby become liable to the penalty the law inflicts upon such offences; such as forfeiture of life, confiscation of lands, etc. etc. And I do hereby further declare all indented servants, negroes, or others (apertaining to rebels) free, that are able and willing to bear arms, they joining his majesty's troops as soon as may be, for the more speedily reducing his colony to a proper sense of their duty to his majesty's crown and dignity.

Lord Dunmore's promise of freedom sought to boost British forces and weaken the anti-British cause rather than to aid

NEW-YORK, 21ˢᵗ *April* 1783.

THIS is to certify to whomfoever it may concern, that the Bearer hereof ___ *Cato Ramsay* ___ a Negro, reforted to the Britifh Lines, in confequence of the Proclamations of Sir William Howe, and Sir Henry Clinton, late Commanders in Chief in America; and that the faid Negro has hereby his Excellency Sir Guy Carleton's Permiffion to go to Nova-Scotia, or wherever elfe *He* may think proper. ___

By Order of *Brigadier General Birch,*

Although Americans expected that the peace treaty would allow them to regain slaves who had run away, British negotiators refused, arguing that promises of freedom to African Americans needed to be kept. Boston King and his wife were among the three thousand former slaves whom the British determined had joined their side before peace negotiations began. In New York, they would have been given passes like this one, certifying that they were free to leave with the British troops.

African Americans—only enslaved people belonging to "rebels" were to be released. But, whether by conscious decision or not, the British army provided many blacks with a chance to improve their own condition. One of these slaves was the South Carolinian Boston King. Born in 1760, King was apprenticed to a carpenter when he was sixteen. The British occupation of Charleston allowed King an opportunity to escape his from master. His fight to preserve the freedom he gained led to a number of difficulties with both Americans and Britons who wanted to restrict his liberty. By the time he wrote his memoirs in the late 1790s, King had become a Methodist minister. The following incidents in King's account of his life begin in 1780, when he ran away to the British in Charleston.

They received me readily, and I began to feel the happiness of liberty, of which I knew nothing before, although I was much grieved at first, to be obliged to leave my friends, and reside among strangers. In this situation I was seized with smallpox, and suffered great hardships; for all the blacks affected with that disease, were ordered to be carried a mile from the camp, lest the soldiers should be infected, and disabled from marching. This was a grievous circumstance to me and many others. We lay sometimes a whole day without anything to eat or drink; but Providence sent a man, who belonged to the York volunteers whom I was acquainted with, to my relief. He brought me such things as I stood need of; and by the blessing of the Lord I began to recover.

By this time, the English left the place [December 13, 1782], but as I was unable to march with the army, I expected to be taken by the enemy. However when they came, and understood that we were ill of the smallpox, they precipitately left us for fear of the infection. Two days after, the wagons were sent to convey us to the English army.

King suffered a number of other setbacks during his efforts to remain free, including the fortunately unsuccessful attempt of a deserting British officer to re-enslave him. After this incident, King settled in British-occupied New York City.

Here I endeavored to follow my trade, but for want of tools was obliged to relinquish it, and enter into service[as a servant]. But the wages were so low that I was not able to keep myself in clothes, so that I was under the necessity of leaving my master and going to another. I stayed with him four months, but he never paid me, and I was obliged to leave him also, and work about the town until I was married. A year after I was taken very ill, but the Lord raised me up again in about five weeks. I then went out in a pilotboat. We were at sea eight days, and had only provisions for five, so that we were in danger of starving. On the ninth day we were taken by an American whaleboat. I went on board them with a cheerful countenance, and asked for bread and water, and made very free with them. They carried me to Brunswick [New Brunswick, New Jersey], and used me very well. Notwithstanding which, my mind was sorely distressed at the thought of being again reduced to slavery, and separated from my wife and family; and at the same time it was exceeding difficult to escape from my bondage. . . . Sometimes I thought, if it was the will of God that I should be a slave, I was ready to resign myself to his will; but at other times I could not find the least desire to content myself in slavery."

King was finally able to walk from New Jersey to nearby Staten Island, New York, during low tide, at a time when the British guards were not carefully patrolling the boundary between American- and British-held territories.

When I arrived at New York, my friends rejoiced to see me once more restored to liberty, and joined me in praising the Lord for his mercy and goodness. . . . the horrors and devastation of war happily terminated [three years later], and peace was restored between America and Great Britain, which diffused universal joy among all parties, except us, who had escaped from slavery, and taken refuge in the English army; for a report prevailed at New York, that all the slaves, in number 2000, were to be delivered up to their masters, although some of them had been three or four years among the English. This dreadful rumor filled us all with inexpressible anguish and terror, especially when we saw our old masters coming from Virginia, North Carolina, and other parts, and seizing upon their slaves in the streets of New York, or even dragging them out of their beds. Many of the slaves had very cruel masters, so that the thoughts of returning home with them embittered life to us. For some days we lost our appetite for food, and sleep departed from our eyes. The English had compassion upon us in the day of distress, and issued out a proclamation that all slaves should be free, who had taken refuge in the British lines, and claimed the sanction and privileges of the proclamations respecting the security and protection of Negroes. In consequence of this, each of us received a certificate from the commanding officer at New York, which dispelled all our fears, and filled us with joy and gratitude. Soon after, ships were fitted out, and furnished with every necessary for conveying us to Nova Scotia. We arrived at Birchtown in the month of August, where we all safely landed. Every family had a [p]lot of land, and we exerted all our strength in order to build comfortable huts before the cold weather set in.

Like African Americans, Native Americans could not count on either side to support their interests fully. Most of the 200,000 Indians who lived east of the Mississippi River, like most white Americans early in the war, sought to remain neutral. When Native Americans were forced to make a decision, almost all chose to side with the British. Perhaps as many as 13,000 Native Americans fought on the British side, while many fewer aided the Americans. To neutralize this advantage, the Revolutionaries made a number of forays into Indian country. Perhaps the most important of these was Major General John Sullivan's 1779 attack on the Iroquois in New York. Four of the six nations in that confederacy had sided with the British.

One of the people who suffered from the Sullivan expedition was an extraordinary woman with European ancestors

An Indian Plea for Peace

The Ohio River Valley, along with New York and the South, was one of the major theaters of fighting between Indians and colonists. Doonyontat, a leader of the Wyandot tribe (sometimes known as the Hurons) made this speech to the American colonel Daniel Brodhead in 1779, ritually confirming the peace agreement between the two. Strings of different colored wampum were presented to the Americans at specific points in the oration.

Brother, listen to me!

When I look around me, I see the bones of our nephews lie scattered and unburied.

Brother, I gather up the bones of all our young men on both sides, in this dispute, without any distinction of party.

Brother, I have now gathered up all the bones of our relations on both sides, and will bury them in a large deep grave, and smooth it over so that there shall not be the least sign of bones, or any thing to raise any grief or anger in our minds hereafter. . . .

Brother, I now tell you that I have forever thrown off my Father the English, and will never give him any assistance; and there are some amongst all the nations that think the same things that I do, and I wish they would all think so. . . .

Brother, you now listen to me, and one favour I beg of you is that when you drive away your enemies you will allow me to continue in possession of my property, which if you grant will rejoice me.

and Indian loyalties. Mary Jemison was born on a ship while her parents were on their way from Ireland to Pennsylvania, When she was fifteen, she was captured by Shawnee and French soldiers. After two women belonging to the Seneca nation (part of the Iroquois Confederacy) ritually adopted her as their sister, she quickly became part of the Indian community. Jemison moved to upstate New York with the two women around 1762. In Jemison's account of her life, she describes the results of the Sullivan expedition of 1779. Despite the difficulties of the war, Jemison survived two Native-American husbands and told her story to a writer in the early 1820s. She lived until 1833.

At that time I had three children who went with me on foot, one who rode on horse back, and one whom I carried on my back.

Our corn was good that year; a part of which we had gathered and secured for winter.

In one or two days after the skirmish at Connissius lake, Sullivan and his army arrived at Genesee river, where they destroyed every article of the food kind that they could lay their hands on. A part of our corn they burnt, and threw the remainder into the river. They burnt our houses, killed what few cattle and horses they could find, destroyed our fruit trees, and left nothing but the bare soil and timber. But the Indians had eloped [left] and were not to be found.

This British print shows a meeting between the British agent Sir William Johnson and Native Americans. One of the key colonial figures in the complex and troubled relationship between the two groups, Johnson lived on the New York frontier with the Iroquois. He died in 1774, but the connections he helped build ensured that the Iroquois would largely refuse to support the Revolutionaries.

Having crossed and recrossed the river, and finished the work of destruction, the army marched off to the east. Our Indians saw them move off, but suspecting that it was Sullivan's intention to watch our return, and then to take us by surprize, resolved that the main body of our tribe should hunt where we then were, till Sullivan had gone so far that there would be no danger of his returning to molest us.

This being agreed to, we hunted continually till the Indians concluded that there could be no risk in our once more taking possession of our lands. Accordingly we all returned; but what were our feelings when we found that there was not a mouthful of any kind of sustenance left, not even enough to keep a child one day from perishing with hunger.

The weather by this time had become cold and stormy; and as we were destitute of houses and food too, I immediately resolved to take my children and look out for myself, without delay. With this intention I took two of my little ones on my back, bade the other three follow, and the same night arrived on the Gardow flats, where I have ever since resided. . . .

The snow fell about five feet deep, and remained so for a long time, and the weather was extremely cold; so much so indeed, that almost all the game upon which the Indians depended for subsistence, perished, and reduced them almost to a state of starvation through that and three or four succeeding years. When the snow melted in the spring, deer were found dead upon the ground in vast numbers; and other animals, of every description, perished from the cold also, and were found dead, in multitudes. Many of our people barely escaped with their lives, and some actually died of hunger and freezing.

One of the soldiers on the Sullivan expedition was Lieutenant Erkuries Beatty. Beatty's father, like Jemison's parents, had emigrated from Ireland. But Beatty took a different side during the war. Serving in the Continental Army throughout the Revolution, he was present at both Valley Forge and Saratoga. His diary of his experiences in upstate New York near where Jemison lived reveals the cruelty practiced by both sides during an encounter between the Patriots and the Indians. It notes the deliberate destruction of the food of entire villages and the torture of combatants.

Kanadasgo Wensday 8th [September 1779]. This morning came out orders that the men was to remain here all Day & for the Men to

GEORGE WASHINGTON PRESIDENT. 1792.

The Revolution led to a more aggressive assault on Indian control of land. As the United States increased its domination of eastern Indians, it often presented medals to their leaders bearing the image of the current President. This medal, given to the Grand Sachem of the Iroquois in 1792, pictures George Washington sharing a pipe of peace with a Native American. In the background, a wooden house and a working farmer suggest the federal government's goal of encouraging Indians to take up a life of settled agriculture. Despite an official national policy of voluntary change, Native Americans such as the Iroquois were increasingly pushed off their old lands.

The Revolution was devastating to Native Americans. In its aftermath, the chiefs of the Iroquois, Shawnee, Cherokee, Chickasaw, Choctaw, and Loup nations told the French governor of St. Louis in 1784: "That event was for us the greatest blow that could have been dealt us, unless it had been our total destruction."

Brothers: You remember when you first came over the great waters, I was great and you was little—very small. I then took you in for a friend, and kept you under my arms, so that no one might injure you; since that time we have ever been true friends; there never has been any quarrel between us. But now our conditions have changed; you are become great and tall; you reach up to the clouds; you are seen round the world; and I am become small, very little; I am not so high as your heel. Now you take care of me, and I look to you for protection.

—From a speech by Captain Solomon Uhhaaunauwaunmut, the Chief Sachem of the Stockbridge Indians, to the American Congress, April 11, 1775

Clean their pieces likewise for all the sick lame &c to return to Tyoga properly officered; aft. 10 oClock Major Parr with the Rifle Corps & the Cohoun was going up the lake to a little town called Kushay to Destroy it. I with a number of others went Volunteers and got there about 12 oClock found it about 8 Miles from Camp and the town opposite to where we lay two nights ago, the town consisted of about 15 houses tolerable well built and all together we got here 5 horses and a great number of Potatoes Apples Peaches cucumbers watermelons fowls &c and found a great Quantity of corn here which we went about to Destroy, after burning the houses. . . .

Tuesday 14th. The whole Army was under arms this morning an hour before Day & remained so till sunrise; about 7 oClock fatigue parties was sent out to Destroy Corn which was there in great Abundance and beans . . . arrived at Chenesee Town which is the largest we have yet seen; it lies in a Crook of [the] River on extraordinary good land about 70 houses very compact and very well built and about the same number of out houses in Cornfields &c: on entering the town we found the body of Lt. Boyd and another Rifle Man in a most terrible mangled condition they [were] both stripped naked and their heads Cut off and the flesh of Lt. Boyds head was intirely taken of[f] and his eyes punched out. the other mans hed was not there. they were stab[b]ed I supose in 40 Different places in the body with a spear and great gashes cut in their flesh with knifes, and Lt. Boyds Privates were nearly cut of[f] & hanging down, his finger and Toe nails was bruised of[f] and the Dogs had eat part of their Shoulders away likewise a knife was Sticking in Lt. Boyds body[.] They [were] immediately buried with the honour of war.

Wensday 15th. The whole army went out this morning 6 oClock to destroy corn and was out till 12 oClock, there was here the greatest quantity of corn & beans here of any of the towns some of it we husked and threw in the River the rest we Carried to the houses & burnd the whole we totally destroyed. about 10 oClock we Recd. orders to begin our march home which we did leaving the towns in flames.

The Fortunes—and Misfortunes—of War

The memoir of Private Joseph Plumb Martin is one of the most vivid pieces written by any participant in the conflict.

Here he recalls his experiences at Valley Forge in late 1777. The winter in southeastern Pennsylvania was one of the worst during the Revolution. Soldiers suffered extraordinary hardships, especially during the early parts of the winter.

And after a few days more maneuvering we at last settled down at a place called "the Gulf" [so named on account of a remarkable chasm in the hills]; and here we encamped some time. And here we had liked to have encamped forever—for starvation here riot-ed in its glory. But lest the reader should be disgusted by hearing so much said about "starvation," I will give something that, per-haps, may in some measure alleviate his ill humor.

While we lay here, there was a Continental Thanksgiving ordered by Congress, And as the army had all the cause in the world to be particularly thankful, if not for being well off, at least that it was no worse, we were ordered to participate in it. We had nothing to eat for two or three days previous, except what the trees of the fields and forests afforded us. But we must now have what Congress said, a sumptuous Thanksgiving to close the year of high living we had now nearly seen brought to a close. Well, to add something extraordinary to our present stock of provi-sions, our country, ever mindful of its suffering army, opened her sympathizing heart so wide, upon this occasion, as to give us something to make the world stare. And what do you think it was, reader? Guess. You cannot guess. I will tell you; it gave each and every man *half* a *gill* of rice and a *tablespoonful* of vinegar!! . . . [1 gill = 1/4 pint]

The army was now not only starved but naked. The greatest part were not only shirtless and barefoot, but destitute of all other clothing, especially blankets. I procured a small piece of raw cowhide and made myself a pair of moccasins, which kept my feet (while they lasted) from the frozen ground. . . . The only alterna-tive I had was to endure this inconvenience or to go barefoot, as hundreds of my companions had to, till they might be tracked by their blood upon the rough frozen ground. . . .

I had experienced what I thought sufficient of the hardships of a military life the year before, although nothing in comparison to what I had suffered the present campaign. We were now absolute-ly in danger of perishing in the midst of a plentiful country. We then had but little and often nothing to eat for days together; but now we had nothing and saw no likelihood of any betterment of our condition. . . .

In the nineteenth century, the difficulties of the Continental Army at Valley Forge became widely commemorated as a symbol of the sacrifices of the Revolution. This 1874 engraving recalls the scene.

Eighteenth-century Europeans often viewed Arabs as vigorous and hearty but unsympathetic to the suffering of other people.

We arrived at the Valley Forge in the evening [December 18]. It was dark. There was no water to be found and I was perishing with thirst. I searched for water till I was weary and came to my tent without finding any. Fatigue and thirst, joined with hunger, almost made me desperate. I felt at that instant as if I would have taken victuals or drink from the best friend I had on earth by force. I am not writing fiction, all are sober realities. Just after I arrived at my tent, two soldiers, whom I did not know, passed by. They had some water in their canteens which they told me they had found a good distance off, but could not direct me to the place as it was very dark. I tried to beg a draught of water from them but they were as rigid as Arabs. At length I persuaded them to sell me a drink for three pence, Pennsylvania currency, which was every cent of property I could then call my own.

I lay here two nights and one day and had not a morsel of anything to eat all the time, save half of a small pumpkin, which I cooked by placing it upon a rock, the skin side uppermost, and making a fire upon it. By the time it was heat through I devoured it with as keen an appetite as I should a pie made of it at some other time.

As the war dragged on and initial enthusiasm died away, fewer people with other options were willing to serve. New recruits, whether they enlisted voluntarily or were drafted, increasingly came from the poorer parts of society. Many of these soldiers and sailors were young, in their late teens and twenties, and sometimes even younger. Andrew Sherburne was only thirteen when he entered the Continental Navy, where like many, he served alongside his relatives. His enthusiasm suggests the excitement that many people felt, at least at the start of their military service. The Continental Navy had only a small force. Larger state fleets and privateers—privately owned ships given permission by the United States government to attack British shipping and share in the profits—made a greater impression upon the enemy. As Sherburne's father recognized, life on privateers or naval vessels was dangerous. Sherburne himself was captured and released three times. This account of his life, which he wrote in the late 1820s, begins when his family moved back to Portsmouth, New Hampshire, around 1778.

An abundance of new objects was here presented to my view. Ships were building, prizes taken from the enemy unloading, privateers fitting out, standards waved on the forts and batteries, the exercising of soldiers, the roar of cannon, the sound of martial music and the call for volunteers so infatuated me that I was filled with anxiety to become an actor in the scene of war. . . . Though not yet fourteen years of age, like other boys, I imagined myself almost a man. I had intimated to my sister, that if my father would not consent that I should go to sea, I would run away, and go on board a privateer. My mind became so infatuated with the subject, that I talked of it in my sleep and was overheard by my mother. She communicated what she had heard to my father. My parents were apprehensive that I might wander off and go on board some vessel without their consent. At this period it was not an uncommon thing for lads to come out of the country, step on board a privateer, make a cruise and return home, their friends remaining in entire ignorance of their fate until they heard it from themselves. Others would pack up their clothes, take a cheese and a loaf of bread and steer off for the army. There was a disposition in commanders of privateers and recruiting officers to encourage this spirit of enterprise in young men and boys. Though these rash young adventurers did not count the cost, or think of looking at the dark side of the picture, yet this spirit, amidst the despondency of many,

Samuel Reynolds "Moons" the British.

Continental Army soldier David Fremoyer described a comic and tragic incident from his service in New York in 1780–81.

The enemy [under Sir John Johnson] succeeded only in killing one man in the fort [Middle Fort on the Schoharie River]. This was a Samuel Runnels, or Reynolds, who went on top of one of the buildings in the fort and there foolishly and indecently exposed . . . his hind parts to the enemy in contempt of them and there remained, contrary to the admonition of those in the fort, until one of the enemy under cover of some sprouts put up from the bushes and saplings that had been previously cut off crept near enough to shoot and fired at him, the ball just breaking the skin across above one of his eyebrows. This stunned Reynolds, and he fell off the house on the pavement or some stone below on his head and broke his neck.

It was afterwards said that Sir John Johnson, having discovered Reynolds's contempt of them with a spyglass, gave a guinea, half johannes, or some gold coin to an expert marksman to shoot Reynolds, which was accomplished in the manner before related. But for the truth of this story affiant cannot vouch.

Drums, such as this painted one, were means of conveying commands to large groups and essential to military life. Revolutionary War drummers were often boys or teenagers.

John Paul Jones was one of the most important leaders of the small American Navy ("I have not yet begun to fight," he said during one battle). With this broadside, he attempted to recruit sailors for the Raleigh, one of the first warships built in the new nation, optimistically speaking of "an agreeable Voyage." In another advertisement, he promised recruits extra money if they lost an arm or a leg.

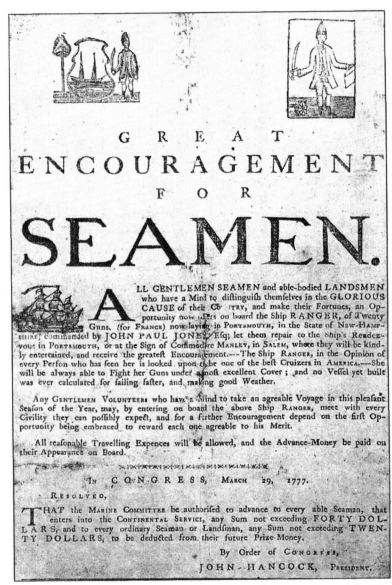

GREAT
ENCOURAGEMENT
FOR
SEAMEN.

ALL GENTLEMEN SEAMEN and able-bodied LANDSMEN who have a Mind to distinguish themselves in the GLORIOUS CAUSE of their Country, and make their Fortunes, an Opportunity now offers on board the Ship RANGER, of Twenty Guns, (for France) now laying in Portsmouth, in the State of New-Hampshire, commanded by JOHN PAUL JONES, Esq; let them repair to the ship's Rendezvous in Portsmouth, or at the Sign of Commodore Manley, in Salem, where they will be kindly entertained, and receive the greatest Encouragement.---The Ship Ranger, in the Opinion of every Person who has seen her is looked upon to be one of the best Cruizers in America.---She will be always able to Fight her Guns under a most excellent Cover; and no Vessel yet built was ever calculated for sailing faster, and making good Weather.

Any Gentlemen Volunteers who have a Mind to take an agreable Voyage in this pleasant Season of the Year, may, by entering on board the above Ship Ranger, meet with every Civility they can possibly expect, and for a further Encouragement depend on the first Opportunity being embraced to reward each one agreable to his Merit.

All reasonable Travelling Expences will be allowed, and the Advance-Money be paid on their Appearance on Board.

In CONGRESS, March 29, 1777.

RESOLVED,

THAT the Marine Committee be authorised to advance to every able Seaman, that enters into the Continental Service, any Sum not exceeding FORTY DOLLARS, and to every ordinary Seaman or Landsman, any Sum not exceeding TWENTY DOLLARS, to be deducted from their future Prize-Money.

By Order of Congress,
JOHN-HANCOCK, President.

enabled our country to maintain a successful struggle and finally achieve her independence.

My father having consented that I should go to sea, preferred the service of congress to privateering. He was acquainted with Capt. Simpson. On board this ship were my two half uncles, Timothy and James Weymouth. Accompanied by my father I visited the rendezvous of the Ranger and shipped as one of her crew. There were probably thirty boys on board this ship. As most of our principal officers belonged to the town, parents preferred this ship as a station for their sons who were about to enter the naval service. Hence most of these boys were from Portsmouth.

Women and the War

Although only men could officially serve in the American armed forces, women also played an important part. As unofficial "camp followers," they provided soldiers with the essential services of cooking, cleaning, and nursing. One of the few such women to leave a written record of her activities was Sarah Osborn. She joined her husband when he was recalled to service in 1780. Here she describes some of her experiences at Yorktown, Virginia, the 1781 battle that convinced the British that their cause was doomed. Osborn dictated this account many years later when she was trying to win a military pension for her husband's service. The clerk who recorded it referred to Osborn as "the deponent."

Deponent took her stand just back of the American tents, say about a mile from the town [of Williamsburg], and busied herself washing, mending, and cooking for the soldiers, in which she was assisted by the other females; some men washed their own clothing. She heard the roar of the artillery for a number of days, and the last night the Americans threw up entrenchments, it was a misty, foggy night, rather wet but not rainy. Every soldier threw up for himself, as she understood, and she afterwards saw and went into the entrenchments. Deponent's said husband was there throwing up entrenchments, and deponent cooked and carried in beef, and bread, and coffee (in a gallon pot) to the soldiers in the entrenchment.

On one occasion when deponent was thus employed carrying in provisions, she met General Washington, who asked her if she "was not afraid of the cannonballs?"

She replied, "No, the bullets would not cheat the gallows," that "It would not do for the men to fight and starve too."

They dug entrenchments nearer and nearer to Yorktown every night or two till the last. While digging that, the enemy fired very heavy till about nine o'clock next morning, then stopped, and the drums from the enemy beat excessively. Deponent was a little way off in Colonal Van Schaik's or the officers marguee [marquee, a large tent]] and a number of officers were present, among whom was Captain Gregg, who, on account of infirmities, did not go out much to do duty.

The drums continued beating, and all at once the officers hurrahed and swung their hats, and deponent asked them, "What is the matter now?"

This portrait of Deborah Sampson appeared in her 1797 memoirs. Five years later, facing ill health and financial difficulties, she gave public lectures in New England and New York. During these lectures she wore a military uniform and performed military drills.

One of them replied, "Are not you soldier enough to know what it means?"

Deponent replied, "No."

They then replied, "The British have surrendered."

Deponent, having provisions ready, carried the same down to the entrenchments that morning, and four of the soldiers whom she was in the habit of cooking for ate their breakfasts.

Perhaps the most well known of the handful of women who fought in the American army was Deborah Sampson. Born in rural Massachusetts in 1760, Sampson had been bound as a servant when she was young. Soon after being released from her term of service, she dressed up as a man and enlisted in the Massachusetts militia. After her true sex was discovered and she was expelled, she enlisted in the Continental Army under the name of Robert Shurtlief. When she was wounded in a battle in New York, she removed a bullet from her thigh herself to avoid being found out by male doctors. When her unit moved to Philadelphia, she contracted a fever. The doctor who treated her finally discovered her identity. He remained quiet, however, and she was discharged at the end of the Revolution in 1783. After marrying Benjamin Gannett, she successfully petitioned for back pay in 1792 and received a government pension in 1805. This 1784 newspaper account seems to be the first published revelation of the story. It takes a generally positive view of Sampson.

New-York, January 10. An extraordinary instance of virtue in a *female soldier*, has occurred lately in the American army, in the Massachusetts line, viz. a lively, comely young nymph, 19 years of age, dressed in man's apparal *[sic]* has been discovered; and what redounds to her honor, she has served in the character of a soldier for near three years undiscovered; during which time she displayed herself with activity, alertness, chastity and valour, having been in several skirmishes with the enemy, and received two wounds; a small shot remaining in her to this day, she was a remarkable vigilant soldier on her post, and always gained the admiration and applause of her officers; was never found in liquor, and always kept company with the most upright and temperate soldiers: For several months this gallantress served with credit as a waiter in a General officer's family [Robert Paterson]; a violent illness (when the troops were at Philadelphia) led to the discovery of her sex; she has since, been honorably discharged from the army with a reward, and sent to her connexions, who, it appears live to the Eastward of Boston, at a place called Munduncook. The cause of her personating a man, it is said, proceeded from the rigour of her parents, who exerted their prerogative, to induce her marriage with a young man she had conceived a great antipathy for, together with her being a remarkable heroine, and warmly attached to the cause of her country, in the service of which, it must be acknowledged, she gained reputation; and no doubt, will be noticed by the compilers of the history of our grand revolution. She passed by the name of Robert Shurtlieff, while in the army, and was borne on the rolls of the regiment as such:—for particular reasons her real name is withheld, but the facts aforementioned are unquestionable and unembellished.

The war affected civilians as well as soldiers. This account of a confrontation between the two groups comes from the letters of the Patriot Eliza Wilkinson. Wilkinson, a young widow, owned a plantation in South Carolina, where these events occurred on morning in June 1780, soon after the British had taken Charleston. That morning a number of horsemen, who turned out to be American soldiers, appeared at the plantation. After some friendly conversation, two of the soldiers, trying to show off, attempted to jump a ditch. One was seriously injured. This account begins just after the soldiers had brought him inside the house.

We were very busy examining the wound when a Negro girl ran in, exclaiming, "O! the King's people are coming! It must be them, for they are all in red!" Upon this cry, the two men that were with us snatched up their guns, mounted their horses and made off, but had not got many yards form the house before the enemy discharged a pistol at them. Terrified almost to death as I was, I was still anxious for my friends' safety. I tremblingly flew to the window, to see if the shot had proved fatal, when, seeing them both safe, "Thank heaven," said I, "they've got off without hurt!"

I'd hardly uttered this when I heard the horses of the inhuman Britons coming in such a furious manner that they seemed to tear up the earth, and the riders at the same time bellowing out the most horrid curses imaginable, oaths and imprecations, which chilled my whole frame. Surely, thought I, such horrid language denotes nothing less than death; but I'd no time for thought. They were up to the house—entered with drawn swords and pistols in their hands. Indeed, they rushed in, in the most furious manner,

Humanity and Justice obliges me to say, that every person with whom I have conversed about Her [Deborah Sampson], & it is not a few, speak of her as a woman of handsome talents, good morals, a dutiful wife, and an affectionate parent. She is now much out of health . . . . She has told me that she has no doubt that her ill health is in consequence of her being exposed when she did a soldier's duty & that while in the army she was wounded.

—Paul Revere supporting a government pension for Deborah Sampson, in an 1804 letter to Congressman William Eustis crying out, "Where're these women rebels?" (pretty language to ladies from the *once famed Britons!*). That was the first salutation!

The moment they espied us, off went our caps (I always heard say none but women pulled caps!). And for what, think you? Why, only to get a paltry stone and wax pin, which kept them on our heads; at the same time uttering the most abusive language imaginable, and making as if they'd hew us to pieces with their swords. But it's not in my power to describe the scene. It was terrible to the last degree; and, what augmented it, they had several armed Negroes with them, who threatened and abused us greatly. They then began to plunder the house of every thing they thought valuable or worth taking; our trunks were split to pieces, and each man, pitiful wretch, crammed his bosom with the contents, which were our apparel, etc., etc., etc.

I ventured to speak to the inhuman monster who had my clothes. I represented to him the times were such we could not replace what they'd taken from us, and begged him to spare me only a suit or two; but I got nothing but a hearty curse for my pains; nay, so far was his callous heart from relenting that, casting his eyes towards my shoes, "I want them buckles," said he, and immediately knelt at my feet to take them out, which, while he was busy about, a brother villain, whose enormous mouth extended from ear to ear, bawled out, "Shares there! I say, shares!" So they divided my buckled between them.

The other wretches were employed in the same manner; they took my sister's ear-rings from her ears; hers, and Miss Samuells's buckles. They demanded her ring from her finger. She pleaded for it, told them it was her wedding ring, and begged they'd let her keep it. But they still demanded it, and, presenting a pistol at her, swore if she did not deliver it immediately, they'd fire. She gave it to them, and, after bundling up all their booty, they mounted their horses. But such despicable figures! Each wretch's bosom stuffed so full they appeared to be all afflicted with some dropsical disorder. Had a party of rebels (as they called us) appeared, we should soon have seen their circumference lessen.

This broadside from Marblehead, Massachusetts, proclaims itself the work of Molly Gutridge, an otherwise unknown woman. Published during the war, probably in 1779, it reveals in primitive verse the difficulties of surviving a long war. Marblehead was a large port town that made its living through the sea at a time when communication between ship and

shore was rare and seafaring an extraordinarily dangerous business. War made these problems more difficult. Gutridge notes missing family members, inflation (thirty-dollar sieves), and shortages (of wood, bread, and meat). "The world," Gutridge suggests, "is now turn'd up-side down." Yet Gutridge also possesses a larger religious perspective on the war, suggesting that God controlled the situation. Her suggestion that the war was a judgment from God was a common view. Although it could be at odds with the view that the Revolution was God's will, the two views were largely complementary since they both suggested that God actively rewarded or punished communities as well as individuals. The picture of the woman with a gun is taken from a pre-Revolutionary woodcut, but it points out that the home front (represented more directly in the other illustration) was also part of the Revolution and that a woman could be, as Gutridge identified herself, a "daughter of liberty."

A New Touch on the Times.
Well adapted to the distressing Situation
    of every Sea-port Town.
By a Daughter of Liberty, living in
    Marblehead.

OUR best beloved they are gone,
We cannot tell they'll e'er return,
For they are gone the ocean wide,
Which for us now they must provide. . . .

It's hard and cruel times to live,
Takes thirty dollars to buy a sieve.

To buy sieves and other things too,
To go thro' the world how can we do,
For times they sure grow worse and worse
I'm sure it sinks our scanty purse. . . .

We can't get fire nor yet food,
Take 20 weight of sugar for two foot of
    wood,
We cannot get bread nor yet meat,
We see the world is nought but cheat.

There was so much Suffering, and so many alarms in our neighborhood in those hard times, that it has always been painful for me to dwell upon them.

—Deposition from an eighty-six-year-old widow of a Revolutionary War soldier applying for a pension, 1840

We cannot now get meat nor bread
By means of which we shake [our head?]
All we can get it is but rice,
And that is of a wretched price. . . .

These times will learn us to be wise,
We now do eat what we despis'd:
I now have something more to say,
We must go up and down the Bay.

To get a fish a-days to fry,
We can't get fat were we to die,
Were we to try all thro' the town,
The world is now turn'd up-side down.

But there's a gracious GOD above,
That deals with us in tender love,
If we be kind and just and true,
He'll set and turn the world anew. . . .

For sin is all the cause of this,
We must not take it then amiss,
Wan't it for our polluted tongues
This cruel war would ne'er begun. . . .

Then gracious GOD now cause to cease
This bloody war and give us peace!
And down our streets send plenty then
With hearts as one we'll say Amen!

MOLLY GUTRIDGE compositio[n,]
Be sure it tis no imposition.

The problems of scarce goods and inflated prices sometimes led to food riots. Some thirty of these crowd actions occurred in the early years of the Revolution. These were not uncontrolled uprisings of the starving but generally orderly affairs directed at merchants who hoarded food or sought to sell it at unreasonable prices. In a letter to her husband John Adams, Abigail Adams describes a July 1777 food riot in Boston. The rioters seized the goods and sold them at an accepted price. Generally, the money was then given to the merchant, although the letter does not specify that here. The victim of this particular action was Nicholas Boylston, one of the city's wealthiest merchants.

I have nothing new to entertain you with, unless it is an account of a New Sort of Mobility which has lately taken the Lead in B[osto]n. You must know that there is a great Scarcity of Sugar and Coffe[e], articles which the Female part of the State are very lo[a]th to give up, especially whilst they consider the Scarcity occasiond by the merchants having secreted a large Quantity. There has been much rout and Noise in the Town for several weeks. Some Stores had been opend by a number of people and the Coffe[e] and Sugar carried into the Market and dealt out by pounds. It was rumourd that an eminent, wealthy, stingy Merchant (who is a Batchelor) had a Hogshead of Coffe[e] in his Store which he refused to sell to the committee under 6 shillings per pound. A Number of Females some say a hundred, some say more assembled with a cart and trucks, marchd down to the Ware House and demanded the keys, which he refused to deliver, upon which one of them seaz[e]d him by his Neck and toss[e]d him into the cart. Upon his finding no Quarter he deliver[e]d the keys, when they tip[pe]d up the cart and discharged him, then opened the Warehouse, Hoisted out the Coffe[e] themselves, put it into the trucks and drove off.

It was reported that he had a Spanking among them, but this I believe was not true. A large concourse of Men stood amaz[e]d silent Spectators of the whole transaction.

SCALE

OF

DEPRECIATION,

Agreeable to an Act of the Commonwealth of Massachusetts to be observed as a Rule for settling the rate of Depreciation on all contracts both publick and private, made on or since the first day of January, 1777——

One Hundred Dollars in Gold and Silver in January 1777, being equal to One Hundred and Five Dollars in the Bills of Credit of the United States.

One thousand seven hundred and seventy-seven.

January,	105	April,	112	July,	125	October,	275
February,	107	May,	115	August,	150	November,	300
March,	109	June,	120	September,	175	December,	310

One thousand seven hundred and seventy-eight.

January,	325	April,	400	July,	425	October,	500
February,	350	May,	400	August,	450	November,	545
March,	375	June,	400	September,	475	December,	634

One thousand seven hundred and seventy-nine.

January,	742	April,	1104	July,	1477	October,	2030
February,	868	May,	1215	August,	1630	November,	2308
March,	1000	June,	1342	September,	1800	December,	2593

One thousand seven hundred and eighty.

| January, | 2934 | February, | 3322 | March, | 3736 | April, | 4000 |

From April 1st, 1780, to April 20th, one Spanish milled dollar was equal to Forty of the old Emission.

April 25th,	42	May 20th,	54	June 20th,	69	Novem. 30th,	74
April 30th,	44	May 25th,	60	August 15th,	70	February 27th	
May 5th,	46	May 30th,	62	Septem. 10th,	71	1781,	75
May 10th,	47	June 10th,	64	October 15th,	72		
May 15th,	49	June 15th,	68	Novem. 10th,	73		

The paper money issued by the Continental Congress during the war quickly lost its value. "Not worth a Continental" remained a common saying long after the fighting had stopped. This Massachusetts broadside traces the currency's rapid and continuing decline. In April 1780, it took $4,000 in Continental money to pay a debt worth $100 in gold or silver.

Benjamin West, an American who had moved to Britain before the war, began this painting of the signing of the treaty that ended the Revolutionary War by painting portraits of the American delegation. From left to right, the figures are John Jay, John Adams, Benjamin Franklin, Henry Laurens, and their secretary, William Temple Franklin. The British commissioners refused to pose for the painting and West never completed it.

Chapter Four

Building Governments

Revolutions in Government

On April 19, 1783, exactly eight years after the Revolution's first battle, Thomas Paine, quoting himself, announced in his pamphlet *The American Crisis*: "The times that tried men's souls, are over." With a peace treaty signed and the fighting ended, Paine declared, "the greatest and completest revolution the world ever knew, [has been] gloriously and happily accomplished." But, Paine went on to say, simply winning the war was not enough. Adjusting to peacetime would be difficult: "pass[ing] from the extremes of danger to safety—from the tumult of war to the tranquillity of peace, though sweet in contemplation, requires a gradual composure of the sense[s] to receive it."

The transition turned out to be even more problematic than Paine predicted. Figuring out how to define liberty—and put it into practice in government and society—was just as difficult as fighting for it. Revolutionary-era Americans experimented widely with different forms of governments on both the state and the national levels. These changes culminated in the United States Constitution written in 1787, creating a full-scale revision of the rules under which the nation was governed. Paine strongly supported this controversial document because it attempted to strengthen the national government. Even in 1783 he had identified the dangers of disunity created by a weak central government as the primary question facing the newly independent country. "Our great national character," he wrote in the pamphlet, is based on "the UNION OF THE STATES." "Our union . . . is the cheapest way of being great—the easiest way of being powerful, and the happiest invention in government which the circumstances of America can admit of." Not all Americans agreed, however. Rather than seeing the "union" as what Paine called the guardian "of our liberty and safety," they worried that it threatened these very values. A strong national government, they feared, might take away their freedom, just as the British government had attempted to do before the Revolution. The complexity of these issues made the tranquility that Paine hoped for difficult to achieve.

The Problems of Peace

Like Paine's April 1783 essay, this letter, sent to the state governments by George Washington two months later, also celebrates the end of the war and warns of a weak national authority. Washington had particular reason to fear the dangers of a political system with a powerless central government. Congress's failure to pay the Continental Army fully had created bitter feelings: Some soldiers had rebelled; some officers had threatened that the army might not disband after the war, raising the possibility of the military gaining political power. Although Washington had skillfully defused these challenges, he foresaw further dangers if the national government was not given greater powers.

Sir: The great object for which I had the honor to hold an appointment in the Service of my Country, being accomplished, I am now preparing to resign it into the hands of Congress, and to return to that domestic retirement, which, it is well known, I left with the greatest reluctance, a Retirement, for which I have never ceased to sigh through a long and painful absence, and in which (remote from the noise and trouble of the World) I meditate to pass the remainder of life in a state of undisturbed repose. But before I carry this resolution into effect, I think it a duty incumbent on me, to make this my last official communication, to congratulate you on the glorious events which Heaven has been pleased to produce in our favor, to offer my sentiments respecting some important subjects . . . and to give my final blessing to that Country, in whose service I have spent the prime of my life, for whose sake I have consumed so many anxious days and watchfull nights, and whose happiness being extremely dear to me, will always constitute no inconsiderable part of my own. . . .

Heaven has crowned all its other blessings [upon America], by giving a fairer oppertunity for political happiness, than any other Nation has ever been favored with. Nothing can illustrate these

Gentleman, you must pardon me. I have grown gray in your service and now find myself growing blind.

—George Washington speaking to Continental Army officers near the end of the Revolution, March 15, 1783

observations more forcibly, than a recollection of the happy con-
juncture of times and circumstances, under which our Republic
assumed its rank among the Nations; The foundation of our
Empire was not laid in the gloomy age of Ignorance and
Superstition, but at an Epocha when the rights of mankind were
better understood and more clearly defined, than at any former
period, the researches of the human mind, after social happiness,
have been carried to a great extent, the Treasures of knowledge,
acquired by the labours of Philosophers, Sages and Legislatures,
through a long succession of years, are laid open for our use, and
their collected wisdom may be happily applied in the
Establishment of our forms of Government; the free cultivation of
Letters, the unbounded extension of Commerce, the progressive
refinement of Manners, the growing liberality of sentiment, and
above all, the pure and benign light of Revelation, have had a
meliorating influence on mankind and increased the blessings of
Society. At this auspicious period, the United States came into
existence as a Nation, and if their Citizens should not be completely free and happy, the fault will be intirely their own.

**Having pointed out the extraordinary times in which the
United States was founded, Washington goes on to warn
that its success was not yet secure. Only a stronger national
government could insure that the Revolution would be a
"blessing" and not a "curse."**

Such is our situation, and such are our prospects: but notwithstanding the cup of blessing is thus reached out to us, notwithstanding happiness is ours, if we have a disposition to seize the
occasion and make it our own; yet, it appears to me there is an
option still left to the United States of America, that it is in their
choice, and depends upon their conduct, whether they will be
respectable and prosperous, or contemptable and miserable as a
Nation; This is the time of their political probation, this is the
moment when the eyes of the whole World are turned upon them,
this is the moment to establish or ruin their national Character
forever, this is the favorable moment to give such a tone to our
Federal Government, as will enable it to answer the ends of its
institution, or this may be the ill-fated moment for relaxing the
powers of Union, annihilating the cement of the Confederation,
and exposing us to become the sport of European politics, which
may play one State against another to prevent their growing
importance, and to serve their own interested purposes. For,

according to the system of Policy the States shall adopt at this moment, they will stand or fall, and by their confirmation or lapse, it is yet to be decided, whether the Revolution must ultimately be considered as a blessing or a curse: a blessing or a curse, not to the present age alone, for with our fate will the destiny of unborn Millions be involved.

The successful conclusion of the war rekindled and extended the rapid growth of a frontier settlement that had begun before the Revolution. Indians resisted the newly independent American government's claim to all the land held by tribes that had sided with Great Britain. But popular demand for land at reasonable prices led both national and state governments to continue pushing Indians off their lands through wars, negotiations, and simple assertion of ownership. Vermont, Ohio, and Kentucky all expanded dramatically in the years after 1783. Kentucky alone boasted 73,000 settlers in 1790, in an area where virtually no white people had lived before the Revolution. This 1785 account about the settlement of Kentucky appeared early the following year in a Connecticut newspaper.

The country abounds with every thing necessary to establish settlements with ease. The forests abound with baffaloe, deer, elk, bears and turkies; the waters are covered with fowl, and the fish are in very great plenty; and in general the climate is very healthy, the ague [chills] and fever are strangers to every part of this river above the falls, and perfect health appears to be the lot of every person inhabiting near these waters: you will easily see I consider this a terrestrial paradise; was I possessed of a good farm in Connecticut I would think I had a good bargain to give it for a like number of acres of this wilderness and cost of transportation. . . .

The population of the country of Kentucky will amaze you; in June, 1779, the whole number of inhabitants amounted to 176 only, and they now exceed 30,000: I have now been 39 days at this post, and there have passed 34 boats for the falls; and now more than one third the boats which come to this country with settlers, go as far down as this place: it is a moderate computation to number 10 to a boat, this gives an addition of 1000 at least in the last 40 days, and I am informed more than one half the settlers come through the wilderness from Virginia. I have not a doubt but 3000 men in arms might be paraded at this place in 12 days if necessary.

It will be as practicable to turn a torrent of water backward, as to prevent the amazing emigration to this country: and like the general collection at the last day, they are of all nations, tongues and languages, from China, from all parts of Europe, from our own country, and every part of America they are gathered.

This 1768 British engraving, based on information from the governor of South Carolina, shows the stages of colonial settlement. On the left, the land is being cleared and a small mill has begun operating. Few Americans would have been able to afford the grand house in the right side of the picture.

Much of the western land being newly settled in the 1780s and 1790s was owned by the federal government, which had received it from the states as part of the negotiations that created the nation's first constitution, the Articles of Confederation. In the years after the war, Congress passed a series of bills that regulated this national domain. This process culminated in the Northwest Ordinance of 1787. Officially titled "An Ordinance for the Government of the Territory of the United States Northwest of the River Ohio," the law defined the government and future status of what became the states of Ohio, Indiana, Michigan, and Wisconsin. Passed by Congress while the United States Constitution was being written, the Ordinance included both a bill of rights and a ban on slavery, which the Constitution did not include. The Ordinance

also ensured that the residents of this area would not become colonists, kept in permanent subordination. Instead, they would become equal in every way to citizens of the original thirteen states. The Ordinance begins by specifying the form of government for each district and the process of changing status from a federal territory to a state.

Be it ordained by the United States in Congress assembled, That the said territory, for the purposes of temporary government, be one district, subject, however, to be divided into two districts, as future circumstances may, in the opinion of Congress, make it expedient. . . .

Be it ordained by the authority aforesaid, That there shall be appointed from time to time by Congress, a governor, whose commission shall continue in force for the term of three years, unless sooner revoked by Congress; he shall reside in the district, and have a freehold estate therein in 1,000 acres of land, while in the exercise of his office. . . . There shall also be appointed a court to consist of three judges, any two of whom to form a court. . . .

The governor and judges, or a majority of them, shall adopt and publish in the district such laws of the original States, criminal and civil, as may be necessary and best suited to the circumstances of the district, and report them to Congress from time to time: which laws shall be in force in the district until the organization of the General Assembly therein, unless disapproved of by Congress; but afterwards the Legislature shall have authority to alter them as they shall think fit. . . .

Previous to the organization of the general assembly, the governor shall appoint such magistrates and other civil officers in each county or township, as he shall find necessary for the preservation of the peace and good order in the same: After the general assembly shall be organized, the powers and duties of the magistrates and other civil officers shall be regulated and defined by the said assembly; but all magistrates and other civil officers not herein otherwise directed, shall, during the continuance of this temporary government, be appointed by the governor. . . .

So soon as there shall be five thousand free male inhabitants of full age in the district, upon giving proof thereof to the governor, they shall receive authority, with time and place, to elect representatives from their counties or townships to represent them in the general assembly: *Provided,* That, for every five hundred free male inhabitants, there shall be one representative, and so on progressively with the number of free male inhabitants shall the right of representation increase, until the number of representatives shall amount to twenty five; after which, the number and proportion of representatives shall be regulated by the legislature. . . .

As soon as a legislature shall be formed in the district, the council and house assembled in one room, shall have authority, by joint ballot, to elect a delegate to Congress, who shall have a seat in Congress, with a right of debating but not voting during this temporary government.

The bill also includes a Bill of Rights guaranteeing the freedoms of residents of the area. These articles also banned slavery and provided for fair dealings with Native Americans.

It is hereby ordained and declared by the authority aforesaid, That the following articles shall be considered as articles of compact between the original States and the people and States in the said territory and forever remain unalterable, unless by common consent, to wit:

Art. 1. No person, demeaning himself in a peaceable and orderly manner, shall ever be molested on account of his mode of worship or religious sentiments, in the said territory.

Art. 2. The inhabitants of the said territory shall always be entitled to the benefits of the writ of *habeas corpus*, and of the trial by jury; of a proportionate representation of the people in the legislature; and of judicial proceedings according to the course of the common law. All persons shall be bailable, unless for capital offenses, where the proof shall be evident or the presumption great. All fines shall be moderate; and no cruel or unusual punishments shall be inflicted. No man shall be deprived of his liberty or property, but by the judgment of his peers or the law of the land; and, should the public exigencies make it necessary, for the common preservation, to take any person's property, or to demand his particular services, full compensation shall be made for the same. And, in the just preservation of rights and property, it is understood and declared, that no law ought ever to be made, or have force in the said territory, that shall, in any manner whatever, interfere with or affect private contracts or engagements, *bona fide*, and without fraud, previously formed.

Art. 3. Religion, morality, and knowledge, being necessary to good government and the happiness of mankind, schools and the means of education shall forever be encouraged. The utmost good faith shall always be observed towards the Indians; their lands and

A rage for emigrating to the western country prevails, and thousands have already fixed their habitations in that wilderness. The Continental Land Office is opened, and the seeds of a great people are daily planting beyond the mountains.
—John Jay, letter to William Bingham, May 1785

habeas corpus

A writ of *habeas corpus* requires that a prisoner be brought before a judge. Literally meaning "produce the body," the writ guards against governments holding people without proper authority."

property shall never be taken from them without their consent; and, in their property, rights, and liberty, they shall never be invaded or disturbed, unless in just and lawful wars authorized by Congress; but laws founded in justice and humanity, shall from time to time be made for preventing wrongs being done to them, and for preserving peace and friendship with them.

Art. 4. The said territory, and the States which may be formed therein, shall forever remain a part of this Confederacy of the United States of America, subject to the Articles of Confederation, and to such alterations therein as shall be constitutionally made; and to all the acts and ordinances of the United States in Congress assembled, conformable thereto. . . .

Art. 5. There shall be formed in the said territory, not less than three nor more than five States. . . .

Art. 6. There shall be neither slavery nor involuntary servitude in the said territory, otherwise than in the punishment of crimes whereof the party shall have been duly convicted: *Provided, always,* That any person escaping into the same, from whom labor or service is lawfully claimed in any one of the original States, such fugitive may be lawfully reclaimed and conveyed to the person claiming his or her labor or service as aforesaid.

Economic Successes and Failures

In this August 1787 speech, Philadelphia businessman and land speculator Tench Coxe celebrates the variety of new economic initiatives springing up in the new nation. These advances, he argues, should be actively encouraged. Historians, like many of Coxe's contemporaries, have often judged the economy of the 1780s in less positive terms. But Coxe insightfully points to two important changes that would shape the next century of American economic life: the expansion of Southern cotton cultivation (still in its infancy in the 1780s) and the growth of manufacturing.

Cotton thrives as well in the southern states, as in any part of the world. The West-India islands and those states raised it formerly, when the price was not half what it has been for years past in Europe. It is also worth double the money in America, which it sold for before the revolution, all the European nations having prohibited the exportation of it from their respective colonies to any foreign country. It is much to be desired, that the southern planters would adopt the cultivation of an article from which the best informed manufacturers calculate the greatest profits, and on which some established factories depend. . . .

Under all the disadvantages which have attended manufacturers and the useful arts, it must afford the most comfortable reflection to every patriotic mind, to observe their progress in the United States and particularly in Pennsylvania. For a long time after our forefathers sought an establishment in this place, then a dreary wilderness, every thing necessary for their simple wants was the work of European hands. How great—how happy is the change. The list of articles we now make ourselves, if particularly enumerated would fatigue the ear, and waste your valuable time. Permit me however, to mention them under their general heads: meal of all kinds, ships and boats, malt liquors, distilled spirits, pot-ash, gun-powder, cordage, loaf-sugar, pasteboard, cards and paper of every kind, books in various languages, snuff, tobacco, starch, cannon, mu[sk]ets, anchors, nails, . . . [Coxe goes on to list nearly fifty other categories of manufactured goods] and several other valuable articles with which the memory cannot furnish us at once.

If the nations of Europe possess some great advantages over us in manufacturing for the rest of the world, it is however clear, that there are some capital circumstances in our favour, when they meet us *in our own markets*. . . .

We must carefully examine the conduct of other countries in order to possess ourselves of their methods of encouraging manufactories and pursue such of them, as apply to our situation, so far as it may be in our power—exempting raw materials, dye stuffs, and certain implements for manufacturing from duty on importation is a very proper measure. Premiums for useful inventions and improvements, whether foreign or American, for the best experiments in any unknown matter, and for the largest quantity of any valuable raw material must have an excellent effect. They would assist the efforts of industry, and hold out the noble incentive of honourable distinction to merit and genius. The state might with great convenience enable an enlightened society, established for the purpose, to offer liberal rewards in land for a number of objects of this nature. . . .

It might answer an useful purpose, if a committee of this society should have it in charge to visit every ship arriving with passengers from any foreign country, in order to enquire what persons they may have on board capable of constructing useful machines, qualified to carry on manufactures, or coming among us with a view to that kind of employment. It would be a great relief and encouragement to those friendless people in a land of strangers,

This model of Eli Whitney's cotton gin (short for engine) was prepared for his patent application. Whitney invented the machine in 1793 in response to the difficulties of cleaning the type of cotton grown in the South. British textile factories, an important part of the developing Industrial Revolution, required much more cotton than ever before in the 1780s and 1790s. The cotton gin made possible a huge expansion of American production—and encouraged the continuation of slavery.

A Call to Arms

One of the leaders of Shays's Rebellion wrote this letter in December 1786 to the townspeople of Boylston, Massachusetts, encouraging them to join the Regulators.

To the good people of bolyston as this is perelous times blood shed and prisoners made by tirants who are a fighting for promotion and to advance their intrest wich will Dest[ro]y the good people of this Land—we that stile ourselves regelators think it is our Duty to stand for our Lives and for our familiys and for our Intrest wich will be taken from us if we Dont Defend them. Therefore we would have you take it into consideration and fly to our assistance and soon as posable in this just and righteous cause as they must be exeration made.

Captain Daniel Shays (left) had been an officer in the Continental Army before he became one of the leaders of the rebellion that came to carry his name. This print from a Boston almanac shows him with another leader of the movement, Job Shattuck.

and would fix many among us whom little difficulties might incline to return.

While some Americans enjoyed relative economic prosperity in the 1780s, othes suffered greatly. Farmers in western Massachusetts were particularly hard-hit by economic difficulties. The state had sharply increased taxes to pay off its war debts. Unable to afford these new levies, many farmers faced the loss of their land at a September 1786 meeting in Worcester County in what was called an "amazing flood of law suits." By then, a number of area residents and farmers had already begun to take the law into their own hands, not only holding meetings and petitioning, but also closing couthouses to prevent legal action. The protests expanded over the next few months; in all over one thousand protesters took up arms in what they called the Regulation and what their opponents called Shays's Rebellion, named after one of its leaders Daniel Shays. An army, hastily organized by the state, defeated the movement in early 1787. This description of the event was written soon afterward by William Manning, an eastern Massachusetts farmer. To Manning, the episode provided an example of his belief that the rich "few" unfairly dominated the "many."

Taxes were extremely high. Some counties were two or three years behind. And with the prices of labor and produce falling very fast, creditors began calling for old debts and saying that they would not take payment in paper money. Those who had money demanded forty or fifty percent for it. And fee officers demanded three or four times so much fees as the law allowed them, and were so crowded with business that sometimes it was hard to get any done. Property was selling almost every day by execution [government seizure] for less than half its value. The jails were crowded with debtors. And with the people being ignorant that all their help lay in being fully and fairly represented in the legislature, many towns neglected to send representatives in order to save the cost—so that the Few only were represented at [the General] court, with an aristocratic [James] Bowdoin as governor at their head.

Under all these circumstances, the people were driven to the greatest extremity. Many counties took to conventions, remonstrances, and petitions to a court where they were not half represented. But not being heard, and in some instances charged with seditious meetings and intentions, under all these circumstances, some counties were so foolish as to stop the courts of justice by force of arms. This shook the government to its foundation. For instead of fatherly counsels and admonitions, the dog of war was let loose upon them, and they were declared in a state of insurrection and rebellion.

In these circumstances, the Few were all alive for the support of the government, and all those who would not be continually crying, "Government, Government," or who dared to say a word against their measures, were called Shaysites and rebels and threatened with prosecutions, etc. But with a large majority of the people thinking that there was blame on both sides, or viewing one side as knaves and the other as fools, it was with great difficulty and delay before a sufficient number could be raised and sent to suppress those who had closed the courts.

But the suppression was done with the loss of but few lives. This put the people in the most zealous searches after a remedy for their grievance. . . . They happily effected it in a few months only by using their privileges as electors.

In Massachusetts, Shays's Rebellion led to a number of measures to relieve economic distress. Political leaders in other states often found a different meaning in the armed uprising. The rebellion that had threatened (unsuccessfully it turned out) to take over the United States arsenal in Springfield seemed to symbolize the weakness of the national government. George Washington wrote to Henry Lee in 1786 about "the clouds that have spread over the brightest morn that ever dawned upon any country." "If [the rebels] have *real* grievances," he advised, "redress them if possible; or acknowledge the justice of them, and your inability to do it in the present moment. If they have not, employ the force of government against them at once. If this is inadequate, *all* will be convinced that the superstructure is bad, or wants support. To be more exposed in the eyes of the world, and more contemptible than we already are, is hardly possible."

Constructing and Reconstructing Governments

After rejecting British rule, the Revolutionaries had to establish new governments to take its place. For a time some states attempted to adapt their old colonial practices, but most eventually created new forms. In the process, the term "constitution" increasingly came to mean not just the ways the government was organized and operated, but a written document that established and regulated these structures. The arguments and experiments that resulted from this period of creating and revising state governments culminated in the controversy over the new national Constitution of 1787.

Pennsylvania made the most radical break from British practices. Rather than following the British practice of divided government (sharing power between the House of Commons, the House of Lords, and the monarch), the new state's 1776 constitution created a single legislative body and a weak collective executive. This plan, drawing upon the ideas in Thomas Paine's immensely popular *Common Sense*, and perhaps upon Paine's personal involvement, attempted to base the government directly upon the will of the people.

The legislature was to be made up of a single house with its members elected annually. Legislative proceedings were open to all. The executive branch consisted of a committee headed by a "president," a term chosen to suggest someone who presided rather than ruled. The instabilities created by a system with virtually no checks upon a constantly changing legislature quickly made Pennsylvania's new constitution controversial; even Paine himself came to oppose it.

SECTION 1. The commonwealth or state of Pennsylvania shall be governed hereafter by an assembly of the representatives of the freemen of the same, and a president and council, in manner and form following—

SECT. 2. The supreme legislative power shall be vested in a house of representatives of the freemen of the commonwealth of state of Pennsylvania.

SECT. 3. The supreme executive power shall be vested in a president and council. . . .

SECT. 6. Every freeman of the full age of twenty-one years, having resided in this state for the space of one whole year next before the day of election for representatives, and paid public taxes during that time, shall enjoy the right of an elector: Provided always, that sons of freeholders of the age of twenty-one years shall be intitled to vote although they have not paid taxes. . . .

SECT. 8. No person shall be capable of being elected a member to serve in the house of representatives of the freemen of this commonwealth more than four years in seven.

SECT. 9. The members of the house of representatives shall be chosen annually by ballot. . . .

SECT. 13. The doors of the house in which the representatives of the freemen of this state shall sit in general assembly, shall be and remain open for the admission of all persons who behave decently, except only when the welfare of this state may require the doors to be shut.

SECT. 14. The votes and proceedings of the general assembly shall be printed weekly during their sitting, with the yeas and nays, on any questions, vote or resolution, where any two members require it, except when the vote is taken by ballot; and when the yeas and nays are so taken every member shall have a right to insert the reasons of his vote upon the minutes, if he desires it.

SECT. 15. To the end that laws before they are enacted may be more maturely considered, and the inconvenience of hasty determinations as much as possible prevented, all bills of public nature

Dangers of a Single-House System

Benjamin Rush was one of the earliest and strongest critics of the Pennsylvania Constitution. In 1777, he complained in a pamphlet "Observations Upon the Present Government of Pennsylvania" about the single-house system.

In the second section, "the supreme legislature is vested in a 'single' House of Representatives of the Freemen of the Commonwealth." By this section we find, that the supreme, absolute, and uncontrouled power of the whole State is lodged in the hands of *one body* of men. Had it been lodged in the hands of one man, it would have been less dangerous to the safety and liberties of the community. Absolute power should never be trusted to man. It has perverted the wisest heads, and corrupted the best hearts in the world. I should be afraid to commit my property, liberty and life to a body of angels for one whole year. The Supreme Being alone is qualified to possess supreme power over his creatures. It requires the wisdom and goodness of a Deity to controul, and direct it properly.

shall be printed for the consideration of the people, before they are read in general assembly the last time for debate and amendment; and, except on occasions of sudden necessity, shall not be passed into laws until the next session of assembly. . . .

SECT. 42. Every foreigner of good character who comes to settle in this state, having first taken an oath or affirmation of allegiance to the same, may purchase, or by other just means acquire, hold, and transfer land or other real estate; and after one year's residence, shall be deemed a free denizen thereof, and entitled to all the rights of a natural born subject of this state. . . .

SECT. 47. In order that the freedom of the commonwealth may be preserved inviolate forever, there shall be chosen by ballot by the freemen in each city and county respectively . . . in the year one thousand seven hundred and eighty-three, and . . . in every seventh year thereafter, two persons in each city and county of this state, to be called the COUNCIL OF CENSORS; who shall meet together on the second Monday of November next ensuing their election. . . . And whose duty it shall be to enquire whether the constitution has been preserved inviolate in every part; and whether the legislative and executive branches of government have performed their duty as guardians of the people, or assumed to themselves, or exercised other or greater powers than they are intitled to by the constitution: They are also to enquire whether the public taxes have been justly laid and collected in all parts of this commonwealth, in what manner the public monies have been disposed of, and whether the laws have been duly executed.

The Massachusetts revolutionary John Adams had been one of the most active advocates of independence. He found proposals to place all power in the hands of a single legislature frightening. Such a system, Adams believed, ignored another lesson taught by the Revolution, the dangers of ambitious leaders and uncontrolled power. In this section from his 1776 pamphlet *Thoughts on Government,* Adams argues for a mixed form of government that includes a second branch of the legislature and balances the power of the different parts of the government. Adams's ideas became an important influence on American constitutional thinking. Four years later, Adams helped write the widely copied constitution of Massachusetts that put his ideas into practice.

We ought to consider what is the end of government, before we determine which is the best form. Upon this point all speculative

John Adams appears as a great statesman in this portrait by John Singleton Copley. Adams posed for the portrait in London after the war ended. The document Adams holds in his right hand probably represents the peace treaty. In the left background, Britannia, the symbolic persona of England, holds out an olive branch, a sign of peace.

Algernon Sidney and the others named were seventeeth- and early-eighteenth-century English writers who argued for increasing the people's role in government.

politicians will agree, that the happiness of society is the end of government, as all divines and moral philosophers will agree that the happiness of the individual is the end of man. From this principle it will follow, that the form of government which communicates ease, comfort, security, or, in one word, happiness, to the greatness number of persons, and in the greatest degree, is the best. . . .

A man must be indifferent to the sneers of modern Englishmen, to mention in their company the names of Sidney, Harrington, Locke, Milton, Nedham, Neville, Burnet, and Hoadly. . . . The wretched condition of this country, however, for ten or fifteen years past, has frequently reminded me of their principles and reasonings. They will convince any candid mind, that there is no good government but what is republican. That the only valuable part of the British constitution is so; because the very definition of a republic is "an empire of laws, and not of men." That, as the republic is the best of governments, so that particular arrangement of the powers of society, or, in other words, that form of government which is best contrived to secure an impartial and exact execution of the laws, is the best of republics. . . .

As good government is an empire of laws, how shall your laws be made? In a large society inhabiting an extensive country, it is impossible that the whole should assemble to make laws. This first necessary step, then, is to depute power from the many to a few of the most wise and good. . . .

The principal difficulty lies, and the greatest care should be employed, in constituting this representative assembly. It should be in miniature an exact portrait of the people at large. It should think, feel, reason, and act like them. That it may be the interest of this assembly to do strict justice at all times, it should be an equal representation, or, in other words, equal interests among the people should have equal interests in it. . . .

I think a people cannot be long free, or ever happy, whose government is in one assembly. My reasons for this opinion are as follow:—

1. A single assembly is liable to all the vices, follies, and frailties of an individual; subject to fits of humor, starts of passion, flights of enthusiasm, partialities, or prejudice, and consequently productive of hasty results and absurd judgments. And all these errors ought to be corrected and defects supplied by some controlling power.

2. A single assembly is apt to be avaricious, and in time will not scruple to exempt itself from burdens, which it will lay, without compunction, on its constituents.

CONSTITUTION

or

FRAME of GOVERNMENT,

Agreed upon by the DELEGATES of the People of the State of MASSACHUSETTS-BAY,

IN

CONVENTION,

begun and held at *Cambridge* on the First of *September*, 1779,

AND

Continued by Adjournments to the Second of *March*, 1780,

To be submitted to the Revision of their Constituents, in Order to the compleating of the same, in Conformity to their Amendments, at a Session to be held for that Purpose, on the First Wednesday in *June* next ensuing.

BOSTON: STATE of MASSACHUSETTS-BAY,

Printed by BENJAMIN EDES & SONS, in State-Street. M,DCC,LXXX,

This edition of the proposed constitution of Massachusetts, originally drafted by John Adams, was printed in 1780 in preparation for ratification by the people. Like some of the later state constitutions—and the national constitution of 1787—the Massachusetts document was written by a special convention called for the purpose. Forming a specially-elected body solely to write a constitution removed some of the problems that results from allowing the legislature to write a document that, at least in theory, created the legislature itself. That very situation had helped to defeat the Massachusetts constitution proposed in 1778.

3. A single assembly is apt to grow ambitious, and after a time will not hesitate to vote itself perpetual. This was one fault of the Long Parliament; but more remarkably of Holland . . . .

4. A representative assembly, although extremely well qualified, and absolutely necessary, as a branch of the legislature, is unfit to exercise the executive power, for want of two essential properties, secrecy and dispatch.

5. A representative assembly is still less qualified for the judicial power, because it is too numerous, too slow, and too little skilled in the laws.

6. Because a single assembly, possessed of all the powers of government, would make arbitrary laws for their own interest, execute all laws arbitrarily for their own interest, and adjudge all controversies in their own favor.

But shall the whole power of legislation rest in one assembly? Most of the foregoing reasons apply equally to prove that the legislative power ought to be more complex; to which we may add, that if the legislative power is wholly in one assembly, and the executive in another, or in a single person, these two powers will oppose and encroach upon each other, until the contest shall end in war, and the whole power, legislative and executive, be usurped by the strongest.

The judicial power, in such case, could not mediate, or hold the balance between the two contending powers, because the legislative would undermine it. And this shows the necessity, too, of giving the executive power a negative upon the legislative, otherwise this will be continually encroaching upon that.

To avoid these dangers, let a distinct assembly be constituted, as a mediator between the two extreme branches of the legislature, that which represents the people, and that which is vested with the executive power.

Elective Despotism

Virginia's constitution did not grant as much power to a single legislature as Pennsylvania's. But Thomas Jefferson, who served as Virginia's governor during the Revolution, still believed his state's system was dangerous. He argues in his 1785 book, Notes on the State of Virginia, *that despotism is not always the result of a dictatorial king or governor.*

All the powers of government, legislative, executive, and judiciary, result to the legislative body. The concentrating these in the same hands is precisely the definition of despotic government. It will be no alleviation that these powers will be exercised by a plurality of hands, and not by a single one. 173 despots would surely be as oppressive as one. Let those who doubt it turn their eyes to the republic of Venice. As little will it avail us that they are chosen by ourselves. An *elective despotism* was not the government we fought for; but one which should not only be founded on free principles, but in which the powers of government should be so divided and balanced among several bodies of magistracy, as that no one could transcend their legal limits, without being effectually checked and restrained by the others.

Many of the new state constitutions established during the Revolution included lists of the rights enjoyed by their citizens. The most influential of these documents was the Declaration of Rights approved by the Virginia legislature in June 1776. Originally drafted by the planter George Mason, the Declaration drew heavily on the English Declaration of Rights prepared during the Glorious Revolution of 1688. An early version of the Virginia document in turn became an important source for the wording of the American Declaration of Independence. The final version was copied by a number of state constitutions and used to formulate the Bill of Rights.

SECTION 1. That all men are by nature equally free and independent, and have certain inherent rights, of which, when they enter into a state of society, they cannot, by any compact, deprive or divest their posterity; namely, the enjoyment of life and liberty, with the means of acquiring and possessing property, and pursuing and obtaining happiness and safety.

SEC. 2. That all power is vested in, and consequently derived from, the people; that magistrates are their trustees and servants, and at all times amenable to them.

SEC. 3. That government is, or ought to be, instituted for the common benefit, protection, and security of the people, nation, or community; of all the various modes and forms of government, that is best which is capable of producing the greatest degree of happiness and safety, and is most effectually secured against the danger of maladministration; and that, whenever any government shall be found inadequate or contrary to these purposes, a majority of the community hath an indubitable, inalienable, and indefeasible right to reform, alter or abolish it, in such manner as shall be judged most conducive to the public weal.

SEC. 4. That no man, or set of men, are entitled to exclusive or separate emoluments or privileges from the community, but in consideration of public services; which, not being descendible, neither ought the offices of magistrate, legislator, or judge to be hereditary.

SEC. 5. That the legislative and executive powers of the State should be separate and distinct from the judiciary; and that the members of the two first may be restrained from oppression by feeling and participating the burdens of the people, they should, at fixed periods, be reduced to a private station, return into that body from which they were originally taken, and the vacancies be supplied by frequent, certain, and regular elections, in which all, or any part of the former members, to be again eligible, or ineligible, as the laws shall direct.

SEC. 6. That elections of members to serve as representatives of the people, in assembly, ought to be free; and that all men, having sufficient evidence of permanent common interest with, and attachment to, the community, have the right of suffrage, and cannot be taxed or deprived of their property for public uses, without their own consent, or that of their representatives so elected, nor bound by any law to which they have not, in like manner, assembled, for the public good.

SEC. 7. That all power of suspending laws, or the execution of laws, by any authority, without consent of the representatives of the people is injurious to their rights, and ought not to be exercised.

SEC. 8. That in all capital or criminal prosecutions a man hath a right to demand the cause and nature of his accusation, to be confronted with the accusers and witnesses, to call for evidence in his favor, and to a speedy trial by an impartial jury of twelve men of his vicinage, without whose unanimous consent he cannot be found guilty; nor can he be compelled to give evidence against himself; that no man be deprived of his liberty, except by the law of the land or the judgement of his peers.

SEC. 9. That excessive bail ought not to be required, nor excessive fines imposed, nor cruel and unusual punishments inflicted.

SEC. 10. That general warrants, whereby any officer or messenger may be commanded to search suspected places without evidence of a fact committed, or to seize any person or persons not named, or whose offense is not particularly described and supported by evidence, are grievous and oppressive, and ought not to be granted.

SEC. 11. That in controversies respecting property, and in suits between man and man, the ancient trial by jury is preferable to any other and ought to be held sacred.

SEC. 12. That the freedom of the press is one of the greatest bulwarks of liberty and can never be restrained but by despotic governments.

SEC. 13. That a well-regulated militia, composed of the body of the people, trained to arms, is the proper, natural, and safe defense of a free State; that standing armies, in time of peace, should be avoided, as dangerous to liberty; and that in all cases the military should be under strict subordination to, and be governed by, the civil power.

SEC. 14. That the people have a right to uniform government; and therefore, that no government separate from, or independent of the government of Virginia, ought to be erected or established within the limits thereof.

SEC. 15. That no free government, or the blessings of liberty, can be preserved to any people, but by a firm adherence to justice, moderation, temperance, frugality, and virtue, and by frequent recurrence to fundamental principles.

SEC. 16. That religion, or the duty which we owe to our Creator, and the manner of discharging it, can be directed by reason and conviction, not by force or violence; and therefore all men are equally entitled to the free exercise of religion, according to the dictates of conscience; and that it is the mutual duty of all to practice Christian forbearance, love, and charity towards each other.

Reconstituting the Federal Government

James Madison was such an influential figure in the Constitutional Convention held in 1787 that he has been called "the Father of the Constitution." Only thirty-six years old at the time of the convention, Madison had prepared extensively for the meeting. His proposals for change, known as

A Flawed System

In February 1787, three months before the Constitutional Convention began, James Madison wrote of the inadequacies of the national government under the Articles of Confederation.

Indeed the Present System neither has nor deserves advocates; and if some very strong props are not applied, will quickly tumble to the ground. No money is paid into the public Treasury; no respect is paid to the federal authority. Not a single State complies with the requisitions; several pass them over in silence, and some positively reject them. The payments ever since the peace have been decreasing, and of late fall short even of the pittance necessary for the Civil list of the Confederacy. It is not possible that a government can last long under these circumstances.

the Virginia Plan, became the basis of the delegates' discussion. In this letter, written to Thomas Jefferson in October 1787, only a little more than a month after the convention ended, Madison explains some of the basic assumptions that guided him and the other delegates.

You will herewith receive the result of the Convention, which continued its Session till the 17th. of September. I take the liberty of making some observations on the subject which will help to make up a letter, if they should answer no other purpose.

It appeared to be the sincere and unanimous wish of the Convention to cherish and preserve the Union of the States. No proposition was made, no suggestion was thrown out, in favor of a partition of the Empire into two or more Confederacies.

It was generally agreed that the objects of the Union could not be secured by any system founded on the principle of a confederation of sovereign States. A *voluntary* observance of the federal law by all the members, could never be hoped for. A *compulsive* one could evidently never be reduced to practice, and if it could, involved equal calamities to the innocent & the guilty, the necessity of a military force both obnoxious & dangerous, and in general, a scene resembling much more a civil war, than the administration of a regular Government.

Hence was embraced the alternative of a Government which instead of operating, on the States, should operate without their intervention on the individuals composing them: and hence the change in the principle and proportion of representation.

The ground-work being laid, the great objects which presented themselves were 1. to unite a proper energy in the Executive and a proper stability in the Legislative departments, with the essential characters of Republican Government. 2. to draw a line of demarkation which would give to the General Government every power requisite for general purposes, and leave to the States every power which might be most beneficially administered by them. 3. to provide for the different interests of different parts of the Union. 4. to adjust the clashing pretensions of the large and small States. Each of these objects was pregnant with difficulties. The whole of them together formed a task more difficult than can be well conceived by those who were not concerned in the execution of it. Adding to these considerations the natural diversity of human opinions on all new and complicated subjects, it is impossible to consider the degree of concord which ultimately prevailed as less than a miracle.

When the Constitutional Convention completed its work, its president, George Washington, sent a copy of the document to Congress requesting careful consideration. "That it will meet the full and entire Approbation of every State is not perhaps to be expected. But each will doubtless consider that had her Interests been alone consulted the Consequences might have been particularly disagreeable or injurious to others. . . . That it may promote the lasting Welfare of that Country so dear to us all and secure her Freedom and Happiness is our most ardent wish."

Almost as soon as the proceedings of the Philadelphia convention were made known, its plans for strengthening the central government aroused immediate and strong opposition. To go into effect, the new document needed to be ratified by conventions in each state. The Constitution's supporters soon began referring to themselves as "Federalist," leading their opponents to be called "Antifederalists." To encourage the election of pro-Constitution delegates to New York's ratifying convention, Alexander Hamilton quickly organized the publication of what came to be called *The Federalist Papers*. In all, Hamilton, working with James Madison and John Jay before he became too sick to continue, prepared eighty-five essays. The pieces, now seen as classic discussions of American political science, originally appeared three times a week in New York newspapers. They were widely reprinted. In this part of the opening essay, dated October 27, 1787, Hamilton explains in broad terms the arguments for the new Constitution.

After an unequivocal experience of the inefficacy of the subsisting F[e]deral Government, you are called upon to deliberate on a new Constitution for the United States of America. The subject speaks its own importance; comprehending in its consequences, nothing less than the existence of the UNION, the safety and welfare of the parts of which it is composed, the fate of an empire, in many respects, the most interesting in the world. It has been frequently remarked, that it seems to have been reserved to the people of this country, by their conduct and example to decide the important question, whether societies of men are really capable or not, of establishing good government from reflection and choice, or whether they are forever destined to depend, for their political constitutions, on accident and force. If there be any truth in the remark, the crisis, at which we are arrived, may with propriety be regarded as the aera in which that decision is to be made; and a wrong election of the part we shall act, may, in this view, deserve to be considered as the general misfortune of mankind.

This idea will add the inducements of philanthropy to those of patriotism to heighten the solicitude, which all considerate and good men must feel for the event. Happy will it be if our choice should be directed by a judicious estimate of our true interests, unperplexed and unbiassed by considerations not connected with the public good. But this is a thing more ardently to be wished,

Both the Declaration of Independence and the United States Constitution were approved in Pennsylvania's State House, now known as Independence Hall.

than seriously to be expected. The plan offered to our deliberations affects too many particular interests, innovates upon too many local institutions, not to involve in its discussion a variety of objects foreign to its merits, and of views, passions and prejudices little favourable to the discovery of truth. . . .

Ambition, avarice, personal animosity, party opposition, and many other motives, not more laudable than these, are apt to operate as well upon those who support as upon those who oppose the right side of a question. Were they not even these inducements to moderation, nothing could be more illjudged than that intolerant spirit, which has, at all times, characterised political parties. . . .

And yet however just these sentiments will be allowed to be, we have already sufficient indications, that it will happen in this as in all former cases of great national discussion. A torrent of angry and malignant passions will be let loose. . . . An enlightened zeal for the energy and efficiency of government will be stigmatized, as the off-spring of a temper fond of despotic power and hostile to the principles of liberty. . . . [I]t will be equally forgotten, that the vigour of government is essential to the security of liberty . . . .

In the course of the preceeding observations I have had an eye, my Fellow Citizens, to putting you upon your guard against all attempts, from whatever quarter, to influence your decision in

In this woodcut celebrating the ratification of the Constitution, two cherubs display the now-united states, represented by pillars, as an angel blows the trumpet of fame.

a matter of the utmost moment to your welfare by any impressions other than those which may result from the evidence of truth. You will, no doubt, at the same time, have collected from the general scope of them that they proceed from a source not unfriendly to the new Constitution. Yes, my Countrymen, I own to you, that, after having given it an attentive consideration, I am clearly of opinion, it is your interest to adopt it. I am convinced, that this is the safest course for your liberty, your dignity, and your happiness. . . .

I propose in a series of papers to discuss the following interesting particulars—*The utility of this UNION to your political prosperity—The insufficiency of the present Confederation to preserve that Union—The necessity of a government at least equally energetic with the one proposed to the attainment of this object—The conformity of the proposed constitution to the true principles of republican government—Its analogy to your own state constitution—*and lastly, *The additional security, which its adoption will afford to the preservation of that species of government, to liberty and to property./*

In the progress of this discussion I shall endeavour to give a satisfactory answer to all the objections which shall have made their appearance that may seem to have any claim to your attention.

It may perhaps be thought superfluous to offer arguments to prove the utility of UNION, a point, no doubt, deeply engraved on the hearts of a great body of the people in every state, and one, which it may be imagined has no adversaries. But the fact is, that we already hear it whispered in the private circles of those who oppose the new constitution, that the Thirteen States are of too great extent for any general system, and that we must of necessity resort

A nation, without a national government, is, in my view, an awful spectacle.

—Alexander Hamilton, arguing for the Constitution in the *Federalist Papers*, 1788

to separate confederacies of distinct portions of the whole. . . . For nothing can be more evident, to those who are able to take an enlarged view of the subject, than the alternative of an adoption of the new Constitution, or a dismemberment of the Union.

One of the most comprehensive Antifederalist indictments of the proposed Constitution was Mercy Otis Warren's February 1788 pamphlet, *Observations on the New Constitution, and on the Federal and State Conventions*. As did most commentators on both sides, Warren, an accomplished writer of plays, poems, and essays, published this piece anonymously. And like many Antifederalists, she later changed her mind about the new document. Her 1805 *History of the Rise, Progress, and Termination of the American Revolution* strongly supported the Constitution.

[1.] . . . [A]nnual election is the basis of responsibility.—Man is not immediately corrupted, but power, without limitation, or ameanability, may endanger the brightest virtue—whereas a frequent return to the bar of their constituents is the strongest check against the corruptions to which men are liable. . . . But it is unnecessary to dwell long on this article, as the best political writers have supported the principles of annual elections with a precision that cannot be confuted, though they may be darkned by the sophistical arguments that have been thrown out with design, to undermine all the barriers of freedom.

2. There is no security in the profered system, either for the rights of conscience, or the liberty of the press. . . .

3. There are no well defined limits of the judiciary powers, they seem to be left as a boundless ocean . . . it would be an Herculean labour to attempt to describe the dangers with which they are replete.

4. The executive and the legislative are so dangerously blended as to give just cause of alarm. . . .

5. The abolition of trial by jury in civil causes.—This mode of trial, the learned Judge Blackstone observes, "has been coeval with the first rudiments of civil government, that property, liberty and life, depend on maintaining in its legal force the constitutional trial by jury." . . .

6. Though it has been said by Mr. *Wilson*, and many others, that a standingarmy is necessary for the dignity and safety of America, yet freedom revolts at the idea, when the . . . despot, may draw out his dragoons to suppress the murmurs of a few. . . .

James Warren, Mercy Otis Warren's husband and a fellow Antifederalist, argued that the Constitution was as dangerous as British rule: "The revolution which separated the United States from Great-Britain was not more important to the liberties of America, than that which will result from the adoption of the new system. The *former* freed us from a *foreign subjugation,* and there is too much reason to apprehend, that the *latter* will reduce us to a *federal domination.*"

James Wilson of Pennsylvania, a strong supporter of a more powerful national government, was one of the most influential delegates at the Constitutional Convention.

Mercy Otis Warren belonged to a prominent Massachusetts political family. Although she could not hold public office, she played a significant part in public affairs through her conversations, correspondence, and other writings. In this engraving, based on a painting made in 1763, Warren is portrayed as a young woman.

It is hoped this country may yet be governed by milder methods than are usually displayed beneath the bannerets of military law.—Standing armies have been the nursery of vice, and the bane of liberty. . . .

7. Notwithstanding the delusory promise to guarantee a republican form of government to every state in the union—If the most discerning eye could discover any meaning at all in the engagement, there are no resources left for the support of internal government, or the liquidation of the debts of the state. Every source of revenue is in the monopoly of Congress. . . .

8. As the new Congress are [e]mpowered to determine their own salaries, the requisitions for this purpose may not be very moderate, and the drain for public monies will probably rise past all calculation. . . .

9. There is no provision for a rotation, nor any thing to prevent the perpetuity of office in the same hands for life; which by a little well timed bribery, will probably be done, to the exclusion of men of the best abilities from their share in the offices of government. . . .

10. The inhabitants of the United States, are liable to be dragged from the vicinity of their own country, or state, to answer to the litigious or unjust suit of an adversary, on the most distant borders of the continent: In short, the appelate jurisdiction of the supreme federal court, includes an unwarrantable stretch of power over the liberty, life, and property of the subject, through the wide continent of America.

11. One Representative to thirty thousand inhabitants is a very inadequate representation . . . .

12. If the sovereignty of America is designed to be elective, the circumscribing the votes to only ten electors in this state, and the same proportion in all the others, is nearly tantamount to the exclusion of the voice of the people in the choice of their first magistrate. It is vesting the choice solely in an aristocratic junto, who may easily combine in each State to place at the head of the union the most convenient instrument for despotic sway.

13. A senate chosen for six years, will in the most instances, be an appointment for life, as the influence of such a body over the minds of the people, will be coequal to the extensive powers with which they are vested, and they will not only forget, but be forgotten by their constituents; a branch of supreme legislature thus set beyond all responsibility, is totally repugnant to every principle of a free government.

14. There is no provision by a bill of rights to guard against the dangerous encroachments of power in too many instances to be named. . . .

[T]he rights of individuals ought to be the primary object of all government, and cannot be too securely guarded by the most explicit declarations in their favor. . . .

15. The difficulty, if not impracticability, of exercising the equal and equitable powers of government by a single legislature over an extent of territory that reaches from the Mississippi to the Western lakes, and from them to the Atlantic ocean, is an insuperable objection to the adoption of the new system. . . .

16. It is an indisputed fact, that not one legislature in the United States had the most distant idea when they first appointed members for a convention, entirely commercial, or when they afterwards authorised them to consider on some amendments of the federal union, that they would, without any warrant from their constituents, presume on so bold and daring a stride, as ultimately to destroy the state governments, and offer a *consolidated system*. . . .

17. The first appearance of the article which declares the ratification of nine states sufficient for the establishment of the new system, wears the face of dissention, is a subversion of the union of the confederated states, and tends to the introduction of anarchy and civil convulsions. . . .

18. The mode in which this constitution is recommended to the people to judge without either the advice of Congress, or the legislatures of the several states, is very reprehensible—it is an attempt to force it upon them before it could be thoroughly understood, and may leave us in that situation, that in the first moments of slavery the minds of the people, agitated by the remembrance of their lost liberties, will be like the sea in a tempest, that sweeps down every mound of security.

A Federalist Appeals to George Washington

In the early stages of the debate over the Constitution, Gouverneur Morris, an active Federalist and a key contributor to the convention, wrote a letter to George Washington explaining that his support was vital to the process.

I have observed that your name to the new Constitution has been of infinite service. Indeed I am convinced that if you had not attended the Convention, and the same paper had been handed out to the world, it would have met with a colder reception, with fewer and weaker advocates, and with more and more strenuous opponents. As it is, should the idea prevail that you would not accept of the Presidency, it would prove fatal in many parts.

Chapter Five

The Limits of Liberty

Revolutions in Society and Culture

This piece of needlework from the 1770s relates the Biblical story of Absalom, the son of King David, in a way that echoes the plight of the colonies before the Revolution. While Absalom, trapped in a tree by his long hair, is executed by the commander Joab, dressed significantly in a red coat—the father uncaringly plays a harp.

I n October 1776, four months after Virginia's Declaration of Rights had proclaimed the liberties of its citizens, members of the Presbyterian church in Hanover County complained to the state's legislature that they were still denied those rights. Americans were now "casting off the yoke of tyranny" imposed by the British. Yet Presbyterians were still oppressed by the "spirit of domination, prejudice, or bigotry" that continued in Virginia. Although they were "dissenters" who did not belong to the Episcopal Church (what had been the Church of England before the Revolution) they still had to pay taxes to support it. This situation seemed particularly unfair in relatively recently settled counties like Hanover. Dissenters there were forced to pay "the heavy burdens" of buying land to support the ministers, paying their salaries, and building churches, even though "there [were] very few Episcopalians."

Having to pay for ministers they did not want to hear and for churches they did not want to attend had not been unusual. For centuries, governments in Britain and other European countries had "established" a single church, requiring residents to pay tax money to support it, accept its religious beliefs, and often even attend its services. As the Virginia Presbyterians suggested, however, the Revolution's ideals of liberty and equality inspired many Americans to challenge this long-established pattern. "In this enlightened age, and in a land where all . . . are united in the most strenuous efforts to be free," the Presbyterians declared, "we hope and expect that our representatives will cheerfully concur in removing every species of religious, as well [as] civil bondage." In fact, their petition argued, political and religious freedom were closely connected: "every argument for civil liberty, gains additional strength when applied to liberty in the concerns of religion."

Ten years later, in 1786, Virginia passed the Statute for Religious Freedom. This legislation declared that people should not be taxed to support churches without their consent—and more important, that state support of religion was wrong and even dangerous. Nearly all the states in the new nation also separated church and state. Many of the issues and situations that underlay this change had developed in the colonial period. But only the power of Revolutionary ideas had made it possible.

As the Hanover County Presbyterians recognized in 1776, liberty and equality also applied to other areas than politics. In the following years arguments for liberty and equality were used to attack a broad range of inequalities, including the practice of slavery and the role of women. By today's standards, the results were mixed. Neither African Americans nor women achieved full equality. But within their eighteenth-century context the changes were often dramatic. The language of liberty, rights, and equality the Revolution helped to establish as principles of social as well as political life provided a continuing source of inspiration for future generations to confront other forms of injustice.

The Religious Revolution

Religion in America had been distinctive long before the dispute between Britain and its colonies developed. From the time of the Pilgrims and the Puritans, many of Europe's most radical religious movements had taken refuge in America and often flourished there. Even before 1700, Pennsylvania and Rhode Island allowed their residents to believe and worship freely. Nearly all other colonies, however, had created an "established" church that received tax money and other forms of preferential treatment. This system faced greater problems in the mid-eighteenth century, as religious life became more diverse. In Virginia, the Church of England (sometimes called the Anglican Church) had been the only established religious body. After 1750, Presbyterian and Baptist churches grew substantially. The Revolutionary ideals of liberty and equality created urgency and gave broader significance to the complaints of these groups about their second-class status.

Americans during the Revolutionary years increasingly supported the idea of religious liberty. But beyond stopping prosecution of people for believing or worshipping differently, the precise meaning of the concept remained unclear.

This 1769 British political cartoon shows New Englanders' harsh reaction to calls for a Church of England bishop in America—and links the opposition to calls for liberty and greater participation in government. As the bishop is pushed away from the dock, the crowd holds volumes of radical political writings (including those of John Locke). A monkey begging at the front suggests that church officials asked for too much money.

Many Americans still feared that removing state support for churches would be dangerous, weakening the churches and the values they taught, perhaps even threatening the moral foundations of society. One popular solution for reconciling liberty and support for religion was to continue to collect taxes for religious purposes but to distribute the money to the groups designated by each taxpayer. The great orator Patrick Henry introduced this "general assessment" plan into the Virginia legislature in 1784. Titled "A Bill Establishing a Provision for Teachers of the Christian Religion," the measure seemed to enjoy wide support, but it was defeated the following year by a coalition of religious liberals, led by James Madison, and religious minorities, led by the Presbyterians.

Whereas the general diffusion of Christian knowledge hath a natural tendency to correct the morals of men, restrain their vices, and preserve the peace of society; which cannot be effected without a competent provision for learned teachers, who may be thereby enabled to devote their time and attention to the duty of instructing such citizens, as from their circumstances and want of education, cannot otherwise attain such knowledge; and it is judged that such provision may be made by the Legislature, without counteracting the liberal principle heretofore adopted and intended to be preserved by abolishing all distinctions of pre-eminence amongst the different societies or communities of Christians;

Be it therefore enacted by the General Assembly, That for the support of Christian teachers, per centum on the amount, or _____ in the pound on the sum payable for tax on the property within this Commonwealth, is hereby assessed, and shall be paid by every person chargeable with the said tax at the time the same shall become due; and the Sheriffs of the several Counties shall have power to levy and collect the same in the same manner and under the like restrictions and limitations, as are or may be prescribed by the laws for raising the Revenues of this State.

And be it enacted, That for every sum so paid, the Sheriff or Collector shall give a receipt, expressing therein to what society of Christians the person from whom he may receive the same shall direct the money to be paid, keeping a distinct account thereof in the books. The Sheriff of every County, shall, on or before the _____ day of _____ in every year, return to the Court, upon oath, two alphabetical lists of the payments to him made, distinguishing in columns opposite to the names of the persons who shall have paid the same, the society to which the money so paid was by

Like the Virginia Presbyterians, Massachusetts Baptist leader Isaac Backus linked the cause of religious freedom to the struggle against the British. He wrote in a 1773 pamphlet, "The great importance of a general union through this country in order to the preservation of our liberties has often been pleaded for with propriety, but how can such a union be expected so long as that dearest of all rights, equal liberty of conscience, is not allowed?"

But our rulers can have authority over such natural rights only as we have submitted to them. The rights of conscience we never submitted, we could not submit. We are answerable for them to our God. The legitimate powers of government extend to such acts only as are injurious to others. But it does me no injury for my neighbour to say there are twenty gods, or no god. It neither picks my pocket nor breaks my leg.

—Thomas Jefferson, *Notes on the State Virginia* (1787)

them appropriated; and one column for the names where no appropriation shall be made. . . . And the Sheriff, after deducting five per centum for the collection, shall forthwith pay to such person or persons as shall be appointed to receive the same by the Vestry, Elders, or Directors, however denominated of each such society, the sum so stated to be due to that society. . . .

And be it further enacted, That the money to be raised by virtue of this Act, shall be by the Vestries, Elders, or Directors of such religious society, appropriated to a provision for a Minister or Teacher of the Gospel of their denomination, or the providing places of divine worship, and to none other use whatsoever; except in the denominations of Quakers and Menonists [Mennonites], who may receive what is collected from their members, and place it in their general fund, to be disposed of in a manner which they shall think best calculated to promote their particular mode of worship.

And be it enacted, That all sums which at the time of payment to the Sheriff of Collector may not be appropriated by the person paying the same, shall be accounted for with the Court in manner as by this Act is directed; and after deducting for his collection, the Sheriff shall pay the amount thereof (upon account certified by the Court to the Auditors of Public Accounts, and by them to the Treasurer) into the public Treasury, to be disposed of under the direction of the General Assembly, for the encouragement of seminaries of learning within the Counties whence such sums shall arise, and to no other use or purpose whatsoever.

THIS ACT shall commence, and be in force, from and after the ____ day of ____ in the year ____.

Having defeated the general assessment plan in 1785, James Madison pushed through what became known as the Virginia Statute for Religious Freedom the following year. Written by Thomas Jefferson in 1777, the act declared that government should not have control over religious beliefs. Jefferson considered the statute so important that he wanted his authorship noted on his tombstone.

I. WHEREAS Almighty God hath created the mind free; that all attempts to influence it by temporal punishments or burthens, or by civil incapacitations, tend only to beget habits of hypocrisy and meanness, and are a departure from the plan of the Holy author of our religion, who being Lord both of body and mind, yet chose not to propagate it by coercions on either, as was in his

A BILL *for establishing* RELIGIOUS FREEDOM, *printed for the consideration of the* PEOPLE.

WELL aware that the opinions and belief of men depend not on their own will, but follow involuntarily the evidence proposed to their minds, that Almighty God hath created the mind free, and manifested his Supreme will that free it shall remain, by making it altogether insusceptible of restraint: That all attempts to influence it by temporal punishments or burthens, or by civil incapacitations, tend only to beget habits of hypocrisy and meanness, and are a departure from the plan of the holy author of our religion, who being Lord both of body and mind, yet chose not to propagate it by coercions on either, as was in his Almighty power to do, but to extend it by its influence on reason alone: That the impious presumption of legislators and rulers, civil as well as ecclesiastical, who, being themselves but fallible and uninspired men, have assumed dominion over the faith of others, setting up their own opinions and modes of thinking, as the only true and infallible, and as such, endeavouring to impose them on others, hath established and maintained false religions over the greatest part of the world, and through all time: That to compel a man to furnish contributions of money for the propagation of opinions which he disbelieves and abhors, is sinful and tyrannical: That even the forcing him to support this or that teacher of his own religious persuasion, is depriving him of the comfortable liberty of giving his contributions to the particular pastor whose morals he would make his pattern, and whose powers he feels most persuasive to righteousness, and is withdrawing from the Ministry those temporal rewards which, proceeding from an approbation of their personal conduct, are an additional incitement to earnest and unremitting labour for the instruction of mankind: That our civil rights have no dependance on our religious opinions, any more than on our opinions in physicks or geometry: That therefore the proscribing any citizen as unworthy the publick confidence, by laying upon him an incapacity of being called to offices of trust and emolument, unless he profess or renounce this or that religious opinion, is depriving him injuriously of those privileges and advantages to which, in common with his fellow citizens he has a natural right: That it tends also to corrupt the principles of that very religion it is meant to encourage, by bribing with a monopoly of wordly honours and emoluments, those who will externally profess and conform to it: That though indeed these are criminal who do not withstand such temptation, yet neither are those innocent who lay the bait in their way: That the opinions of men are not the object of civil government, nor under its jurisdiction: That to suffer the civil Magistrate to intrude his powers into the field of opinion, and to restrain the profession or propagation of principles on supposition of their ill tendency, is a dangerous fallacy, which at once destroys all religious liberty; because he being of course Judge of that tendency will make his own opinions the rule of judgment, and approve or condemn the sentiments of others only as they shall square with, or differ from his own: That it is time enough for the rightful purposes of civil government for its officers to interfere when principles break out into overt acts against peace and good order: And finally, that truth is great and will prevail if left to herself; that she is the proper and sufficient antagonist to errour, and has nothing to fear from the conflict, unless by human interposition, disarmed of her natural weapons, free argument and debate; errours ceasing to be dangerous when it is permitted freely to contradict them

WE the General Assembly of *Virginia* do enact, that no man shall be compelled to frequent or support any religous Worship place or Ministry whatsoever, nor shall be enforced, restrained, molested, or burthened in his body or goods, nor shall otherwise suffer on account of his religious opinions or belief, but that all men shall be free to profess, and by argument to maintain their opinions in matters of religion, and that the same shall in no wise diminish, enlarge, or affect their civil capacities.

AND though we well know that this Assembly, elected by the people for the ordinary purposes of legislation only, have no power to restrain the acts of succeeding Assemblies, constituted with powers equal to our own, and that therefore to declare this act irrevocable would be of no effect in law; yet we are free to declare, and do declare, that the rights hereby asserted are of the natural rights of mankind, and that if any act shall be hereafter passed to repeal the present, or to narrow its operation, such act will be an infringement of natural right.

This is the earliest known printing of the Virginia Statute for Religious Freedom. This draft was published in 1779 in order to encourage public discussion of the measure. The final version passed in 1786.

Almighty power to do; that the impious presumption of legislators and rulers, civil as well as ecclesiastical, who being themselves but fallible and uninspired men, have assumed dominion over the faith of others, setting up their own opinions and modes of thinking as the only true and infallible, and as such endeavouring to impose them on others, hath established and maintained false religions over the greatest part of the world, and through all time; that to compel a man to furnish contributions of money for the propagation of opinions which he disbelieves, is sinful and tyrannical; that even the forcing him to support this or that teacher of his own religious persuasion, is depriving him of the comfortable liberty of giving his contributions to the particular pastor whose morals he would make his pattern, and whose powers he feels most persuasive to righteousness, and is with-drawing from the ministry those temporary rewards, which pro-ceeding from an approbation of their personal conduct, are an additional incitement to earnest and unremitting labours for the instruction of mankind; that our civil rights have no dependence on our religious opinions, any more than our opinions in physics or geometry; that therefore the proscribing any citizen as unwor-thy the public confidence by laying upon him an incapacity of being called to offices of trust and emolument, unless he profess or renounce this or that religious opinion, is depriving him injuri-ously of those privileges and advantages to which in common with his fellow-citizens he has a natural right; that it tends only to corrupt the principles of that religion it is meant to encourage, by bribing with a monopoly of worldly honours and emoluments, those who will externally profess and conform to it; that though indeed these are criminal who do not withstand such temptation, yet neither are those innocent who lay the bait in their way; that to suffer the civil magistrate to intrude his powers into the field of opinion, and to restrain the profession or propagation of princi-ples on supposition of their ill tendency, is a dangerous fallacy, which at once destroys all religious liberty, because he being of course judge of that tendency will make his opinions the rule of judgment, and approve or condemn the sentiments of others only as they shall square with or differ from his own; that it is time enough for the rightful purposes of civil government, for its offi-cers to interfere when principles break out into overt acts against peace and good order; and finally, that truth is great and will pre-vail if left to herself, that she is the proper and sufficient antago-nist to error, and has nothing to fear from the conflict, unless by human interposition disarmed of her natural weapons, free argu-ment and debate, errors ceasing to be dangerous when it is per-mitted freely to contradict them.

After a long introduction that justifies the need for religious liberty, the Statute continues with provisions calling for com-plete freedom of religious belief and worship. The final sec-tion seeks to balance two of Jefferson's strongly held convictions, a faith in unchanging universal principles of lib-erty and a belief that the rules accepted by previous genera-tions could not bind their successors without their consent.

II. *Be it enacted by the General Assembly,* that no man shall be compelled to frequent or support any religious worship, place or ministry whatsoever, nor shall be enforced, restrained, molested, or burthened in his body or goods, nor shall otherwise suffer on account of his religious opinions or belief; but that all men shall be free to profess, and by argument to maintain, their opinion in matters of religion, and that the same shall in no wise diminish, enlarge or affect their civil capacities.

III. And though we well know that this assembly, elected by the people for the ordinary purposes of legislation only, have no power to restrain the acts of succeeding assemblies, constituted with powers equal to our own, and that therefore to declare this act to be irrevocable would be of no effect in law; yet as we are free to declare, and do declare, that the rights hereby asserted are of the natural rights of mankind, and that if any act shall hereafter be passed to repeal the present, or to narrow its operation, such act will be an infringement of natural right.

A group of Baptists holds a service alongside the Schuylkill River in Pennsylvania. In the water, a minister baptizes a new member. Although they had been present in the early colonies, Baptists (who believed that people should be baptized only as adults) did not become a significant force within American Christianity until the middle of the eighteenth century.

Changing Ways of Worship

Rationalists such as James Madison and Thomas Jefferson, who believed that specific differences of religious belief were relatively unimportant, were only part of the coalition that supported the separation of church and state in Virginia. Just as important, and much more numerous, were the often more humble members of religious groups outside the old established churches. To them, religious beliefs were too important to be controlled by government. These new "evangelical" groups gained increasing popularity in the Revolutionary period. By the early part of the next century, the Baptists and the Methodists had become America's largest denominations. These evangelical faiths were particularly appealing because they welcomed new members and stressed religious feelings rather than specific doctrines. These three 1766 letters by the Episcopal minister Reverend Devereux Jarret describe the emotional power of the new religious forms. Although Jarrett worried about excessive emotionalism, he worked closely with Virginia's Methodists while they were still part of the Anglican Church. The Methodists created their own church organization after the war.

In this 1819 French engraving preachers address a crowd at a Methodist camp meeting. Increasingly common in the post-Revolutionary south, the camp meeting brought together people from many localities for preaching and religious services.

May 2, 1776. Rev. and Dear Brother,—Yesterday I preached at B.'s chapel, to a crowded and attentive audience. Afterward the Methodists held their love-feast: during which, as many as pleased rose, one after another, and spoke, in few words, of the goodness of God to their souls. Before three had done speaking (although they spoke but few words) you might see a solemn sense of the presence of God visible on every countenance, while tears of sorrow or joy were flowing from many eyes. Several testified to the consolation they had received: some believed they were perfected in love. When the passions of the people were rising too high, and breaking through all restraint, the preacher gently checked them by giving out a few verses of a hymn. When most of the congregation went away, some were so distressed with a sense of their sins, that they could not be persuaded to leave the place. Some lively Christians stayed with them, and continued in prayer for the space of two hours, till fifteen mourners were enabled to rejoice in God their Saviour; and some careless creatures of the politer sort, who would needs go in to see what this strange thing meant, felt an unusual power, so that, like Saul among the prophets, they fell down on their knees, and cried for mercy among the rest. O may they still continue to pray till God has given them another heart!

May 3, 1776. Last night three or four score [fifty to eighty] of my neighbours met together to keep a watch-night: at which it is the custom to spend three or four hours in religious exercises, and to break up at twelve. Such was the distress of those that were convinced of sin, that they continued in prayer all night, and till two hours after sunrise. Here also fourteen or fifteen received a sense of pardon: so that in two days thirty of my own parish have been justified, besides others of other parishes.

Indeed I do not take it for granted that all are justified who think they are so. Some I fear are mistaken. But I shall judge better of this when I see the fruits.

May 7, 1776. I have no doubt but the work now carrying on is genuine: yet there are some circumstances attending it which I disliked—such as loud outcries, tremblings, fallings, convulsions. . . .

There is another thing which has given me much pain—the praying of several at one and the same time. Sometimes five or six, or more, have been praying all at once, in several parts of the room, for distressed persons. Others were speaking by way of exhortation: so that the assembly appeared to be all in confusion, and must seem to one at a little distance, more like a drunken rabble than the worshippers of God. I was afraid, this was not doing all things in decency and order. . . . But this is a delicate point. It requires much wisdom to allay the wild, and not damp the sacred fire.

The African-American religious pioneer Richard Allen was born into slavery in 1760 but was allowed to buy his freedom out of his earnings after his Delaware master became a Methodist. Allen also converted and became a traveling Methodist minister, speaking to both black and white Americans. By 1786, he had become the leader of a group of African Americans in Philadelphia affiliated with St. George's Methodist Church, known as the Free African Society of Philadelphia. The group, although they had continued to meet at St. George's, had already held some separate services and had been making plans to build their own church in 1792 when, as this account by Allen suggests, the racial prejudices of the leaders at St. George became painfully clear. When the group later decided to become part of the Episcopal Church, Allen disagreed with the decision. He assembled a new congregation at the Bethel Church, where he established the nation's first African-American denomination, the African Methodist Episcopal Church.

A number of us usually attended St. George's church in Fourth street; and when the colored people began to get numerous in attending the church, they moved us from the seats we usually sat on, and placed us around the wall, and on Sabbath morning we went to church and the sexton stood at the door, and told us to go in the gallery. He told us to go, and we would see where to sit. We expected to take the seats over the ones we formerly occupied below, not knowing any better. We took those seats; meeting had begun, and they were nearly done singing, and just as we got to the seats, the Elder said, "Let us pray." We had not been long upon our knees before I heard considerable scuffling and loud talking. I raised my head up and saw one of the trustees, H—— M——, having hold of the Rev. Absalom Jones, pulling him off his knees, and saying, "You must get up, you must not kneel here." Mr. Jones

Although Richard Allen and other African Americans founded Bethel Church in the 1790s, white Methodists continued to claim control over it. In 1816 church members legally established their right to control its property and its activities. That same year, Richard Allen and others formed the African Methodist Episcopal Church. With Allen as its first bishop, the new denomination provided a structure that allowed African-American congregations in other localities to direct their own institutions.

Methodists and Slavery

The early leaders of the Methodist movement often boldly challenged racial prejudices, although later Methodists accepted slavery and racial division as their organization grew larger and more established. Richard Allen's master, Sterling Sturgis, became a Methodist and an opponent of slavery because of the work of the white Methodist minister Freeborn Garrettson. Garrettson's memoir discusses some of his early 1777 attempts to reach out to African Americans and to attack slavery.

In September I went to North-Carolina, . . . [where] my exercises were very great, particularly respecting the slavery, and hard usage of the poor afflicted negroes. Many times did my heart ache on their account, and many tears run down my cheeks, both in Virginia and Carolina, while exhibiting a crucified Jesus to their view; and I bless God that my labours were not in vain among them. I endeavoured frequently to inculcate the doctrine of freedom in a private way, and this procured me the ill will of some, who were in that unmerciful practice. I would often set apart times to preach to the blacks, and adapt my discourse to them alone; and precious moments have I had. While many of their sable faces were bedewed with tears, their withered hands of faith were stretched out.

replied . . . "Wait until prayer is over, and I will get up and trouble you no more." With that he beckoned to one of the other trustees, Mr. L— S—, to come to his assistance. He came, and went to William White to pull him up. By this time prayer was over, and we all went out of the church in a body, and they were no more plagued with us in the church. This raised a great excitement and inquiry among the citizens, in so much that I believe they were ashamed of their conduct. But my dear Lord was with us, and we were filled with fresh vigor to get a house erected to worship God in. . . . Here was the beginning and rise of the first African church in America.

"Mother" Ann Lee, founder of the Shakers, moved to America from England just before the Revolution to escape religious oppression. She set up a congregation in Niskeyuna, New York, near Albany, that became the United Society of Believers in Christ's Second Appearing. The group became known as the Shakers because of the dances that formed an important part of their worship. At its height, several thousand members lived in the more than twenty Shaker communities in Ohio, Kentucky, New York, and New England. This success was extraordinary for a group that rejected both marriage and sexual activity and considered their founder, a woman who never learned to read or write, the female counterpart of Jesus. The official history of the early church, published in 1816, tells these stories about its earliest American converts.

While Mother and her little family were laboring in the wilderness of Neskeyuna, and preparing themselves for the opening of the gospel, they were little noticed or-known, even by the neighboring inhabitants. But in the spring of the year 1780, God, in his providence, opened the way for the commencement of that great and mighty work, which they had long been waiting to see, and which, shortly after, filled the whole neighboring country with anxiety and alarm.

The first intelligence concerning this little Church of Christ, was received by the inhabitants of New-Lebanon, and its vicinity, in the month of March. Enquiries were soon after made, and people began to visit the Church from different places, particularly from New-Lebanon. When they came to see Mother and the Elders, they were filled with wonder and admiration at the great power and operations which they were under and the clear

One of the earliest Shaker communities—aside from the first community established in Niskeyuna, New York—met in New Lebanon, New Hampshire. The society there built this meeting house in 1785. Men and women entered by separate doors.

and pointed plainness of their testimony against all sin, and every evil work.

The gifts and operations of the Holy Ghost were evident among them. Shaking, trembling, speaking in unknown tongues, prophesying and singing melodious songs, were gifts with which they seemed continually to be filled; with many other signs and operations, which showed the mighty power of God, and pointed out the particular sins and abominations which those who came to see them had committed. Even the very thoughts of the heart were plainly and particularly pointed out; insomuch that many feared and trembled in their presence, while others ran to get out of the way, lest their sins should be told them.

Many enquiries were made concerning their religion and doctrines, of which the following is a short specimen. The people enquired of Mother and the Elders, the cause of their maintaining such a singular faith and manner of life. They replied, that they had been laboring, for years, in the work of the regeneration, and had actually risen with Christ, and did travel with him, in the resurrection; and related considerable of their experience. . . .

To the married people, Mother said, "You must forsake the marriage of the flesh, or you cannot be married to the Lamb, nor have any share in the resurrection of Christ: for those who are counted worthy to have part in the resurrection of Christ, neither marry nor are given in marriage; but are like unto the angels."

As this story about two male converts suggests, Ann Lee and the group she founded challenged common expectations about roles of women and men. In a time when religious groups taught the subordination of women, Shakers followed a woman they called "Mother." Later communities had women as well as men among their leaders.

Joseph Meacham and Calvin Harlow were among the first that visited this little Church, for the purpose of searching out the truth of their religion. After much conversation, and many critical enquiries, in all which they received plain and satisfactory answers, Joseph sent Calvin to Mother with the following observation and query, namely: "Saint Paul says, Let your women keep silence in the Churches; for it is not permitted unto them to speak; but they are commanded to be under obedience, as also saith the law. And if they will learn any thing, let them ask their husbands at home: for it is a shame for a woman to speak in the Church. How do you reconcile this with the Apostle's doctrine?"

Mother answered, "The order of man, in the natural creation, is a figure of the order of God in the spiritual creation. As the order of nature requires a man and a woman to produce offspring; so, where they both stand in their proper order, the man is the first, and the woman the second in the government of the family. He is the father and she the Mother; and all the children, both male and female, must be subject to their parents; and the woman, being second, must be subject to her husband, who is the first; but when the man is gone, the right of government belongs to the woman: So is the family of Christ.

This answer opened a vast field of contemplation to Joseph, and filled his mind with great light and understanding concerning the spiritual work of God. He clearly saw that the new creation could not be perfect in its order, without a father and a mother: That as the natural creation was the offspring of a natural father and mother; so the spiritual creation must be the offspring of a spiritual father and mother.

He saw Jesus Christ to be the Father of the spiritual creation, who was now absent; and he saw Ann Lee to be the Mother of all who were now begotten in the regeneration; and she being present in the body, the power and authority of Christ on earth, was committed to her; and to her appertained the right of leading, directing, and governing all her spiritual children.

Liberty, But Not for All

The Revolutionary years were extremely important in the history of African Americans. Like state support of religion, slavery had been almost universally accepted in colonial America. But the ideals of the Revolution—rights, liberty, and equality—put slavery on the defensive. By the end of the eighteenth century, all Northern states had either ended slavery completely or established a program to end it gradually. Even in the South, many prominent figures spoke out against it. Unfortunately, slavery would not end quickly in the South. It grew stronger there and prejudice against African Americans continued, in other parts of the country.

In 1779, during the middle of the war for American independence, twenty New Hampshire slaves petitioned the state legislature asking for their freedom. One of the signers, Prince Whipple, had served in the Continental Army, perhaps even at George Washington's celebrated crossing of the

Delaware River. The initial reaction to their complaints was not warm, although he and other African Americans made the same arguments about rights and God-given liberty made by white Patriots who attacked British rule. The state legislature did not consider their petition. The *New-Hampshire Gazette* printed it in July 1780, saying it did so "for the amusement of our readers." The situation changed eventually and the state ended slavery after the war.

The petition of *Nero Brewster*, and others, natives of Africa, now forcibly detained in slavery, in said state, most humbly sheweth, That the God of Nature gave them life and freedom, upon terms of the most perfect equality with other men; that freedom is an inherent right of the human species, not to be surrendered, but by consent, for the sake of social life; that private or public tyranny and slavery, are alike detestable to minds conscious of the equal dignity of human nature; that in power and authority of individuals, derived solely from a principle of coercion, against the wills of individuals, and to dispose of their persons and properties, consists the compleatest idea of private and political slavery; that all men being amenable to the Deity for the ill improvement of the blessings of his providence, they hold themselves in duty bound, strenuously to exert every faculty of their minds, to obtain that blessing of freedom which they are justly entitled to from the donation of the beneficent Creator; that thro' ignorance & brutish violence of their native country men, and by sinister designs of others, (who ought to have taught them better) & by the avarice of both, they, while but children, and incapable of self-defence, whose infancy might have prompted protection, were seized, imprisoned, and transported from their native country, where, (tho' ignorance and inchristianity prevailed) they were born free to a country, where (tho' knowledge, christianity and freedom, are their boast) they are compelled, and their unhappy posterity, to drag on their lives in miserable servitude.—Thus, often is the parent's cheek wet for the loss of a child, torn by the cruel hand of violence from her aking bosom! Thus, often, and in [va]in, is the infant's sigh,

Like Emmanuel Leutze's painting George Washington Crossing the Delaware, *which is better known today, Thomas Sully's earlier 1819 depiction of the same event also includes an African-American soldier, presumably the New Hampshire slave Prince Whipple. Whipple was set free during the war.*

How many [good slaves] have there been, and now are in this Province, who have had every Day of their Lives embittered with this most intollerable Reflection, That, let their Behaviour be what it will, neither they, nor their Children to all Generations, shall ever be able to do, or to possess and enjoy any Thing, no, not even Life itself, but in a Manner as the Beasts that perish.

We have no Property! We have no Wives! No Children! We have no City! No Country! But we have a Father in Heaven.

—Petition of Boston slaves to Governor Hutchinson, January 6, 1773

for the nurturing care of it's bereaved parent! and thus, do the ties of nature and blood, become victims, to cherish the vanity and luxury of a fellow-moral! Can this be right? Forbid it gracious Heaven! . . .

Therefore, your humble slaves most devoutly pray, for the sake of injured liberty, for the sake of justice, humanity, and the rights of mankind; for the honor of religion, and by all that is dear, that your honors would graciously interpose in our behalf, and enact such laws and regulations as in your wisdom you may think proper, whereby we may regain our liberty and be rank'd in the class of free agents, and that the name of SLAVE may no more be heard in a land gloriously contending for the sweets of freedom; and your humble slaves as in duty bound will ever pray.

Portsmouth, Nov. 12, 1779

A more direct attack on the contradictions between Revolutionary ideals and slavery appeared on the tombstone in Concord, Massachusetts, of John Jack, a slave who had purchased his freedom shortly before his death in 1773. The moving inscription on his grave was presumably written by Daniel Bliss, the executor of his estate. Bliss's awareness of the tensions between Revolutionary ideals and everyday reality probably came not only from his friendship with Jack, but also from his own loyalty to the Crown in a town that was moving toward Revolution.

God wills us free; man wills us slaves.
I will as God wills; God's will be done.
Here lies the body of
JOHN JACK
a native of Africa who died
March 1773 aged about 60 years
Tho' born in a land of slavery,
He was born free.
Tho' he lived in a land of liberty,
He lived a slave.
Till by his honest, tho' stolen labors,
He acquired the source of slavery,
Which gave him his freedom;
Tho' not long before
Death, the great tyrant
Gave him his final emancipation,
And set him on a footing with kings.

Tho' a slave to vice,
He practiced those virtues
Without which kings are but slaves.

**The growing sense of the contradiction between slavery and
Revolutionary ideals encouraged all the Northern states to
end the practice by the end of the century. The process varied
from state to state. In Massachusetts, court decisions played
the key role. The most notable case involved the prosecution
of Nathaniel Jennison for assaulting the African-American
Quock Walker. Jennison defended himself by asserting his
rights as Walker's owner. In the final court case, *Commonwealth* v. *Jennison*, held before the Massachusetts Supreme
Court in 1784, Chief Justice William Cushing gave these
instructions to the jury, telling them that slavery violated
the state's constitution. Although the jury followed Cushing's advice and ordered Walker freed, for a number of years
African Americans in Massachusetts often had to turn to
individual lawsuits to gain their freedom.**

As to the doctrine of slavery and the right of Christians to hold
Africans in perpetual servitude, and sell and treat them as we do our
horses and cattle, that (it is true) has been heretofore countenanced
by the Province Laws formerly, but nowhere is it expressly enacted or established. It has been a usage—a usage which took its origin from the practice of some of the European nations, and the regulations of the British government respecting the then Colonies,
for the benefit of trade and wealth. But whatever sentiments have

In this 1792 painting made for the Library
Company of Pennsylvania, the figure of
Liberty, with her liberty cap (on a staff
beside her) as a sign of freedom, sits surrounded by the symbols of learning. A
broken chain at Liberty's feet suggests the
end of slavery in Pennsylvania, and before
her freed African Americans express their
gratitude. The celebration of freedom in the
background takes place around a liberty
pole, a pre-Revolutionary symbol of
Patriotic ideals.

> *We expect great things from men who have made such a noble stand against the designs of their fellow-men to enslave them*
> —Petition by four slaves to the Massachusetts General Court, 1773

formerly prevailed in this particular or slid in upon us by the example of others, a different idea has taken place with the people of America, more favorable to the natural rights of mankind, and to that natural, innate desire of Liberty, which the Heaven (without regard to color, complexion, shape of noses-features) has inspired all the human race. And upon this ground our Constitution of Government, by which the people of this Commonwealth have solemnly bound themselves, sets out with declaring that all men are born free and equal—and that every subject is entitled to liberty, and to have it guarded by the laws, as well as life and property—and in short is totally repugnant to the idea of being born slaves. This being the case, I think the idea of slavery is inconsistent with our own conduct and Constitution; and that there can be no such thing as perpetual servitude of a rational creature, unless his liberty is forfeited by some criminal conduct or given up by personal consent or contract.

About a month after America declared its independence, Henry Laurens, a South Carolinian planter and merchant, wrote this letter to his son explaining his opposition to slavery. Laurens owned slaves and had at one time been a slave trader. In this 1776 letter, he blames England for introducing the practice of slavery into America, an argument that Thomas Jefferson had also made in an early draft of the Declaration of Independence. During the war Laurens served as the president of the Continental Congress, was captured by the British, and acted as a negotiator during the peace process. He estimated that his wartime losses added up to the huge sum of £40,000. Such financial losses were widespread in the South. These difficulties helped discourage many southern slaveholders from doing much about their new awareness of the evils of slavery. Like Jefferson, Laurens neither freed his slaves nor did much to end slavery in general.

My Negroes . . . all to a Man are strongly attached to me, so are all of mine in this Country, hitherto not one of them has attempted to desert on the contrary those who are more exposed hold themselves always ready to fly from the Enemy in case of a sudden descent—many hundreds of that Colour have been stolen & decoyed by the Servants of King George the third—Captains of British Ships of War & Noble Lords have busied themselves in such inglorious pilferage to the disgrace of their Master & disgrace of their Cause.—these Negroes were first enslaved by the

English—Acts of Parliament have established the Slave Trade in favour of the home residing English & almost totally prohibited the Americans from reaping any share of it—Men of War Forts Castles Governors Companies & Committees are employed & authorized by the English Parliament to protect regulate & extend the Slave Trade—Negroes are brought by English Men & sold as Slaves to Americans—British Liverpoole Manchester Birmingham &c. &c. live upon the Slave Trade—the British Parliament now employ their Men of War to steal those Negroes from the Americans to whom they had sold them, pretending to set the poor wretches free but basely trepan [kidnap] & sell them into ten fold worse Slavery in the West Indies, where probably they will become the property of English-Men again & of some who sit in Parliament; what meanness! what complicated wickedness appears in this scene! O England, how changed! how fallen!

You know my Dear Sir. I abhor Slavery, I was born in a Country where Slavery had been established by British Kings & Parliaments as well as by the Laws of that Country Ages before my existence, I found the Christian Religion & Slavery growing under the same authority & cultivation—I nevertheless disliked it—in former days there was no combatting the prejudices of Men supported by Interest, the day I hope is approaching when from principles of gratitude as well justice every Man will strive to be foremost in shewing his readiness to comply with the Golden Rule; not less than £20000 Stg. [Sterling] would all my Negroes produce if sold at public Action tomorrow I am not the Man who enslaved them. they are indebted to English Men for that favour, nevertheless I am devising means for manumitting [freeing] many of them & for cutting off the entail of Slavery—great powers oppose me, the Laws & Customs of my Country, my own & the avarice of my Country Men—What will my Children say if I deprive them of so much Estate? these are difficulties but not insuperable

I will do as much as I can in my time & leave the rest to a better hand. I am not one of those . . . who dare trust in Providence for defence & security of their own Liberty while they enslave & wish to continue in Slavery, thousands who are as well intitled to freedom as themselves.

No American's opinions about slavery have been more fully examined than Thomas Jefferson. Author of the Declaration of Independence and the third President of the United States, Jefferson was also a slave holder and, many scholars believe, the father of at least one child with a slave. Two

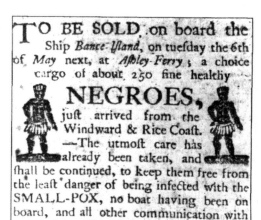

Though Henry Laurens turned against slavery around the time of the Revolution, he and his partners had sold thousands of African Americans before he left the slave trade in the 1760s. This advertisement from a Charleston, South Carolina, newspaper announces the arrival of a new slave ship.

Washington and Slavery

Almost alone among the major southern Revolutionary leaders, George Washington freed his slaves, but only after his death. In a letter written to John Francis Mercer in 1786, he declared:

I never mean (unless some peculiar circumstances should compel me to it) to possess another slave by purchase; it being among my first wishes to see some plan adopted by the Legislature in which slavery in this Country may be abolished by slow, sure & imperceptible degrees.

of his key statements on the subject appear in his *Notes on the State of Virginia*, a book written over a number of years in the early 1780s. These passages reveal the tensions in Jefferson's attitudes. Like a number of other southern leaders of the time, he was opposed to slavery, viewing it as a violation of the human rights that lay at the heart of the new nation's ideals. At the same time, however, Jefferson was also reluctant to admit the equality of African Americans—and reluctant to push very hard for an end to slavery.

A page from Thomas Jefferson's memorandum book from 1773. In this one-month period, he records both the buying (January 21) and selling (January 29) of slaves.

I advance it therefore as a suspicion only, that the blacks, whether originally a distinct race, or made distinct by time and circumstances, are inferior to the whites in the endowments both of body and mind. It is not against experience to suppose, that different species of the same genus, or varieties of the same species, may possess different qualifications. Will not a lover of natural history then, one who views the gradations in all the races of animals with the eye of philosophy, excuse an effort to keep those in the department of man as distinct as nature formed them? The unfortunate difference of colour, and perhaps of faculty, is a powerful obstacle to the emancipation of these people. Many of their advocates, while they wish to vindicate the liberty of human nature, are anxious also to preserve its dignity and beauty. . . . Among the Romans [who enslaved whites] emancipation required but one effort. The slave, when made free, might mix with, without staining the blood of his master. But with us a second is necessary, unknown to history. When freed, he is to be removed beyond the reach of mixture. . . .

The whole commerce between master and slave is a perpetual exercise of the most boisterous passions, the most unremitting despotism on the one part, and degrading submissions on the other. Our children see this, and learn to imitate it; . . . The man must be a prodigy who can retain his manners and morals undepraved by such circumstances. . . . And can the liberties of a nation be thought secure when we have removed their only firm basis, a conviction in the minds of the people that these liberties are of the gift of God? That they are not to be violated but with his wrath? Indeed I tremble for my country when I reflect that God is just:

that his justice cannot sleep for ever: that considering numbers, nature and natural means only, a revolution of the wheel of fortune, an exchange of situation, is among possible events: that it may become probable by supernatural interference! The Almighty has no attribute which can take side with us in such a contest.

Boston resident Prince Hall was a beneficiary of the Revolutionary changes in African-American life—and a victim of its limitations. Freed before the Revolution, he became a leader of Boston's African-American community and the founder of an African-American Masonic organization that still exists today. Hall's religious faith and the changes he had already experienced made him optimistic about the future. But he was also fully aware of the racial problems around him. In this 1797 address to African-American Masons in Boston, he describes the abuses and oppression suffered by black Americans even in a region where slavery had ended.

Among these numerous sons and daughters of distress, I shall begin with our friends and brethren; and first, let us see them dragge'd from their native country by the iron hand of tyranny and oppression, from their dear friends and connections, with weeping eyes and aching hearts, to a strange land and strange people, whose tender mercies are cruel; and there to bear the iron yoke of slavery & cruelty till death as a friend shall relieve them. . . . But God can and will change their conditions, and their hearts too; and let Boston and the world know, that He hath no respect of persons; and that that bulwark of envy, pride, scorn and contempt, which is so visible to be seen in some and felt, shall fall, to rise no more. . . .

Let us seek those things which are above, which are sure, and stedfast, and unchangeable, and at the same time let us pray to Almighty God, while we remain in the tabernacle, that he would give us the grace of patience and strength to bear up under all our troubles, which at this day God knows we have our share. Patience I say, for were we not possess'd of a great measure of it you could not bear up under the daily insults you meet with in the streets of Boston; much more on public days of recreation, how are you shamefully abus'd, and that at such a degree that you may truly be said to carry your lives in your hands, and the arrows of death are flying about your heads; helpless old women have their clothes torn off their backs, even to the exposing of their nakedness . . . . 'Twas said by a gentleman who saw that filthy behaviour in the common, that in all the places he had been in, he never saw so cruel behaviour in all his life, and that a slave in the West-Indies, on Sunday or holidays enjoys himself and friends without any molestation. Not only this man, but many in town who hath seen their behaviour to you, and that without any provocation—twenty or thirty cowards fall upon one man—have wonder'd at the patience of the Blacks: 'tis not for want of courage in you, for they know that they dare not face you man for man, but in a mob, which we despise, and had rather suffer wrong than to do wrong, to the disturbance of the community and the disgrace of our reputation: for every good citizen doth honor to the laws of the State where he resides.

My brethren, let us not be cast down under these and many other abuses we at present labour under: for the darkest is before the break of day. My breathren, let us remember what a dark day it was with our African brethren six years ago, in the French West-Indies. Nothing but the snap of the whip was heard from morning to evening; hanging, broken on the wheel, burning, and all manner of tortures inflicted on those unhappy people for nothing else but to gratify their masters pride, wantonness, and cruelty: but blessed be God, the scene is changed; they now confess that God hath no respect of persons, and therefore receive them as their friends, and treat them as brothers. Thus doth Ethiopia begin to stretch forth her hand, from a sink of slavery to freedom and equality.

Honorable Daughters of America

Just as the Revolution sparked opposition to slavery and state support of religion, it also provoked discussion about the role of women. The Revolutionary ideal of equality provided a new means of challenging the widespread belief that women were inferior to men. As in the debate about slavery, the Revolutionary-era discussions about women's status did not completely change older ideas and systems. Furthermore, it was primarily concerned with the position of white women of middle- or upper-class status, women who were generally not forced into employment outside the household. But the Revolution created new ways of thinking about the role of women and new opportunities for education that formed the basis of nineteenth-century feminist demands for women's rights.

Abigail Smith grew up in a wealthy family as the daughter of a Massachusetts minister. Like many other women of

"Surely we [women] may have sense enough to give our opinions to commend or discommend such actions as we may approve or disapprove; without being reminded of our spinning and household affairs as the only matters we are capable of thinking or speaking of with justness and propriety."
—Eliza Wilkinson, a letter to a friend, South Carolina, 1782

the time, she received no formal schooling. She took full advantage, however, of reading and interacting with her learned family members. In 1764, she married the lawyer John Adams, who became a leader in the movement for independence—and later President of the United States. The Revolution was a difficult time for both of them. From 1774 to 1784, while John was away serving in various official positions, Abigail Adams ran both the household and the family farm. During their separation, the two wrote each other regularly. The most well-known exchange between the two concerned women's legal rights.

In her letter on March 31, 1776, Abigail raises this issue just months before independence, using the language of the Revolutionary debate about tyranny, representation, and rebellion to argue for greater legal protection for women. The resulting interchange reveals not only the close personal relationship between the two, but also the ways that discussion of women's rights challenged older ways of thinking.

Just before he left on a diplomatic mission to France in 1778, John Adams gave this locket to his wife, Abigail. It contained some of his hair and bore an image of a woman on shore watching a ship, a reminder of their own situation. The inscription on the shield reads: "I yield whatever is is right." The repeated "is" may be a mistake or a reference to the poet Alexander Pope's early-eighteenth-century assertion of the morality of the universe, "whatever is, is right."

I long to hear that you have declared an independancy—and by the way in the new Code of Laws which I suppose it will be necessary for you to make I desire you would Remember the Ladies, and be more generous and favourable to them than your ancestors. Do not put such unlimited power into the hands of the Husbands. Remember all Men would be tyrants if they could. If perticuliar care and attention is not paid to the Laidies we are determined to foment a Rebelion, and will not hold ourselves bound by any Laws in which we have no voice, or Representation.

That your Sex are Naturally Tyrannical is a Truth so thoroughly established as to admit of no dispute, but such of you as wish to be happy willingly give up the harsh title of Master for the more tender and endearing one of Friend. Why then, not put it out of the power of the vicious and the Lawless to use us with cruelty and indignity with impunity. Men of Sense in all Ages abhor those customs which treat us only as the vassals of your Sex. Regard us then as Beings placed by providence under your protection and in immitation of the Supreem Being make use of that power only for our happiness.

John Adam's reply on April 15 also links the idea of women's legal rights to the Revolutionary struggle, but stresses the danger of uncontrolled power in the hands of the ruled.

As to your extraordinary Code of Laws, I cannot but laugh. We have been told that our Struggle has loosened the bands of Government every where. That Children and Apprentices were disobedient—that schools and Colledges were grown turbulent—that Indians slighted their Guardians and Negroes grew insolent to their Masters. But your Letter was the first Intimation that another Tribe more numerous and powerfull than all the rest were grown discontented.—This is rather too coarse a Compliment but you are so saucy, I wont blot it out.

Depend upon it, We know better than to repeal our Masculine systems. Altho they are in full Force, you know they are little more than Theory. We dare not exert our Power in full Latitude. We are obliged to go fair, and softly, and in Practice you know We are the subjects. We have only the Name of Masters, and rather than give up this, which would compleatly subject Us to the Despotism of the Peticoat, I hope George Washington, and all our brave Heroes would fight. . . . I begin to think the Ministry as deep as they are wicked. After stirring up Tories, Landjobbers, Trimmers, Bigots, Canadians, Indians, Negroes, Hanoverians, Hessians, Russians, Irish Roman Catholicks, Scotch Renegadoes, at last they have stimulated . . . to demand new Priviledges and threaten to rebell.

Abigail Adams's May 7 response reaffirms their relationship, but continues to stress the value of legal reform for women.

I can not say that I think you very generous to the Ladies, for whilst you are proclaiming peace and good will to Men, Emancipating all Nations, you insist upon retaining an absolute power over Wives. But you must remember that Arbitrary power is like most other things which are very hard, very liable to be broken—and notwithstanding all your wise Laws and Maxims we have it in our power not only to free ourselves but to subdue our Masters, and without violence throw both your natural and legal authority at your feet—
"Charm by accepting, by submitting sway
Yet have our Humour most when we obey."
I thank you for several Letters which I have received since I wrote Last. They alleviate a tedious absence, and I long earnestly for a Saturday Evening, and experience a similar pleasure to that which I used to find in the return of my Friend upon that day after a week[']s absence. The Idea of a year dissolves all my Phylosophy.

Like Abigail Adams, Judith Sargent Murray grew up without a formal education. Murray's series of essays published in the *Massachusetts Magazine* during the early 1790s under the title "The Gleaner" (and reprinted as a book by that name in 1798) contain a number of discussions about the status of women. In this selection, Murray celebrates the increasing ability of middle- and upper-class women to gain the formal education that she had been denied. These new opportunities, Murray predicts, would lead to a growing recognition of women's abilities. Yet she still believes that they would continue to act as wives and mothers—roles, she argues, that would be enhanced rather than weakened by greater education. Murray's emphasis on gender equality helped to articulate ideals that would become central to the nineteenth-century movement for women's rights.

And, first, by way of exordium, I take leave to congratulate my fair country-women, on the happy revolution which the few past years has made in their favour; that in these infant republics, where, within my remembrance, the use of the needle was the principal attainment which was thought *necessary* for a woman, the lovely proficient is now permitted to appropriate a moiety of her time to studies of a more elevated and elevating nature. Female academies are every where establishing, and right pleasant is the appellation to my ear.

Yes, in this younger world, "the Rights of Women" begin to be understood; we seem, at length, determined to do justice to THE SEX; and, improving on the opinions of a Wollstonecraft, we are ready to contend for the *quantity*, as well as *quality*, of mind. The younger part of the female world have now an inestimable prize put into their hands; and it depends on the rising generation to refute a sentiment, which, still retaining its advocates, grounds its arguments on the incompatibility of the present enlarged plan of female education, with those necessary occupations, that must ever be considered as proper to the department and comprised in the duties of a judiciously instructed and elegant woman; and, if our daughters will combine their efforts, converts to the new regulations will every day multiply among us. To argue against facts, is indeed contending with both wind and tide; and, borne down by accumulating examples, conviction of the utility of the present plans will pervade the public mind, and not a dissenting voice will be heard.

The British author Mary Wollstonecraft wrote *A Vindication of the Rights of Women* in 1792 to argue that women deserved equal rights and opportunities. It was much discussed—and heavily criticized—in England and America. Mary Wollstonecraft Shelley, her daughter, wrote the popular novel *Frankenstein*.

In 1770, John Singleton Copley painted this portrait of nineteen-year-old Judith Sargent Murray, who was born into a wealthy Massachusetts family. Her 1798 book, The Gleaner, attracted advance orders from George Washington, Mercy Otis Warren, and John Adams, who agreed to allow the book to be dedicated to him.

I may be accused of enthusiasm; but such is my confidence in THE SEX, that I expect to see our young women forming a new era in female history. . . .

It is true, that every faculty of their minds will be occasionally engrossed by the most momentous concerns; but as often as *necessity* or *propriety* shall render it incumbent on them, they will *cheerfully* accommodate themselves to the more *humble duties* which their situation imposes. When their sphere of action is enlarged, when they become wives and mothers, they will fill with honour the parts alloted them. Acquainted, theoretically, with the nature of their species, and experimentally with themselves, they wil not expect to meet, in wedlock, with those faultless beings, who so frequently issue, armed at all points, from the teeming brain of the novelist. They will learn properly to estimate; they will look, with pity's softest eye, on the natural frailties of those whom they elect partners for life; and they will regard their virtues with that sweet complacency, which is ever an attendant on a predilection founded on love, and happily combining esteem. As mothers, they will assume with alacrity their arduous employment, and they will cheerfully bend to its various departments. They will be primarily solicitous to fulfil, in *every instance*, whatever can *justly* be denominated *duty*; and those intervals, which have heretofore been devoted to frivolity, will be appropriated to pursuits, calculated to inform, enlarge, and sublime the soul—to contemplations, which will ameliorate the heart, unfold and illumine the understanding, and gradually render the human being an eligible candidate for the society of angels.

Such, I predict, will be the daughters of Columbia [America]; and my gladdened spirit rejoices in the prospect. A sensible and informed woman—companionable and serious—possessing also a facility of temper, and united to a congenial mind—blest with competency—and rearing to maturity a promising family of children—Surely, the wide globe cannot produce a scene more truly interesting. See! the virtues are embodied—the domestic duties appear in their place, and they are all fulfilled—morality is systematized by religion, and sublimed by devotion—every movement is the offspring of elegance, and their manners have received the highest polish. . . . Such is the family of reason—of reason, cultivated and adorned by literature.

The idea of the incapability of women, is, we conceive, in this *enlightened age,* totally *inadmissible;* and we have concluded, that establishing the *expediency* of admitting them to share the blessings of equality, will remove every obstacle to their advancement. In proportion as nations have progressed in the arts of civilization, the value of THE SEX hath been understood, their rank in the scale of being ascertained, and their consequence in society acknowledged.

The debate about women's activities during the Revolutionary period led many people to express, more clearly than ever before, the idea that the roles of men and women placed them in parallel and distinct areas of life—men in the public worlds of business and politics, women in the household. In the nineteenth century, this view became known as the doctrine of separate spheres. This idea pointed both to equality, by arguing that women played important roles, and inequality, by continuing to justify women's exclusion from public life and paid employment. An anonymous New York author elaborated this argument in a 1788 article titled "An Address to the Ladies" that appeared in *American Magazine*.

One sex is formed for the more hardy exercises of the Council, the field and the laborious employments of procuring subsistence. The other, for the superintendence of domestic concerns, and for diffusing bliss thro social life. When a woman quits her own department, she offends her husband, not merely because she obtrudes herself upon *his* business, but because she departs from that sphere which is assigned *her* in the order of society—because she neglects *her* duty and leaves *her own* department vacant. The same remark will apply to the man who visits the kitchen and gets the name of a *Betty*. The same principle which excludes a man from an attention to domestic business, excludes a woman from law, mathematics and astronomy. Each sex feels a degree of pride in being best qualified for a particular station, and a degree of resentment when the other encroaches upon their privilege. This is acting conformably to the constitution of society.

One of the primary arguments for expanding women's education came from the increased importance accorded to child-rearing. In this 1791 magazine piece, "On the Supposed Superiority of the Masculine Understanding," an anonymous author argues that raising children is a greater public service than the traditionally more valued activities of politics and business. Behind this argument that motherhood is an

When Thomas Jefferson's daughter Martha married in 1790, he gave her this traditional advice about the role of women: "The happiness of your life depends now on the continuing to please a single person. To this all other objects must be secondary."

During the Revolutionary years, Americans increasingly celebrated the mother's role in child rearing. In this image from an 1804 children's book, a mother breast feeds a baby while fondly looking at an older child. An alphabet book rests on the floor.

important part of public life lay a belief that a republican government, dependent upon the character of the people rather than the will of an individual, requires citizens who are morally strong—and that childhood is the time to establish proper moral habits. Like many people who supported greater standing for women in this period, the author argues for expanding women's public influence but does not demand full political participation.

The mind of man no sooner expands itself into action, than it is impressed with the passions of vanity, and a love of power. . . .

From these, and various combining circumstances, we may trace the source of that assumption of superiority, by which the men claim an implicit obedience from our sex: a claim which they support on the vain presumption of their being assigned the most important duties of life, and being intrusted by nature with the guardianship and protection of women. Let the daily victims of their infidelity speak how worthy they are of the boasted title of protectors. But it is in us that Heaven hath reposed its supreme confidence; to us it hath assigned the care of making the first impressions on the infant minds of the whole human race, a trust of more importance than the government of provinces, and the marshalling of armies; as on the first impression depends more than on the discipline of the schools, the grave lectures of divines, or the future terrors of the laws. . . .

The daily follies committed by men, leave it unnecessary to prove the imbecillity of their *minds*; and as to what strength of *body* they possess superior to the women, this may be chiefly attributed to the exercise permitted and encouraged in their youth; but forbidden to us, even to a ridiculous degree.

In 1787, an anonymous woman calling herself "a Daughter of America" published a pamphlet in Boston. The tract, Women Invited to War, argues that women need to attack immorality publicly. The author's argument that women have an important role in activities that were usually assigned to men suggests the ways that religious activities in these years provided new justification for women's involvement and leadership.

O ye ladies of honour, worthy women, and honourable daughters of America,—Although it is our lot to live in a time of remarkable difficulty, trouble and danger; a time wherein we have heard the confused noise of the warrior, and seen garments rolled in blood: yet blessed be God, we have had the honour and favour of seeing our friends and brethren exert themselves valiantly in the defence of life and liberty. . . .

But alas! my dear friends, there is another powerful enemy spread through America, and is daily increasing among us, and threatens our destruction. This enemy has done more harm already, than all the armies of Britain have done or ever will be able to do. This dangerous and ruining enemy that is in the midst of us, has almost got the victory over America, and we shall all be destroyed or brought into captivity, if the women as well as the men, do not oppose, resist, and fight against this destructive enemy. . . .

Now if any of you inquire, saying, What enemy is this by whom we are in danger of being destroyed?

I answer, Truly my friends, we are in great danger of being overcome and destroyed by SIN, which is the worst of all enemies. . . .

But it may be, some will enquire, saying, Is not the Female the inferior sex, and shall inferiors set out before their superiors, in this great and important affair?—To which it may be replied, that in this spiritual warfare, an inferior may go before a superior without acting contrary to the rules of religion, decency or good manners. And as to one sex being superior to the other, let it be considered that our first parents were made, the one as well as the other of them, in the image of GOD, and that they had equal dominion over the creatures: And as some writers have observed, The Woman was not made out of Man's head to rule him, nor out of his feet to be trampled upon by him, but of his side, to be equal. Though it is acknowledged, that as the Man was first formed, and as the Woman was first in the transgression, therefore the male is in civil respects to be considered as the superior sex. But still, in the rights of religion and conscience, and in point of salvation, there is neither male nor female, but all are one in Christ, and joint-heirs of the promise: for with God there is no respect of persons. And therefore the superiority of the Male can be no bar to hinder the Female from being either the first engaged, or more zealous and courageous in proceeding in this spiritual warfare. And the Women as well as the Men, are invited to inlist themselves into the . . . cause of Christ, that they be strong in the Lord, and in the power of his might.

Besides, the first impressions upon the minds of children are generally derived from the women. Of how much consequence, therefore, is it in a republic, that they should think justly upon the great subject of liberty and government!

—Benjamin Rush's essay, "Thoughts Upon the Mode of Education, Proper in a Republic," 1786

Chapter Six

Paul Revere
Craftsman of the Revolution

In John Singleton Copley's portrait, painted in the late 1760s when Revere was about thirty-five years old, Revere is depicted as a working silversmith. Looking thoughtfully out a window— the reflection appears on the silver he is holding—Revere is preparing to engrave a teapot. His open shirt and vest reveal him as a what was then called a "middling" man, one clearly successful but not wealthy enough or with sufficient free time to be a leisured gentleman.

Popular culture today remembers Paul Revere as a man on horseback riding through the night and crying "The British are coming! The British are coming!" His ride warned the Patriot militias and minutemen of the advance of British troops on Lexington and Concord, helping to assemble the Patriots and setting off the first battle of the American Revolution. But Revere may have been just as important when he was not on horseback. He was also one of the finest—perhaps *the* finest—silversmith in America, an important (although less impressive) engraver, and a pioneering manufacturer, whose boilers powered some of the world's first working steamboats, whose copper sheets covered ships and the Massachusetts capitol dome, and whose bells still ring from many New England churches.

Revere is also significant for what he was not. Unlike many other Revolutionary leaders, he did not belong to a prominent family. Instead, he was the son of an immigrant and received only a short formal education before becoming an apprentice. Furthermore, Revere's military service did not bring him glory; it ended in public failure and court-martial, a trial before a military court. He received neither the Continental Army commission nor the office in federal government he had hoped for. Although in later life he became quite well-to-do, he remained a craftsman who worked with his hands well into his seventies. When Revere died in 1818, Bostonians recognized his importance but they did not always consider his April 1775 ride the most significant event of his life. The fullest newspaper obituary failed even to mention it.

The Making of an Artisan

Paul Revere's father, Apollos Rivoire, moved from France to Boston in 1716 at age fourteen and apprenticed with John Coney, one of America's most accomplished silversmiths. By the late 1720s, Rivoire had become known as "Paul" and had Americanized his last name to "Revere." Though his son, born in 1734, became wealthier and more prominent than his father, he remained a "mechanic," the eighteenth-century term for an artisan or craftsman. As he explained in 1782, "I am not rich, but I am in good circumstances."

Revere's father made this cream pot between 1740 and 1754 for his sister-in-law, Mary Hitchborn. Revere's Hitchborn relatives were more prosperous than his Revere family. Benjamin Hitchborn, one of Paul Revere's cousins, attended Harvard and became a state representative and senator. By contrast, Revere, who as a boy lived for a time in a house rented from the Hitchborns, received little formal education. After attending public school (probably for fewer than seven years) he learned the craft of silversmithing as an apprentice in his father's shop.

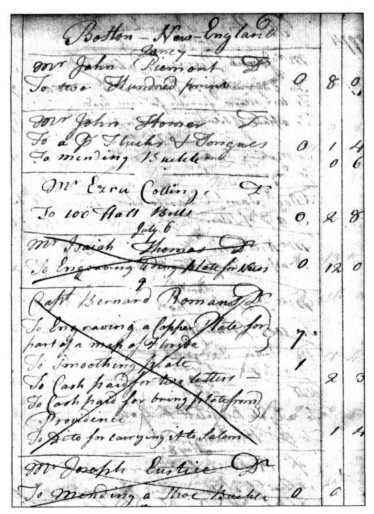

This day book served as Paul Revere's working account book in which he noted his business activities. As bills were paid, Revere crossed them out. This page reveals the range of Revere's business, noting engraving, selling prints, fixing shoe buckles, and making a pair of silver tongs. Although he did not, as legend suggests, make a set of dentures for George Washington, he did clean teeth and attach false ones. In 1776, Revere's dental work for General Joseph Warren allowed him to identify Warren's body after the British had thrown it into an unmarked grave in the Battle of Bunker Hill.

This may be the teapot which Revere is working on in the Copley portrait. The complexity of its lines, particularly in the handle and spout, shows the ornate rococo style that became fashionable as Revere moved into middle age. Revere's taste and craftsmanship made him an important silversmith not only in Boston, where local silversmiths sometimes turned to him for help with their more demanding projects, but in all the American colonies.

The skills involved in creating silver could also be used for other purposes. In the 1760s, Revere began engraving prints and illustrations. In 1770, he engraved the title page and the songs for The New England Psalm Singer, the first book of music printed in America written solely by an American composer. Since colorists could not yet print music with movable type, each page had to be separately engraved. In this illustration, the men are sitting around a circular table and the music fittingly is in a circular shape—since the music is itself a round (like "Row, Row, Row Your Boat").

Revere and his first wife, Sarah, bought this house in the North End of Boston in February 1770, only a month before the Boston Massacre. They moved again in 1780 to a three-story brick house that no longer stands. Sarah died in early 1773, not long after giving birth to her eighth child, six of whom lived past infancy. This photograph shows the earlier house as it appeared near the beginning of the twentieth century. It is now the only seventeenth-century house remaining in Boston.

Like many eighteenth-century widowers with children, Paul Revere quickly married again to Rachel Walker. Perhaps the event was the occasion for this miniature portrait made on ivory. They had eight children together. All told, Revere even-tually had fifty-two grandchildren.

The Making of a Revolutionary

When British soldiers learned that the man on horseback they had stopped on the night of April 18, 1775, was Paul Revere, they immediately identified him as a "damned Rebel." British soldiers as well as Boston civilians would have known Revere's name. Although he was never a primary leader of the resistance against Britain, his services to the Revolutionary cause ranged from engraving the most important image of the Boston Massacre and participating in the Boston Tea Party to organizing a group to spy on British soldiers.

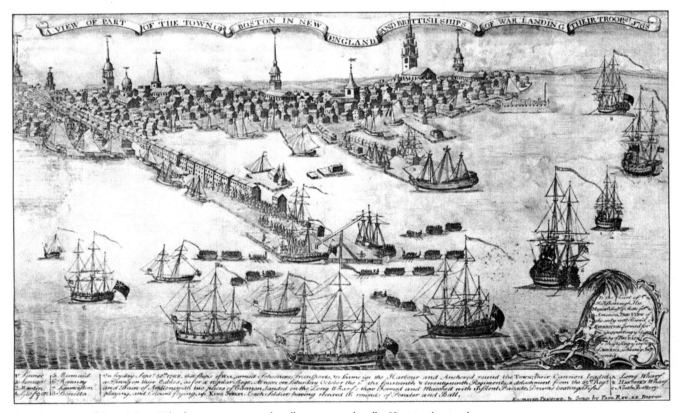

Revere's engraving of Boston's Long Wharf was as important politically as it was culturally. His print showing the 1768 arrival of British troops appeared in 1770, just after the Boston Massacre led to their removal. The picture's political message is ambiguous. The dedication on the bottom right of the picture notes that the troops were "supporting the dignity of BRITAIN & chastising the insolence of AMERICA." The caption at the bottom, however, notes that the troops marched into town "with insolent Parade." The print also portrays the city where Revere lived virtually all his life. The troops arrived on Long Wharf, one of many places in the busy seaport where ships could dock, unload, and load. The wharf continues to the State House up King Street, the ceremonial center of the city and the site of the 1770 Boston Massacre. Many of the public meetings opposing British measures took place in Fanueil Hall, the smaller building with the cupola to the right of the State House. Farther in the same direction is the city's North End, the part of town where Revere was born and worked. The second church from the right is Old North Church, where lanterns were hung the night before the battles of Lexington and Concord to signal the British movement. Revere's ride began in Charlestown, shown here as the grassy area in the right background.

In 1768, Boston citizens commissioned Revere to make this punch bowl to commemorate the ninety-two members of the Massachusetts House who refused to renounce their protest against the Townshend Acts. The choice of Revere recognized not only his artistic skill but also his commitment to the resistance.

Engrav'd Printed & Sold by PAUL REVERE Boston

This print of the Boston Massacre of March 1770 is Revere's most famous engraving and, except for his midnight ride five years later, his best-known contribution to the coming of the Revolution. Rather than showing the angry and chaotic mob that gathered on King Street that night, Revere pictures a carefully arranged group of soldiers firing on a peaceful group of citizens. The original composition came from another artist, who angrily protested it being copied without his permission. Revere added a "Butcher's Hall" sign to the Customs House where the shooting took place.

The Midnight Ride

Revere's famous "midnight ride" in April 1775 was not the only time he rode for the Patriot cause. He served as a messenger for the Patriots as early as 1773. Through his trips to Philadelphia, New York, and Portsmouth, New Hampshire, Revere helped build the connections between Patriots that made the Revolution possible. Despite this important early contribution, Revere's wartime experience was not a happy one. He failed to receive a commission to the Continental Army he had hoped for, becoming instead first a major and then a colonel in the Massachusetts militia. Colonel Revere commanded the troops on Castle Island (located in Boston Harbor) for several years. He also participated in several military expeditions. The last, a 1779 attack on the British in Maine, ended badly. After a chaotic retreat, a superior officer accused Revere of insubordination, disobeying orders, and even cowardice. Revere resigned his commission, but actively defended himself for three years before being cleared of all charges.

Revere carried this pass signed by the Boston Patriot leader James Otis when he took a message to the Continental Congress in November 1775, seven months after fighting broke out in Lexington and Concord.

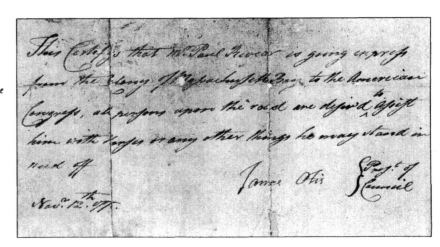

After his role in the battles of Lexington and Concord, Revere could not return to Boston. He spent the following year in Watertown, engraving the state's paper money and serving as a messenger for the Revolutionary cause. This is the back of a 1776 bill by Revere that shows a Patriot using his sword "in defence of American Liberty." In the figure's other hand is the Magna Charta (or Magna Carta), the origin of British freedoms. The front of the bill was individually signed and numbered by members of the Massachusetts House to discourage counterfeiting.

After arriving in Lexington after his midnight ride, Revere attempted to continue to Concord but was captured by British soldiers. He was later released, without his horse, about a mile out of Lexington. When he had made his way back to Lexington, John Hancock's clerk asked him to help hide this trunk, which was filled with Hancock's papers, so that they would not be taken by the British.

The Post-Revolutionary Businessman

"Man is a restless animal," wrote Paul Revere in a letter in 1804. He may have been thinking of himself. In the years after the Revolution, Revere established a variety of new businesses that made him not just an artisan but a successful and well-to-do businessman. Increasing public leadership accompanied Revere's business success. He served as the county coroner and from 1795 to 1797 as the Grand Master of the Massachusetts Grand Lodge of Masons, the men's fraternal order he had joined in the 1760s.

Despite the expansion of his other businesses, Revere continued to craft silver into the new century. His post-Revolutionary production often followed the new, less ornate "neoclassical" style inspired by Greek examples.

After his military service ended in 1779, Revere moved aggressively into other businesses. He operated a hardware store for a half-dozen years after 1783. In 1788 he established the iron foundry in the Boston's North End advertised on this trade card. The factory's biggest productions were cannons for ships and bells for a number of New England churches.

Revere's most important post-Revolutionary business was the factory he established in 1800, the first American mill to produce sheet copper. Helped by a grant from the United States government, the factory produced the metal used to recopper the hull of the Constitution. Revere also made the copper that still covers the dome of the Massachusetts State House and built boilers for some of the pioneering steamboats built by the inventor Robert Fulton.

This drawing, perhaps by Revere himself, shows his house and copper mills in Canton, Massachusetts, outside Boston. Although Revere kept a house in Boston, he spent increasing amounts of time in the countryside as he grew older.

Chapter Seven

The Living Revolution

The Revolution Remembered

S peaking on the Fourth of July, 1833, the Massachusetts lawyer and politician, Robert Rantoul, Jr., declared the American Revolution "the dividing point in the history of mankind." "It is," he noted, "the moment of the political regeneration of the world . . . the end from which the new order of things is to be reckoned." The very nature of government had changed: "Before [the Revolution] came the governments of force; after it, come, and shall come in long succession, the governments of opinion. They who wielded the sword had hitherto directed the fate of nations: the Fourth of July, seventeen hundred and seventy-six, announced the principle of self-government, and hereafter nations shall follow no guidance but the mastery of mind."

As Rantoul suggests, the American Revolution *was* revolutionary, an observation that people in both America and elsewhere have been making for more than two hundred years after the Revolution. But, despite Rantoul's deep admiration of the Revolution and the ideals it spurred, he possessed an ambiguous relationship with it. He strongly supported religious liberty and broader education, ideals that were closely identified with the Revolutionary generation, even when they were controversial. But he was also an enthusiastic supporter of the Democratic party, even though Revolutionary-era leaders had strongly condemned political parties as threats to the commitment to the common good they believed was necessary for the republic's survival. Rantoul also attacked the death penalty and supported labor unions—issues that had hardly been raised in the years before the Constitution.

The complexity of Rantoul's relationship to the Revolution and its ideals is not unusual. Memories and celebrations are always shaped by

In 1776, after the first reading of the Declaration of Independence in New York City, Patriots pulled down the statue of King George III from its pedestal on Bowling Green, melting it down to make bullets. In the 1790s, many people called for a statute of Washington to take its place. This 1798 print shows one such proposal. In the background is an image of Bowling Green with the empty pedestal in the left foreground. Unlike the British king, who had been portrayed as a Roman dressed in a toga and mounted on a horse, the American President appears in modern military dress and holds a written document inscribed "Friends and Fellow Citizens."

their context. As a central part of American identity, the Revolution has been perceived and represented in various ways. Several primary themes, however, have remained important. Many Americans celebrate the founding and the founders as the origin of their nation and the source of its unity. Other Americans have found the Revolution an inspiring source of ideals that challenge injustices. Just as important, the power of the Revolutionary past to influence the present has not been limited to Americans. Many people outside the United States have also seen the Revolutionary period as a source of powerful political ideals.

From a broader, more global perspective, however, it is more difficult to accept Rantoul's argument that the Revolution was the single most important event in human history. But the widespread use of its ideals and symbols over the course of two centuries and by many more nations suggests its continuing significance.

Commemorations and Celebrations

In 1817, John Adams complained of Americans' lack of interest in the founding of their country. Writing to John Trubull, he noted, "I See no disposition to celebrate or remember, or even Curiosity to enquire into the Characters, Actions, or Events of the Revolution." Adams's concern partly represented his disappointment that he was not remembered with the same awe and affection granted some other Revolutionary leaders. But his complaint was not simply personal. It also identified a particular dilemma in America's commemoration of its founding. Until the 1810s, the Revolution was a living memory for most Americans, an event they or people close to them had experienced directly. That connection was fading by the time of Adams's complaint. Soon afterward, it became clear that a conscious effort would be needed to keep these memories alive. The result was the renewed interest that Adams had longed for.

As these developments suggest, memory and commemoration of the Revolution did not arise automatically. They were created and reshaped by people in particular circumstances. Since the founding of the nation, Americans have celebrated the Revolution in variety of ways and a variety of styles.

In 1783, as the Revolution was winding down and American victory finally seemed secure, Ezra Stiles, President of Yale College, celebrated George Washington in an address

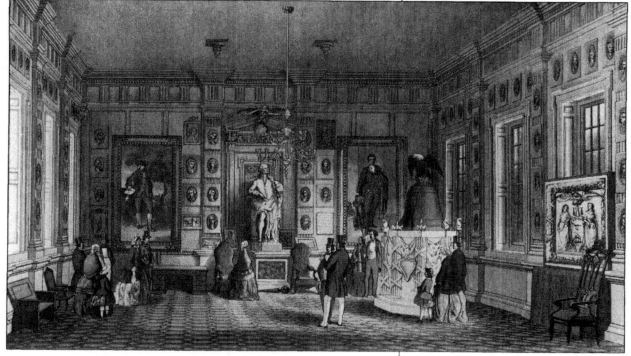

to the governor and the newly assembled legislature of Connecticut. Stiles portrayed General Washington as an instrument of God and the heir to the kings and heroes of classical and Biblical times.

O WASHINGTON! how do I love thy name! how have I often adored and blessed thy God, for creating and forming thee the great ornament of human kind! upheld and protected by the Omnipotent, by the Lord of Hosts, thou hast been sustained and carried through one of the most arduous and most important wars in all history. The world and posterity will, with admiration, contemplate thy deliberate, cool, and stable judgment, thy virtues, thy valour and heroic achievements, as far surpassing those of a CYRUS, whom the world loved and adored. The sound of thy fame shall go out into all the earth, and extend to distant ages. Thou has convinced the world of the BEAUTY OF VIRTUE—for in thee this BEAUTY shines with distinguished lustre. . . . something is there so singularly glorious and venerable thrown by heaven about thee, that not only does thy country love thee, but our very enemies stop the madness of their fire in full volley, stop the illiberality of their slander, at thy name, as if rebuked from heaven with a *touch not mine anointed*, and do my HERO *no harm!* Thy fame is of sweeter perfume than arabian spices in the gardens of

By the 1850s, when this print was published, the room in Philadelphia's Independence Hall where the Declaration had been debated and accepted had become a shrine to the Revolution. In addition to the Liberty Bell, the room contained numerous portraits, a statue of Washington, and a large painting of Lafayette.

According to the Bible, the ancient Persian King Cyrus delivered the Jews from captivity in Babylon.

Did anybody ever see Washington naked! It is inconceivable. He had no nakedness, but, I imagine, was born . . . with his clothes on and his hair powdered, and made a stately bow on his first appearance in the world.
—Nathaniel Hawthorne,
The French and Italian Notebooks, 1858

[P]ersia. . . . [L]istening angels shall catch the oduor, waft it to heaven, and perfume the universe.

The most popular early biography of Washington was written by the Reverend Mason Locke Weems. "Parson Weems" first wrote what came to be called *The Life of Washington* in 1800, soon after Washington died in late 1799. Over the next ten years, and in nearly as many editions of the biography, Weems expanded his short pamphlet into a book. What had originally been a celebration of Washington as a hero came to be a portrait of Washington as a man, certainly a great man, but one whose greatness was seen largely in his private life. The most famous part of the book, the cherry tree incident, illustrates this theme. Although historians believe that it was invented by Weems, the story was still a powerful one in its time, drawing upon the images of the supportive parent and the angelic child that were increasingly celebrated in the nineteenth century. Less than a decade after Washington's death, Weems presented a world of fervent emotions and sentimentality that was very different from the reserved and dignified self-presentation of the real Washington.

Never did the wise Ulysses take more pains with his beloved Telemachus, than did Mr. Washington with George, to inspire him with an *early love of truth.* "Truth, George," (said he), " is the loveliest quality of youth. I would ride fifty miles, my son, to see the little boy whose heart is so *honest,* and his lips so *pure,* that we may depend on every word he says. O how lovely does such a child appear in the eyes of every body! . . .

"But, Oh! how different, George, is the case with the boy who is so given to lying, that nobody can believe a word he says! He is looked at with aversion wherever he goes, and parents dread to see him come among their children. Oh, George! my son! rather than see you come to this pass, dear as you are to my heart, gladly would I assist to nail you up in your little coffin, and follow you to your grave. Hard, indeed, would it be to me to give up my son, whose little feet are always so ready to run about with me, and whose fondly looking eyes and sweet prattle makes so large a part of my happiness: but still I would give him up, rather than see him a common liar."

"Pa," (said George very seriously), do I ever tell lies?

"No, George, I *thank God* you do not, my son; and I rejoice in the hope you never will. At least, you shall never, from me, have cause to be guilty of so shameful a thing. Many parents, indeed, even compel their children to this vile practice, by barbarously beating them for every little fault; hence, on the next offence, the little terrified creature slips out a *lie!* just to escape the rod. But as to yourself, George, you know I have *always* told you, and now tell you again, that, whenever by accident you do anything wrong, which must often be the case, as you are but a poor little boy yet, without *experience* or *knowledge*, you must never tell a falsehood to conceal it; but come *bravely* up, my son, like a *little man*, and tell me of it: and, instead of beating you, George, I will but the more honour and love you for it, my dear."

In Grant Wood's 1939 painting, Parson Weems lifts a curtain to reveal a scene from his story of Washington and the cherry tree. Wood mocks the story's sentimentality and Americans' deification of Washington by picturing the young boy with the older man's face.

This, you'll say, was sowing good seed!—Yes, it was: and the crop, thank God, was, as I believe it ever will be, where a man acts the true parent, that is, the *Guardian Angel*, by his child.

The following anecdote is a *case in point.* It is too valuable to be lost, and too true to be doubted; for it was communicated to me by the same excellent lady to whom I am indebted for the last.

"When George," said she, "was about six years old, he was made the wealthy master of a *hatchet!* of which, like most little boys, he was immoderately fond, and was constantly going about chopping every thing that came in his way. One day, in the garden, where he often amused himself hacking his mother's peasticks, he unluckily tried the edge of his hatchet on the body of a beautiful young English cherry-tree, which he barked so terribly, that I don't believe the tree ever got the better of it. The next morning the old gentleman finding out what had befallen his tree, which, by the by, was a great favourite, came into the house; and with much warmth asked for the mischievous author, declaring at the same time, that he would not have taken five guineas for his tree. Nobody could tell him anything about it. Presently George and his hatchet made their appearance. *George, said his father, do you know who killed that beautiful little cherry tree yonder in the garden?* This was a *tough question;* and George staggered under it for a moment; but quickly recovered himself: and looking at his father, with the sweet face of youth brightened with the inexpressible charm of

These two illustrations reflect shifting views of George Washington. Edward Savage painted The Washington Family (top) *in the 1790s. This picture of Washington with his wife, her children, and a slave in attendance quickly became a popular image. In 1845, a new print adapted the Savage picture to reflect changes in style and taste of its time. The later version (bottom) not only removed the slave, but also presents the Washington family as a domestic couple surrounded by flowers and fashionable wallpaper.*

all-conquering truth, he bravely cried out, "*I can't tell a lie, Pa; you know I can't tell a lie. I did cut it with my hatchet.*"—*Run to my arms, you dearest boy,* cried his father in transports, *run to my arms; glad am I, George, that you killed my tree; for you have paid me for it a thousand fold. Such an act of heroism in my son, is more worth than a thousand trees, though blossomed with silver, and their fruits of purest gold.*

It was in this way, by interesting at once both his *heart* and *head*, that Mr. Washington conducted George with great ease and pleasure along the happy paths of virtue."

Two of the key figures of the Revolution, John Adams and Thomas Jefferson, died on the same day on July 4, 1826, the fiftieth anniversary of the Declaration of Independence. The moment seemed symbolic to Americans, who were

increasingly aware of the passing of the Revolutionary generation. Remembering those events would require deliberate action. One of the people to take up this task was Abraham Lincoln. In 1838, he gave an address at the Springfield, Illinois, Lyceum. Although he was only twenty-nine years old at the time, this lecture helped to establish his reputation as a speaker and a political figure. Responding to the lynching of an African American accused of murder in St. Louis, Lincoln warned of the dangers of disregarding laws. This disrespect could actually destroy the nation, the future president suggested, partly because a new generation that had not participated in America's founding was taking power. Only respect for the work of the Revolutionary generation could save America from ruin.

I do not mean to say, that the scenes of the revolution *are now or ever will* be entirely forgotten; but that like every thing else, they must fade upon the memory of the world, and grow more and more dim by the lapse of time. In history, we hope, they will be read of, and recounted, so long as the bible shall be read;— but even granting that they will, their influence *cannot be* what it heretofore has been. Even then, they *cannot be* so universally known, nor so vividly felt, as they were by the generation just gone to rest. At the close of that struggle, nearly every adult male had been a participator in some of its scenes. The consequence was, that of those scenes, in the form of a husband, a father, a son or brother, a *living history was* to be found in every family— a history bearing the indubitable testimonies of its own authenticity, in the limbs mangled, in the scars of wounds received, in the midst of the very scenes related—a history, too, that could be read and understood alike by all, the wise and the ignorant, the learned and the unlearned.—But *those* histories are gone. They *can* be read no more forever. They *were* a fortress of strength; but, what invading foeman could *never do*, the silent artillery of time *has done*; the leveling of its walls. They are gone. They *were* a forest of giant oaks; but the all-resistless hurricane has swept over them, and left only, here and there, a lonely trunk, despoiled of its verdure, shorn of its foliage; unshading and unshaded, to murmur in a few more gentle breezes, and to combat with its mutilated limbs, a few more ruder storms, then to sink, and be no more.

They *were* the pillars of the temple of liberty; and now, that they have crumbled away, that temple must fall, unless we, their descendants, supply their places with other pillars, hewn from the

I regret that I am now to die in the belief that the useless sacrifice of themselves by the generation of 1776, to acquire self-government and happiness to their country, is to be thrown away by the unwise and unworthy passions of their sons.
—Thomas Jefferson, letter to John Holmes, April 22, 1820

Who shall write the history of the American revolution? Who can write it? Who will ever be able to write it?
—John Adams from his letter to Thomas Jefferson and Thomas McKean, July 30, 1815

Paul Revere became an increasingly significant part of Revolutionary mythology in the years after Henry Wadsworth Longfellow's poem "Paul Revere's Ride" was published. He is pictured here in a romantic 1882 print.

solid quarry of sober reason. Passion has helped us; but can do so no more. It will in future be our enemy. Reason, cold, calculating, unimpassioned reason, must furnish all the [materials] for our future support and defence. Let those materials be moulded into *general intelligence,* [sound] *morality,* and in particular, *a reverence for the constitution and laws;* and, that we improved to the last; that we remained free to the last; that we revered his name to the last; [that], during his long sleep, we permitted no hostile foot to pass over or desecrate [his] resting place; shall be that which to le[arn the last] trump shall awaken our WASH[INGTON].

[Upon these] let the proud fabric of freedom r[est, as the] rock of its basis; and as truly as has been said of the only greater institution, *"the gates of hell shall not prevail against it."*

The poet Henry Wadsworth Longfellow's "Paul Revere's Ride" established its subject as a permanent part of American Revolutionary mythology. But Longfellow's purpose went beyond simply dramatizing an important historical incident. The poem was first published in 1861, on the eve of the Civil War. For Longfellow, who was a strong opponent of slavery, it was another "hour of darkness and peril and need" when, as in 1775, "the fate of a nation" was at stake.

LISTEN, my children, and you shall hear
Of the midnight ride of Paul Revere,
On the eighteenth of April, in Seventy-Five;
Hardly a man is now alive
Who remembers that famous day and year.

He said to his friend, "If the British march
By land or sea from the town to-night,
Hang a lantern aloft in the belfry arch
Of the North Church tower as a signal light, —
One, if by land, and two, if by sea;
And I on the opposite shore will be,
 Ready to ride and spread the alarm
Through every Middlesex village and farm,
For the country-folk to be up and to arm."

Then he said "Good-night!" and with muffled oar
Silently rowed to the Charlestown shore . . . .

Meanwhile, his friend, through alley and street
Wanders and watches with eager ears . . . .

Then he climbed the tower of the church,
Up the wooden stairs, with stealthy tread,
To the belfry-chamber overhead, . . .

Meanwhile, impatient to mount and ride,
Booted and spurred, with a heavy stride
On the opposite shore walked Paul Revere. . . .
And lo! as he looks, on the belfry's height
A glimmer, and then a gleam of light!
He springs to the saddle, the bridle he turns,
But lingers and gazes, till full on his sight
A second lamp in the belfry burns!

A hurry of hoofs in a village street,
A shape in the moonlight, a bulk in the dark,
And beneath, from the pebbles, in passing, a spark
Struck out by a steed flying fearless and fleet;
That was all! And yet, through the gloom and the light,
The fate of a nation was riding that night;
And the spark struck out by that steed, in his flight,
Kindled the land into flame with its heat. . . . .

It was one by the village clock,
When he galloped into Lexington.
He saw the gilded weathercock
Swim in the moonlight as he passed,
And the meeting-house windows, blank and bare,
Gaze at him with a spectral glare,
As if they already stood aghast
At the bloody work they would look upon.

It was two by the village clock,
When he came to the bridge in Concord town.
He heard the bleating of the flock,
And the twitter of birds among the trees,
And felt the breath of the morning breeze
Blowing over the meadows brown.
And one was safe and asleep in his bed
Who at the bridge would be first to fall,
Who that day would be lying dead,
Pierced by a British musket-ball.

You know the rest. In the books you have read,
How the British Regulars fired and fled, —

I set off upon a very good Horse; it was then about 11 o'Clock, and very pleasant. After I had passed Charlestown Neck . . . I saw two men on Horse back, under a Tree. When I got near them, I discovered they were British officer[s]. One tryed to git a head of Me, and the other to take me. I turn my Horse very quick, and Galloped toward Charlestown neck, and then pushed for the Medford Road . . . . I got clear of him, and went through Medford, over the Bridge, and up to Menotomy. In Medford, I awaked the Captain of the Minute men; and after that, I alarmed almost every House, till I got to Lexington.

—Paul Revere's own account of his ride, from a letter to Jeremy Belknap, 1798

Noise! You'll have noise enough before long. The Regulars are coming out," was Revere's response to the guards when he arrived after his midnight ride at the Lexington house where John Hancock and Samuel Adams were staying.

How the farmers gave them ball for ball,
From behind each fence and farm-yard wall,
Chasing the red-coats down the lane,
Then crossing the fields to emerge again
Under the trees at the turn of the road,
And only pausing to fire and load.

So through the night rode Paul Revere;
And so through the night went his cry of alarm
To every Middlesex village and farm, —
A cry of defiance and not of fear,
A voice in the darkness, a knock at the door,
And a word that shall echo forevermore!
For, borne on the night-wind of the Past,
Through all our history, to the last,
In the hour of darkness and peril and need,
The people will waken and listen to hear
The hurrying hoof-beat of that steed,
And the midnight-message of Paul Revere.

American Anniversaries

The one-hundredth anniversary of American independence in 1876 inspired a surge of interest in the Revolution. The largest formal celebration was the Centennial Exhibition held at Philadelphia. This "world's fair" featured exhibits from across the United States as well as from other countries, attracting almost ten million visitors. William Dean Howells, a widely admired critic and novelist, wrote about his visit to the exposition in the magazine he edited, *The Atlantic Monthly.* He discusses the question of how to refer to the event, comparing it to London's extraordinarily popular Crystal Palace Exposition of 1851.

The Centennial is what every one calls the great fair now open at Philadelphia. "Have you been at the Centennial?" "How do you like the Centennial?" Some politer and more anxious few struggle for logical precision, reflecting that you cannot go to a Centennial, any more than you can go to a Millennial. These entangle themselves in International Exhibition, or talk of the Exposition. The English, who invented it, and have a genius for simplicity (in some things), called the first international exhibition the World's Fair. But this simple and noble name does not quite

Oh, ye Powers! what a roar.
Such was never heard before—
Thundering from shore to shore:
"Uncle Sam's a hundred!"

Cannons boom and trumpets bray,
Fiddles squeak and fountains play—
'Tis his great Centennial day—
"Uncle Sam's a hundred!"

Stalwart men and puny boys,
Maids and matrons swell the noise,
Every baby lifts its voice:
"Uncle Sam's a hundred!"

Nervous folks who dote on quiet,
Though they're half distracted by it,
Can't help mixing in the riot:
"Uncle Sam's a hundred!"

—"Uncle Sam's a Hundred" from
the Centennial Songster, 1876

serve for us, since our World's Fair means the commemoration of our hundredth national anniversary; and so, at last, Centennial is the best name, in spite of its being no name at all.

Writing at a time when "muckraking" investigative journalists were revealing corruption in politics and big business, a number of early-twentieth-century writers argued that the Revolutionaries needed to be "debunked"—cut down to human size. These writers viewed the founding fathers as flawed, frail human beings, rather than virtual gods, and saw the events in which they participated less as heroic myths than as real historical events. The popular and prolific author and screenwriter Rupert Hughes subtitled the first book of his biography of Washington *The Human Being and the Hero*. Although works like this, which appeared in 1926, often seem restrained and respectful from today's perspective, they were extremely controversial at the time. Critics argued that they dishonored the memory of the Revolution—and thus the United States as a whole. Here Hughes discusses the romanticized views of the Revolution that were common during his time.

The recent historians have gone to the sources, the original manuscripts and the actual utterances of the heroes, and have come back with explanations that are probably nearer the truth than could be realized either by the participants themselves, who were too near, or by the next generations, who were too reverent.

To turn history into a revivalist's sermon, as Bancroft and others did, and insist that the Americans of 1776 were a holy people raised up and "chosen to keep guard over the liberties of mankind," and to find in every victory a clear manifestation of God's intervention and in every defeat a proof of his chastising love—is to imply that God did not know what He was about, blundered on all occasions, and came incessantly so close to losing the war to the British that if the wicked French had not come to the rescue, the devil would have carried off the palm.

The sense of sportsmanship, fair play and common honesty also turns the modern historian away from the old school of exalting forefathers by lying about their foes, of proving men demigods by concealing their intense humanity, and of juggling the figures in a manner that would send a poor bookkeeper to the penitentiary.

Some of the most scholarly of recent historians have had to show almost as much heroism as the forefathers revealed, for every

The most famous image from the 1876 centennial was Archibald Willard's painting The Spirit of '76, which was exhibited at the Philadelphia Centennial Exposition. It celebrates the enthusiasm and determination of the American people to achieve independence, symbolized by the row of three men of different ages marching together. The bandage on the middle-aged man (on the right) suggests that he has been wounded. The painting's emphasis on unity and military spirit was particularly meaningful at a time when memories of the Civil War remained fresh.

Emmanuel Leutze created a key image in the heroic tradition in his 1851 painting George Washington Crossing the Delaware. *The immense, almost life-size image portrayed the general on his way to attack the British at Trenton on the day after Christmas, 1777. Leutze highlighted Washington by showing him standing in the boat—a heroic but highly unlikely stance.*

[George Washington] has been considered the least understood of our great men, when in truth he is the best understood. People have thought that they did not understand him because they could not see in him anything that was not in themselves. It was just in that quality that his greatness lay. He was the American common denominator, the average man deified and raised to the *nth* power.

—W. E. Woodward, *George Washington, The Image and the Man*, 1926

effort to lay the plain facts before the public has been met by ferocious accusations of treason and even to the ludicrous charge that they were bought with British gold. It is a sad commentary if Americans have to be bribed by foreigners to tell the truth.

Hughes also attacks previous biographers of Washington for deifying him.

In their fanatic zeal for denaturing this big, blundering, bewildered giant they have done a further injustice to all his contemporaries, of whom they have made either dwarfs or acolytes, and of his sincere adversaries demons of malice and envy.

It is poor patriotism, ridiculous idolatry, and rank dishonestly to rob the host of other strugglers for liberty and progress of their just deserts, and to perpetuate old slanders against his enemies at home and abroad in order to turn Washington into a god. As a god, Washington was a woeful failure; as a man he was tremendous. This is a study of the man.

John Updike, one of the most celebrated and prolific of recent American authors, suggests the continuing difficulty people have coming to terms with Washington. Written during the centennial anniversary of the Civil War in the 1960s, Updike's poem, "February" portrays Abraham Lincoln as godlike. In contrast, Washington appears as a troubled political and military figure.

More than great successes, we love great failures.
Lincoln is Messiah; he, merely Caesar.
He suffered greatness like a curse.
He fathered our country, we feel, without great joy.

This 1976 letter to advice columnist Ann Landers complains of one overly enthusiastic celebrator of the nation's bicentennial, the 200th anniversary of the Revolution. The garish commemoration at this "super-patriot's" house re-called not only the candles that marked Revolutionary-era celebrations, but also the electric lights of post-World War II Christmas decorations. At that time, patriotic displays could carry political meaning and spark political debates. In the aftermath of the Vietnam War (America had pulled out of that country only three years before), patriotism and the flag had become controversial. Landers responds with another American theme closely connected to the Revolution: the language

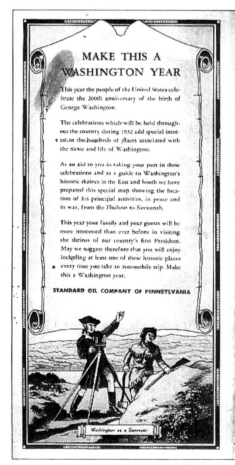

MAKE THIS A WASHINGTON YEAR

This year the people of the United States celebrate the 200th anniversary of the birth of George Washington.

The celebrations which will be held throughout the country during 1932 add special interest to the hundreds of places associated with the name and life of Washington.

As an aid to you in taking your part in these celebrations and as a guide to Washington's historic shrines in the East and South we have prepared this special map showing the location of his principal activities, in peace and in war, from the Hudson to Savannah.

This year your family and your guests will be more interested than ever before in visiting the shrines of our country's first President. May we suggest therefore that you will enjoy including at least one of these historic places every time you take an automobile trip. Make this a Washington year.

STANDARD OIL COMPANY OF PENNSYLVANIA

Washington as a Surveyor

MAP
of the
Principal Events
in the life of
GEORGE WASHINGTON

contributed to the
Bicentennial Celebration
of his birth
by the
**STANDARD OIL COMPANY
OF PENNSYLVANIA**

Washington at Valley Forge

This map, produced for the bicentennial of Washington's birthday in 1932, suggests the mixture of commerce and patriotism that became common in the twentieth century. The Standard Oil Company distributed the map at gas stations, celebrating the Revolutionary figure and encouraging the use of cars.

*Had Washington Lived in
these days
He'd say with all the Rest
"I cannot, will not tell a lie,
Duke's Durham is the Best."*
—Twentieth-century
tobacco advertising card

of rights and privacy that was also gaining significance during the late twentieth century.

Dear Ann Landers: I am just as enthusiastic about the Bicentennial
as the next person, but the lunatics who live across the street have
made our neighborhood the laughing stock of the town. People
come from miles around just to look.

They painted their house red, white, and blue. Five flagpoles
in the front yard fly Old Glory from dawn till dusk. Last week
they put up three huge papier mache figures: Betsy Ross sewing a
flag; George Washington crossing the Delaware, and John
Hancock signing the Declaration of Independence.

There are two enormous neon lights on the front porch that
flash off and on all night long. The message is "Happy Birthday,
U.S.A." We can't get to sleep because the lights shine in our bed-
room window.

The worst is the music. A public-address system blasts the
"Battle Hymn of the Republic," the National Anthem and "God
Bless America" from 6:00 p.m. until midnight.

Yesterday the nut who owns the house was out mowing the
grass in an Uncle Sam costume—fake beard, hat and all.

The traffic jam in front of our place was unbelievable. Our
lawn is a mess. What can we do about this?—We Love America,
Too, But . . .

Dear Love: You can notify the police. Mr. Superpatriot is
infringing on your inalienable right to the pursuit of happiness.
He is also disturbing the peace and creating a public nuisance.
Get going.

The Political Uses of the Revolution

The Revolutionary legacy can be used not only to celebrate
common values, but also to support controversial ones. Like
the less divisive commemorative tradition, this use of the
Revolution goes back to the earliest days of the republic. Celebrations of independence in the 1790s became means of
supporting political parties. Members of the Democratic-
Republican party led by Thomas Jefferson used the Fourth of
July festivities to emphasize Jefferson's important role in the
Declaration of Independence; their opponents, the Federalists, tried less successfully to elevate the birthday of their
hero, George Washington to the same level of importance. In

the nineteenth century some Americans used the Fourth of July to encourage opposition to slavery or the consumption of alcohol. For these partisans, the Revolution was not simply something to be celebrated. It was also a way of recalling the country's central values.

In this humorous story from the 1830s written by the popular author Eliza Leslie, the main character, a sixteen-year-old student named Russel, organizes a revolt against his schoolmaster, Peter Puckeridge. Russel draws up this list of complaints using the Declaration of Independence as a model. The joke is not just that adolescents used the Revolutionary document for their own much smaller purposes, but that—from the boys' perspective—the earlier complaints against tyranny fit their own situation.

When in the course of human events it becomes necessary for the boys of a school to break through the bands that have connected them with the teacher (falsely, meanly, and improperly called their *master*) a decent respect for the opinions of the girls requires them to declare the causes that compel them to a separation.

We hold these truths to be self-evident: that we are in every point of view equal to the man denominated Peter Puckeridge. We can run as fast, we can ride as well: we can shoot much better; and we are no way below him in fishing and trapping. And if any of us are his inferiors in reading, writing and cyphering, (and even this is doubtful) it is only the natural consequences of our youth and inexperience. In all *essential* qualifications we acknowledge no inferiority whatever.

But our causes of complaint are of more serious moment: and after enduring a long train of abuses and vexations, it is our choice, it is our wish, to throw off his government, and declare ourselves independent. . . .

But as no warning has had any effect on him, and as he has not had the grace to retire from office as soon as he knew himself to be unpopular, we therefore absolve ourselves from all allegiance to him and his authority. We throw him off as we would an old coat, and we declare ourselves free and independent of Peter Puckeridge, and that we will never more allow ourselves to be subjected by the frown of his brow, the sharpness of his voice, or the slaps of his ferule. And for the support of this declaration we mutually pledge to each other the heads that can plan, the hearts that can dare, and the hands that can execute.

This 1870 print shows a number of the leading figures in the women's rights movement. Lucretia Mott is at the top. Elizabeth Cady Stanton, the other key figure in the Seneca Falls Women's Rights Convention, appears on the upper right.

The Convention on Women's Rights, held in Seneca Falls, New York, in July 1848, marked the start of the movement for women's rights. To publicize their concerns, the attendees turned to the most famous affirmation of equal rights in American history. The convention's "Declaration of Sentiments," written by Lucrecia Mott, Elizabeth Cady Stanton, and several others, used the form and the language of the Declaration of Independence to argue against the injustices inflicted upon women and for their equality with men.

When, in the course of human events, it becomes necessary for one portion of the family of man to assume among the people of the earth a position different from that which they have hitherto occupied, but one to which the laws of nature and of nature's God entitle them, a decent respect to the opinions of mankind requires that they should declare the causes that impel them to such a course.

We hold these truths to be self-evident; that all men and women are created equal; that they are endowed by their Creator with certain inalienable rights; that among these are life, liberty, and the pursuit of happiness; that to secure these rights governments are instituted, deriving their just powers from the consent of the governed. Whenever any form of Government becomes destructive of these ends, it is the right of those who suffer from it to refuse allegiance to it, and to insist upon the institution of a new government, laying its foundation on such principles, and organizing its powers in such form, as to them shall seem most likely to effect their safety and happiness. Prudence, indeed, will dictate that governments long established should not be changed for light and transient causes; and accordingly all experience hath shown that mankind are more disposed to suffer while evils are sufferable, than to right themselves by abolishing the forms to which they are accustomed. But when a long train of abuses and usurpations, pursuing invariably the same object, evinces a design to reduce them under absolute despotism, it is their duty to throw off such government, and to provide new guards for their future security. Such has been the patient sufferance of the women under this government, and such is now the necessity which constrains them to demand the equal station to which they are entitled.

The history of mankind is a history of repeated injuries and usurpations on the part of man toward woman, having in direct object the establishment of an absolute tyranny over her. To prove this, let facts be submitted to a candid world.

Like its earlier 1776 model, the 1848 Declaration includes a list of violations of liberty, here commited by "man" rather than King George III. Denying women the vote is listed first.

He has never permitted her to exercise her inalienable right to the elective franchise.

He has compelled her to submit to laws, in the formation of which she had no voice.

He has withheld from her rights which are given to the most ignorant and degraded men—both natives and foreigners.

Having deprived her of this first right of a citizen, the elective franchise, thereby leaving her without representation in the halls of legislation, he has oppressed her on all sides.

He has made her, if married, in the eye of the law, civilly dead.

He has taken from her all right in property, even to the wages she earns.

He has made her, morally, an irresponsible being, as she can commit many crimes with impunity, provided they be done in the presence of her husband. In the covenant of marriage, she is compelled to promise obedience to her husband, he becoming, to all intents and purposes, her master — the law giving him power to deprive her of her liberty, and to administer chastisement.

He has so framed the laws of divorce, as to what shall be the proper causes and; in case of separation, to whom the guardianship of the children shall be given, as to be wholly regardless of the happiness of women — the law, in all cases, going upon the false supposition of the supremacy of man, and giving all power into his hands.

After depriving her of all rights as a married woman, if single, and the owner of property, he has taxed her to support a government which recognizes her only when her property can be made profitable to it.

He has monopolized nearly all the profitable employments, and from those she is permitted to follow, she receives but a scanty remuneration. He closes against her all the avenues to wealth and distinction. . . .

He has denied her the facilities for obtaining a thorough education, all colleges being closed against her.

He allows her in Church, as well as State, but a subordinate position, claiming Apostolic authority for her exclusion from the ministry, and, with some exceptions, from any public participation in the affairs of the Church.

He has created a false public sentiment by giving to the world a different code of morals for men and women, by which moral delinquencies which exclude women from society, are not only tolerated, but deemed of little account in man.

He has usurped the prerogative of Jehovah himself, claiming it as his right to assign for her a sphere of action, when that belongs to her conscience and her God.

He has endeavored, in every way that he could, to destroy her confidence in her own powers, to lessen her self-respect and to make her willing to lead a dependent and abject life.

The Declaration of Sentiments ends with a call for women to be granted all the rights of citizenship and a pledge to work towards that goal.

Now, in view of this entire disfranchisement of one-half the people of this country, their social and religious degradation,—in view of the unjust laws above mentioned, and because women do feel themselves aggrieved, oppressed, and fraudulently deprived

See your Declaration, Americans!!! Do you understand your own language?
—David Walker, a freeborn African American, in an 1829 pamphlet, *Appeal in Four Articles, Together with a Preamble to the Colored Citizens of the World*

of their most sacred rights, we insist that they have immediate admission to all the rights and privileges which belong to them as citizens of these United States.

In entering upon the great work before us, we anticipate no small amount of misconception, misrepresentation, and ridicule; but we shall use every instrumentality within our power to effect our object. We shall employ agents, circulate tracts, petition the State and national Legislatures, and endeavor to enlist the pulpit and the press in our behalf. We hope this Convention will be followed by a series of Conventions, embracing every part of the country.

Firmly relying upon the final triumph of the Right and the True, we do this day affix our signatures to this declaration.

On the Fourth of July, 1852, the escaped slave and antislavery leader Frederick Douglass addressed a celebration in Rochester, New York. He used the occasion to tell the crowd that he and other African Americans had no cause to celebrate. Despite the ideals of liberty and equality proclaimed in the Declaration of Independence, slavery continued to exist in the southern United States. Douglass's harsh indictment encouraged his listeners to make the realities of American life live up to the high ideals of the nation's founding. When the Civil War began nine years later, Douglass's writings and advice helped encourage Abraham Lincoln and other Republican leaders to recognize the importance of ending slavery.

Fellow Citizens: Pardon me, and allow me to ask, why am I called upon to speak here today? What have I or those I represent to do with your national independence? Are the great principles of political freedom and of natural justice, embodied in that Declaration of Independence, extended to us? And am I, therefore, called upon to bring our humble offering to the national altar, and to confess the benefits, and express devout gratitude for the blessings resulting from your independence to us?

Would to God, both for your sakes and ours, that an affirmative answer could be truthfully returned to these questions. Then would my task be light, and my burden easy and delightful. For who is there so cold that a nation's sympathy could not warm him? Who so obdurate and dead to the claims of gratitude, that would not thankfully acknowledge such priceless benefits? Who so stolid and selfish that would not give his voice to swell the hallelujahs

As a nation, we began by declaring that '*all men are created equal.*' We now practically read it 'all men are created equal, *except negroes.*' When the Know-Nothings get control, it will read 'all men are created equal, except negroes, *and foreigners, and catholics.*' When it comes to this I should prefer emigrating to some country where they make no pretence of loving liberty—to Russia, for instance, where despotism can be taken pure, and without the base alloy of hypocracy.

[The Know-Nothing Party objected to the influence of immigrants and Catholics]

—In an 1855 letter by Abraham Lincoln to Joshua Speed.

Although the Confederate States of America rejected the Federal Union, it claimed its ideals were rooted in the Revolutionary War. The most powerful symbol of this claim to continuity with the Revolution was the Virginian George Washington. The Confederate's seal shows him as a general on horseback.

Colored men were good enough to fight under Washington. They were not good enough to fight under McClellan. . . . They were good enough to help win American Independence, but they were not good enough to help preserve that independence against treason and rebellion.

—Frederick Douglass, in a speech in New York City given during the Civil War, mocks the Union policy that kept African Americans from serving in the army, February, 1862

Rebels *before,*
Our fathers of yore,
Rebel's *the righteous name*
Washington *bore.*
Why, then, be ours the same.
—"God Save the South,"
Southern Confederate song during the Civil War

of a nation's jubilee, when the chains of servitude had been torn from his limbs? I am not that man. In a case like that, the dumb might eloquently speak, and the "lame man leap like a hare."

But such is not the state of the case. I say it with a sad sense of disparity between us. I am not included within the pale of this glorious anniversary! Your high independence only reveals the immeasurable distance between us. The blessings in which you this day rejoice are not enjoyed in common. The rich inheritance of justice, prosperity, and independence bequeathed by your fathers is shared by you, not by me. The sunlight that brought life and healing to you has brought stripes and death to me. This Fourth of July is *yours,* not *mine.* You may rejoice, I must mourn. To drag a man in fetters into the grand illuminated temple of liberty, and call upon him to join you in joyous anthems, were inhuman mockery and sacrilegious irony. Do you mean, citizens, to mock me, by asking me to speak today? . . .

Fellow Citizens, above your national, tumultuous joy, I hear the mournful wail of millions, whose chains, heavy and grievous yesterday, are today rendered more intolerable by the jubilant shouts that reach them. . . . Standing here, identified with the American bondman, making his wrongs mine, I do not hesitate to declare, with all my soul, that the character and conduct of this nation never looked blacker to me than on this Fourth of July. Whether we turn to the declarations of the past, or to the professions of the present, the conduct of the nation seems equally hideous and revolting. America is false to the past, false to the present, and solemnly binds herself to be false to the future. . . .

What to the American slave is your Fourth of July? I answer, a day that reveals to him more than all other days of the year, the gross injustice and cruelty to which he is the constant victim. To him your celebration is a sham; . . . your sounds of rejoicing are empty and heartless; your denunciation of tyrants, brass-fronted impudence; your shouts of liberty and equality, hollow mockery; your prayers and hymns, your sermons and thanksgivings, with all your religious parade and solemnity, are to him mere bombast, fraud, deception, impiety, and hypocrisy—a thin veil to cover up crimes which would disgrace a nation of savages. There is not a nation of the earth guilty of practices more shocking and bloody than are the people of these United States at this very hour.

Go where you may, search where you will, roam through all the monarchies and despotisms of the Old World, travel through South America, search out every abuse and when you have found the last, lay your facts by the side of the everyday practices of this nation, and you will say with me that, for revolting barbarity and shameless hypocrisy, American reigns without a rival.

Though opponents of the radical left-wing movements of the late nineteenth and early twentieth centuries often accused them of being inspired, influenced, and perhaps directed by foreign ideas and people, their followers often saw the Revolution as a starting point for their thinking. The Socialist Party leader and newspaper editor Daniel De Leon published this version of the Declaration of Independence on July 4, 1895, using Revolutionary language to criticize the injustices created by the development of industry.

Ever since the Revolution, Americans have portrayed George Washington as a religious figure. This poster uses a statue of Washington in prayer at Valley Forge, although there is no historical evidence of this event. The poster was used to advertise a religious rally held in Washington, D.C. in 1980— at a time when conservative Christians were organizing the so-called "religious right" and arguing that America was a particularly Christian country.

When in the course of human progression, the despoiled class of wealth producers becomes fully conscious of its rights and determined to take them, a decent respect to the judgment of posterity requires that it should declare the causes which impel it to change the social order.

More truly can we say of our plutocracy than our forefathers did of the British crown that "its history is one of repeated injuries and usurpations, all having in direct object the establishment of an absolute tyranny over these states." Let the facts speak.

The foundation of the Union was coeval with the birth of the modern system of production by machinery. No sooner was the federal Constitution adopted than the spirit of capitalism began to manifest its absorbing tendency and corrupting influence. Every new invention was looked upon, not as a means of promoting the welfare of all, but as an instrument of private profit. Every tract of fertile land belonging to the states was appropriated by individuals, regardless of the rights of future generations. Every public franchise of any value was given away to "enterprising" persons and companies.

Thus was already formed in those early days, a privileged class, whose wealth was derived from the labor of others; this growing monopoly of the means of production and exchange, by placing a steadily increasing number of disinherited workers in its dependence for employment, strengthened its hold upon the public powers, which it used more and more unscrupulously for its own aggrandizement. . . .

So did the promises and purposes of the Revolution immediately prove abortive. While the fundamental law declared that the

Union was formed "to establish justice, insure domestic tranquillity, promote the general welfare, and secure the blessings of liberty," free scope was given to an economic system replete with injustice, pregnant with the seeds of domestic strife, destructive of every true element of happiness, and fatally tending to class tyranny.

Under that system the value of man, and, therefore, his remuneration, were not to be measured by the extent to which his industry and intelligence benefited his fellows. They were to be gauged by the necessities of his competitors on the "labor market". . . .

Americans, fall into line! Onward to the Cooperative Commonwealth!

To the industrious the tools of industry; to the laborer the fruits of his labor; to mankind the earth!

The American Revolution Beyond America

The significance of the American Revolution went beyond the United States. As the first successful rebellion of a colony against an European empire, a large and successful republic, and as a source of political ideas about liberty, equality, and rights, the American example was widely influential. Ironically, America later opposed many attempts by foreign

Benjamin Franklin became extremely popular in France during his wartime diplomatic mission, partly by virtue of his choice of dress. Although he was a renowned scientist, he rejected the elaborate wigs and fancy clothing of the French court, presenting himself as a simple American. In this 1778 French engraving, a woman crowns him with a laurel wreath, symbolizing his high distinction.

groups to overthrow their colonial rule, looking to the American Revoltion as a model.

The American Revolution took on particular significance in France. Even before the Revolution, French Enlightenment thinkers, with their concern for personal and political liberty, had been deeply interested in America. Benjamin Franklin became a celebrity during his wartime diplomatic mission in the country. When France itself revolted against its king in 1789, many of its leaders looked to the American Revolution as an inspiration. One of the key statements of the early, moderate stage of the French Revolution was "The Declaration of the Rights of Man and Citizen." Issued on August 26, 1789, it was largely written by the French aristocrat Marquis de Lafayette, who had served in the Continental Army and become personally close to George Washington. Lafayette consulted with Thomas Jefferson while he was preparing this document, which drew heavily upon the Virginia Declaration of Rights. Lafayette's declaration became a central statement of the French Revolution and helped spread the ideals of liberty and equality to the rest of Europe and beyond.

The world has its eye upon America. The noble struggle we have made in the cause of liberty, has occasioned a kind of revolution in human sentiment. The influence of our example has penetrated the gloomy regions of despotism, and has pointed the way to inquiries, which may shake it to its deepest foundation. Men begin to ask every where, who is this tyrant, that dares to build his greatness on our misery and degradation? What commission has he to sacrifice millions to the wanton appetites of himself and the few minions that surround his throne?

—A published letter by Alexander Hamilton, "To the Considerate Citizens of New York," 1784

Preamble. The representatives of the French people, organized in National Assembly, considering that ignorance, forgetfulness or contempt of the rights of men are the sole causes of the public miseries and of the corruption of governments, have resolved to set forth in a solemn declaration the natural, inalienable, and sacred rights of men, in order that this declaration, being ever present to all the members of the social body, may unceasingly remind them of their rights and their duties: in order that the acts of the legislative power and those of the executive power may be each moment compared with the aim of every political institution and thereby may be more respected; and in order that the demands of the citizens, grounded henceforth upon simple and incontestable principles, may always take the direction of maintaining the constitution and the welfare of all.

In consequence, the National Assembly recognizes and declares, in the presence and under the auspices of the Supreme Being, the following rights of man and citizen.

1. Men are born and remain free and equal in rights. Social distinctions can be based only upon public utility.

2. The aim of every political association is the preservation of the natural and imprescriptible rights of man. These rights are liberty, property, security, and resistance to oppression.

3. The source of all sovereignty is essentially in the nation; no body, no individual can exercise authority that does not proceed from it in plain terms.

4. Liberty consists in the power to do anything that does not injure others; accordingly, the exercise of the natural rights of each man has for its only limits those that secure to the other members of society the enjoyment of these same rights. These limits can be determined only by law.

5. The law has the right to forbid only such actions as are injurious to society. Nothing can be forbidden that is not interdicted by the law and no one can be constrained to do that which it does not order.

6. Law is the expression of the general will. All citizens have the right to take part personally or by their representatives in its formation. It must be the same for all, whether it protects or punishes. All citizens being equal in its eyes are equally eligible to all public dignities, places, and employments, according to their capacities, and without other distinction than that of their virtues and their talents.

7. No man can be accused, arrested, or detained except in the cases determined by the law and according to the forms that it has prescribed. . . .

8. The law ought to establish only penalties that are strictly and obviously necessary and no one can be punished except in virtue of a law established and promulgated prior to the offense and legally applied.

9. Every man being presumed innocent until he has been pronounced guilty, if it is thought indispensable to arrest him, all severity that may not be necessary to secure his person ought to be strictly suppressed by law.

10. No one ought to be disturbed on account of his opinions, even religious, provided their manifestation does not derange the public order established by law.

11. The free communication of ideas and opinions is one of the most precious of the rights of man; every citizen then can freely speak, write, and print, subject to responsibility for the abuse of this freedom in the cases determined by law.

12. The guarantee of the rights of man and citizen requires a public force; this force then is instituted for the advantage of all and not for the personal benefit of those to whom it is entrusted.

13. For the maintenance of the public force and for the expenses of administration the general tax is indispensable; it

ought to be equally apportioned among all the citizens according to their means.

14. All the citizens have the right to ascertain, by themselves or by their representatives, the necessity of the public tax, to consent to it freely, to follow the employment of it, and to determine the quota, the assessment, the collection, and the duration of it.

15. Society has the right to call for an account from every public agent of its administration.

16. Any society in which the guarantee of the rights is not secured or the separation of powers not determined has no constitution at all.

17. Property being a sacred and inviolable right, no one can be deprived of it unless a legally established public necessity evidently demands it, under the condition of a just and prior indemnity."

In England as well as France, a variety of radical political thinkers at the end of the eighteenth century drew upon American ideals and symbols to argue for greater popular participation in government. The poet Samuel Coleridge, while a college student, boldly proclaimed his allegiance to these ideals by proposing a toast to George Washington in a tavern. Thomas Paine was an even more important figure for

In 1789, King Louis XVI called together the Estates-General, a representative assembly that had not met for many years. The king sought additional taxes for a government whose financial resources had been strained by the cost of supporting the American fight against Great Britain. The demands of the Estates-General, quickly led to a revolution in France as well.

[A]s the British Constitution is the most subtile organism which has proceeded from the womb and the long gestation of progressive history, so the American Constitution is . . . the most wonderful work ever struck off at a given time by the brain and purpose of man.

—William E. Gladstone, British prime minister, article "Kin Beyond The Sea" from *North American Review* 1878

this movement. Although born in England, Paine had first established himself as an important writer and thinker in Philadelphia during the American Revolution before returning to England in 1787. Four years later, he dedicated the first volume of his defense of the French Revolution, *The Rights of Man*, to George Washington, the most famous symbol of the American Revolution. These two English songs from the period celebrate Paine and his ideas.

This song is from Sheffield, where craftsman sang these words to the national anthem (Americans usually sing "My Country, 'tis of thee" to the same tune).

God save great Thomas Paine
His "Rights of Man" to explain
   To every soul.
He makes the blind to see
What dupes and slaves they be
And points out liberty
   From pole to pole.

The other song comes from London.

There was a man whose name was Paine, a man of Common
   Sense,
Who came from Philadelphia here, his knowledge to dispense;
He prov'd that man had equal rights, as equal sons of nature,
Deriv'd by universal grant, from Heaven's Legislature.

He taught, that on the people's will all lawful pow'r depended,
That governors were for the good of the governed intended;
And many other wholesome truths, all form'd on reason's plan,
He wrote within a little book, and call'd it Rights of Man.

When Latin America revolted against Spanish rule in the 1810s and 1820s, the American Revolution, along with the French Revolution, provided a constant point of reference. The central figure in these Latin American revolts was Simon Bolivar. Born in Venezuela, Bolivar played important roles in liberating not only his own country but also Bolivia—which was named after him—Columbia, and Peru. Bolivar had mixed feelings about the example set by the United States. In his address to Venezuela's leaders at the start of the Second National Congress in February 15, 1819,

Bolivar warned against the constitution established by the earlier congress. It was defective, he argued, largely because it followed the American Constitution too closely.

The more I admire the excellence of the federal Constitution of Venezuela, the more I am convinced of the impossibility of its application to our state. And, to my way of thinking, it is a marvel that its prototype in North America endures so successfully and has not been overthrown at the first sign of adversity or danger. Although the people of North America are a singular model of political virtue and moral rectitude; although that nation was cradled in liberty, reared on freedom, and maintained by liberty alone; and—I must reveal everything—although those people, so lacking in many respects, are unique in the history of mankind, it is a marvel, I repeat, that so weak and complicated a government as the federal system has managed to govern them in the difficult and trying circumstances of their past. But, regardless of the effectiveness of this form of government with respect to North America, I must say that it has never for a moment entered my mind to compare the position and character of two states as dissimilar as the English-American and the Spanish-American. Would it not be most difficult to apply to Spain the English system of political, civil, and religious liberty? Hence, it would be even more difficult to adapt to Venezuela the laws of North America. . . .

The first Congress, in its federal Constitution . . . yielded to the ill-considered pleadings of those men from the provinces who were captivated by the apparent brilliance of the happiness of the North American people, believing that the blessings they enjoy result exclusively from their form of government rather than the character and customs of the citizens. In effect, the United States' example, because of their remarkable prosperity, was one too tempting not to be followed. Who could resist the powerful attraction of full and absolute enjoyment of sovereignty, independence, and freedom? Who could resist the devotion inspired by an intelligent government that has not only blended public and private rights but has also based its supreme law respecting the desires of the individual upon common consent? . . .

But no matter how tempting this magnificent federative system might have appeared, and regardless of its possible effect, the Venezuelans were not prepared to enjoy it immediately upon casting off their chains. We were not prepared for such good, for good, like evil, results in death when it is sudden and excessive. Our moral fibre did not then possess the stability necessary to

As for me, the suspicion that I desire to usurp a tyrannical power hangs over my head, a suspicion that troubles many a Colombian heart. Zealous republicans regard me with a secret fear, for history teaches them that men in my position have always been ambitious. In vain does Washington's example rise in my defense, for, in truth, an occasional exception cannot stand up against the long history of a world that has always been oppressed by the powerful.

—Simon Bolivar, letter to the president of the Senate of Colombia, February 6, 1827

American Revolution—and the Vietnamese

In 1927 Ho Chi Minh wrote about the American Revolution in his Road to Revolution:

How is the American revolution distinguished from the Vietnamese revolution?

1. French policy toward Vietnam today is more shameful than English policy was toward America because the French put their grip on everything belonging to our people, hindering our people's labor and other affairs . . . Nonetheless, the Vietnamese people still continue to study the American revolution!

2. In America's declaration of independence, there are these lines: "Under heaven all people have the fight to liberty, the right to defend their lives and the right to earn their living happily. If any government injures the broad masses of its people, the people must bring down that government and build up another one . . . But now the American government does not want anyone to speak about revolution or attack the government!

derive benefits from a wholly representative government; a government so sublime, in fact, that it might more nearly befit a republic of saints.

The Vietnamese Communist leader Ho Chi Minh also admired the American Revolution. During World War II, he fought against the French, who had held Vietnam as a colony, and the Japanese, who had conquered it from the French. When the war ended and France's ability to reassert control of Vietnam seemed uncertain, Ho Chi Minh announced the formation of the Democratic Republic of Vietnam on September 2, 1945. American military officers attended the ceremony as invited guests and a band played "The Star-Spangled Banner." In his public statement, Ho used both the form and the language of the American Declaration of Independence to proclaim the establishment of the new Vietnamese nation. Ho had admired the American Revolution as the first colonial uprising against a European power and he had hoped to gain American support for his country's independence. But his hopes were unrealized. The French soon attempted to retake their colony and America came to their aid. Long after the French left Vietnam in 1954, the United States continued to fight in what became the Vietnam War. Ho Chi Minh was finally victorious in 1975.

"We hold truths that all men are created equal, that they are endowed by their Creator with certain unalienable Rights, among these are Life, Liberty and the pursuit of Happiness." This immortal statement is extracted from the Declaration of Independence of the United States of America in 1776. Understood in the broader sense, this means: "All peoples on the earth are born equal; every person has the right to live to be happy and free."

The Declaration of Human and Civic Rights proclaimed by the French Revolution in 1791 likewise propounds: "Every man is born equal and enjoys free and equal rights." These are undeniable truths. Yet, during and throughout the last eighty years, the French imperialists, abusing the principles of "Freedom, equality and fraternity," have violated the integrity of our ancestral land and oppressed our countrymen. Their deeds run counter to the ideals of humanity and justice.

In the political field, they have denied us every freedom. . . .

They have ruthlessly appropriated our rice fields, mines, forests and raw materials. They have arrogated to themselves the privilege of issuing banknotes, and monopolised all our external commerce. . . .

In the autumn of 1940, when the Japanese fascists, in order to fight the Allies, invaded Indochina and set up new bases of war, the French imperialists surrendered on bended knees and handed over our country to the invaders.

Subsequently, under the joint French and Japanese yoke, our people were literally bled white. . . .

Despite all that, our countrymen went on maintaining, vis-à-vis the French, a humane and even indulgent attitude. After the events of March 9th the Viet Minh League helped many French to cross the borders, rescued others from Japanese prisons and, in general, protected the lives and properties of all the French in their territory.

In Fact, since the autumn of 1940, our country ceased to be a French colony and became a Japanese possession. . . .

The French fled, the Japanese surrendered. Emperor Bao Dai abdicated, our people smashed the yoke which pressed hard upon us for nearly one hundred years, and finally made our Viet Nam an independent country. Our people at the same time overthrew the monarchical regime established tens of centuries ago, and founded the Republic.

For these reasons, we, the members of the Provisional Government representing the entire people of Viet Nam, declare that we shall from now on have no more connections with imperialist France; we consider null and void all the treaties France has signed concerning Viet Nam, and we hereby cancel all the privileges that the French arrogated to themselves on our territory. . . .

A people which has so stubbornly opposed the French domination for more than 80 years, a people who, during these last years, so doggedly ranged itself and fought on the Allied side against Fascism, such a people has the right to be free, such a people must be independent.

For these reasons, we, the members of the Provisional Government of the Democratic Republic of Viet Nam, solemnly declare to the world:

"Viet Nam has the right to be free and independent and, in fact, has become free and independent. The people of Viet Nam decide to mobilise all their spiritual and material forces and to sacrifice their lives and property in order to safeguard their right of Liberty and Independence."

Despite his communist ideology, Ho Chi Minh, seen standing, believed that his fight for an independent Vietnam followed the path laid down by the American Revolution. At a peace conference in 1954, the year this photograph was taken, France surrendered its colonial claim—an action that led to greater American military involvement in the fight against Ho.

Timeline

1763
Seven Years or French and Indian War ends with British defeat of French; Pontiac leads American Indian uprising; Proclamation Line halts colonial settlement west of the Allegheny Mountains

1764
Plantations or Sugar Act is passed

1765
Stamp Act is passed; strong American opposition and boycotts develops: Virginia Resolves pass; Stamp Act Congress convenes

1766
Stamp Act is repealed; Declaratory Act is passed

1767
Townshend Acts are passed; Sons of Liberty reorganize

1768
British troops arrive in Boston; Nonimportation agreements are revived

1770
Boston Massacre; Townshend Acts are repealed

1771
Nonimportation agreements end

1773
Tea Act is passed, Boston Tea Party occurs seven months later

1774
Coercive (Intolerable) Acts are passed; First Continental Congress meets

1775
Paul Revere makes Midnight Ride; Battle of Lexington and Concord is fought; Second Continental Congress meets; George Washington becomes commander in chief of the Continental Army; Battle of Bunker Hill is fought; George III declares colonies in open rebellion; Virginia governor, Lord Dunmore, promises freedom to slaves and indentured servants who join the British forces

1776
Thomas Paine publishes *Common Sense*; British troops leave Boston; Congress recommends establishing governments independent of British rule; Virginia issues Declaration of Rights; Continental Congress votes for independence; British capture New York City; Thomas Paine publishes first issue of *The American Crisis*; Washington crosses Delaware River, wins Battle of Trenton

1777
Vermont constitution forbids slavery; British capture Philadelphia; Americans win battle of Saratoga; Continental Army winters in horrible conditions at Valley Forge, Pennsylvania

1778
French sign public treaties of alliance and trade with America; British capture Savannah

1779
Sullivan expedition attacks Iroquois villages in upstate New York

1780

League of Armed Neutrality in Europe isolates Britain further; Pennsylvania Act for Emancipation begins gradual freeing of slaves; British capture Charleston; Benedict Arnold flees to British; General Nathaniel Greene heads Continental Army in the South

1781

Articles of Confeder-ation ratified; American victory at Battle of Yorktown leads to peace negotiations

1782

Virginia allows slaves to be freed by masters; Provisional Peace Treaty signed in Paris

1783

Discontent peaks among Continental Army officers and soldiers; Congress declares war over and ratifies provisional treaty; Treaty of Paris ends war; British evacuate New York; Washington resigns commission

1784

General Assessment Plan to support reli-gious groups through tax money considered and defeated in Virginia; *Commonwealth v. Jennison* finds slavery illegal in Massachusetts

1785

Thomas Jefferson publishes *Notes on the State of Virginia*

1786

Virginia enacts Statute for Religious Freedom; Shays's Rebellion; Annapolis Convention calls for a convention of all colonies in Philadelphia

1787

Constitutional Convention convenes; Northwest Ordinance passed by Continental Congress organizes what become Ohio, Indiana, Michigan, and Wisconsin; *Federalist Papers* begin appearing in New York newspapers and are widely reprinted; Delaware is first state to ratify the Federal Constitution

1788

New Hampshire is ninth state to ratify the Constitution, making it take effect in all thirteen states; Benjamin Rush writes on physical and mental effects of the Revolution

1789

Elections for new gov-ernment under the Constitution make George Washington first President; Bill of Rights proposed; French Revolution begins; Declaration of the Rights of Man and Citizen pro-claimed in France

1790

Benjamin Franklin dies

1799

George Washington dies

1810

Simon Bolivar begins fight against Spanish control of Latin America, using the American Revolution as an example

1826

Thomas Jefferson and John Adams die

1848

Seneca Falls Convention on Women's Rights uses the Declaration of Independence to pre-pare their "Declaration of Sentiments"

1876

Centennial Exhibition is held at Philadelphia, Pennsylvania

1945

Ho Chi Minh declares the formation of the Democratic Republic of Vietnam, using the Declaration of Independence as a model

1976

Bicentennial celebra-tion of the United States is commemorated

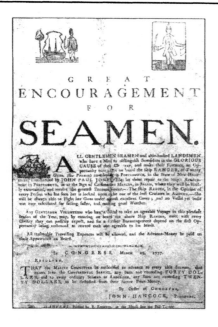

Further Reading

Overviews of Revolutionary Era

Bonwick, Colin. *The American Revolution.* Charlottesville: University Press of Virginia, 1991.

Brown, Richard D. *Major Problems in the Era of the American Revolution, 1760–1791.* 2d ed. Boston: Houghton Mifflin, 2000.

Commager, Henry Steele, and Richard B. Morris, eds. *The Spirit of 'Seventy-six; The Story of the American Revolution as Told by Participants.* Indianapolis: Bobbs-Merrill, 1958.

Countryman, Edward. *The American Revolution.* 2d ed. New York: Hill and Wang, 2002.

Gephart, Ronald M. *Revolutionary America, 1763–1789: A Bibliography.* 2 vols. Washington, D. C.: Library of Congress, 1984.

Greene, Jack P. *Colonies to Nation, 1763–1789: A Documentary History of the American Revolution.* New York: Norton, 1975.

Greene, Jack P., and J. R. Pole, eds. *Blackwell Encyclopedia of the American Revolution.* Cambridge, Mass.: Blackwell, 1991.

Middlekauff, Robert. *The Glorious Cause: The American Revolution, 1763–1789.* New York: Oxford University Press, 1982.

Morgan, Edmund S. *The Birth of the Republic.* 3d ed. Chicago: University of Chicago Press, 1992.

Nash, Gary. *Landmarks of The American Revolution.* New York: Oxford University Press, 2003.

Phillips, Kevin P. *The Cousins' Wars : Religion, Politics, and the Triumph of Anglo-America.* New York: Basic, 1999.

Purcell, L. Edward., *Who Was Who in the American Revolution.* New York: Facts on File, 1993.

Wood, Gordon S. *The American Revolution: A History.* New York: Modern Library, 2002

———. *The Radicalism of the American Revolution.* New York: Knopf, 1992.

The Coming of the Revolution

Bailyn, Bernard. *The Ideological Origins of the American Revolution.* Cambridge: Harvard University Press, 1967.

Christie, Ian R., and Benjamin W. Labaree. *Empire or Independence: A British-American Dialogue on the Coming of the American Revolution.* New York: Norton, 1976.

Holton, Woody. *Forced Founders: Indians, Debtors, Slaves, and the Making of the American Revolution in Virginia.* Chapel Hill: University of North Carolina Press, 1999.

Jensen, Merrill. *The Founding of a Nation; A History of the American Revolution, 1763–1776.* New York : Oxford University Press, 1968.

Labaree, Benjamin. *The Boston Tea Party.* New York: Oxford University Press, 1964.

Maier, Pauline. *From Resistance to Revolution; Colonial Radicals and the Development of American Opposition to Britain, 1765–1776.* New York: Knopf, 1972.

Morgan, Edmund S., and Helen M. Morgan. *The Stamp Act Crisis: Prologue to Revolution.* Rev. ed. New York: Macmillan, 1962.

Young, Alfred Fabian. *The Shoemaker and the Tea Party: Memory and the American Revolution.* Boston: Beacon, 1999.

Zobel, Hiller B. *The Boston Massacre.* New York: Norton, 1970.

The Revolutionary War

Calhoon, Robert M. *The Loyalists in Revolutionary America, 1760–1781.* New York: Harcourt Brace Jovanovich, 1973.

Dann, John C. *The Revolution Remembered: Eyewitness Accounts of the War for Independence.* Chicago: University of Chicago Press, 1983.

Dull, Jonathan R. *A Diplomatic History of the American Revolution.* New Haven: Yale University Press, 1985.

Maier, Pauline. *American Scripture: Making the Declaration of Independence.* New York: Knopf, 1997.

Martin, James Kirby, and Mark Edward Lender. *A Respectable Army: The Military Origins of the Republic, 1763–1789.* Arlington Heights, Ill.: Harlan Davidson, 1982.

Martin, Joseph Plumb. *Private Yankee Doodle: Being a Narrative of Some of the Adventures, Dangers, and Sufferings of a Revolutionary Soldier.* Boston: Little, Brown, 1962.

Mintz, Max M. *The Generals of Saratoga: John Burgoyne and Horatio Gates.* New Haven: Yale University Press, 1990.

Neimeyer, Charles Patrick. *America Goes to War: A Social History of the Continental Army.* New York: New York University Press, 1996.

The Legacy of the Revolution

Kammen, Michael G. *A Machine That Would Go of Itself: The Constitution in American Culture.* New York: Knopf, 1986.

———. *A Season of Youth: The American Revolution and the Historical Imagination.* New York: Knopf, 1978.

Klapthor, Margaret Brown, and Howard Alexander Morrison. *G. Washington: A Figure Upon the Stage.* Washington, D.C.: Smithsonian Institution Press, 1982.

Weems, Mason L. *The Life of Washington.* Edited by Marcus Cunliffe. Cambridge: Harvard University Press, 1962.

American Indians and African Americans

Berlin, Ira ,and Ronald Hoffman, eds. *Slavery and Freedom in the Age of the American Revolution.* Charlottesville: University Press of Virginia, 1983.

Calloway, Colin G. *American Revolution in Indian Country: Crisis and Diversity in Native American Communities.* New York: Cambridge University Press, 1995.

Dowd, Gregory Evans. *A Spirited Resistance: The North American Indian Struggle for Unity, 1745–1815.* Baltimore: Johns Hopkins University Press, 1992.

Frey, Sylvia R. *Water from the Rock : Black Resistance in a Revolutionary Age.* Princeton: Princeton University Press, 1991.

Graymont, Barbara. *The Iroquois in the American Revolution.* Syracuse, N.Y.: Syracuse University Press, 1972.

Kaplan, Sidney, and Emma Nogrady Kaplan. *The Black Presence in the Era of the American Revolution.* Rev. ed. Amherst: University of Massachusetts Press, 1989.

Littlefield, Daniel C. *Revolutionary Citizens: African Americans 1776–1804.* New York: Oxford University Press, 1997.

Nash, Gary B. *Race and Revolution.* Madison, Wis.: Madison House, 1990.

Quarles, Benjamin. *The Negro in the American Revolution.* Chapel Hill: University of North Carolina Press, 1961.

Zilversmit, Arthur. *The First Emancipation: The Abolition of Slavery in the North.* Chicago: University of Chicago Press, 1967.

Politics and the Constitution

Adams, Willi Paul. *The First American Constitutions: Republican Ideology and the Making of the State Constitutions in the Revolutionary Era.* Translated by Robert and Rita Kimber. Chapel Hill: University of North Carolina Press, 1980.

Bernstein, Richard B., and Kym S. Rice. *Are We to Be a Nation? The Making of the Constitution.* Cambridge: Harvard University Press, 1987.

Morris, Richard Brandon. *The Forging of the Union, 1781–1789.* New York: Harper & Row, 1987.

Rakove, Jack N. *James Madison and the Creation of the American Republic.* New York: Longman, 1990.

Rutland, Robert Allen. *The Birth of the Bill of Rights, 1776–1791.* Bicentennial ed. Boston: Northeastern University Press, 1991.

———. *The Ordeal of the Constitution: The Antifederalists and the Ratification Struggle of 1787–1788.* Norman: University of Oklahoma Press, 1966.

Wood, Gordon S. *The Creation of the American Republic.* Chapel Hill: University of North Carolina Press, 1969.

Paul Revere

Brigham, Clarence. *Paul Revere's Engravings.* New York: Atheneum, 1969.

Fischer, David Hackett. *Paul Revere's Ride.* New York: Oxford University Press, 1994.

Forbes, Esther. *Paul Revere and the World He Lived In.* Boston: Houghton Mifflin, 1942.

Paul Revere Memorial Association. *Paul Revere—Artisan, Businessman, and Patriot: The Man Behind the Myth.* Boston: Paul Revere Memorial Association, 1988.

Triber, Jayne E. *A True Republican: The Life of Paul Revere.* Amherst: University of Massachusetts Press, 1998.

Revolutionary Lives

Akers, Charles W. *Abigail Adams, an American Woman.* Boston: Little, Brown, 1980.

Bailyn, Bernard. *The Ordeal of Thomas Hutchinson.* Cambridge, Mass.: Belknap, 1974.

Bernstein, R. B. *Thomas Jefferson.* New York: Oxford University Press, 2003.

Cunliffe, Marcus. *George Washington: Man and Monument.* Rev. ed. Boston: Little, Brown, 1982.

Ellis, Joseph J. *Passionate Sage: The Character and Legacy of John Adams.* New York: Norton, 1993.

Flexner, James Thomas. *Washington, the Indispensable Man.* Boston: Little, Brown, 1974.

Irvin, Benjamin H. *Samuel Adams: Son of Liberty, Father of Revolution.* New York: Oxford University Press, 2002.

Kaye, Harvey J. *Thomas Paine: Firebrand of the Revolution.* New York: Oxford University Press, 2001.

Maier, Pauline. *Old Revolutionaries: Political Lives in the Age of Samuel Adams.* New York: Knopf, 1980.

Morgan, Edmund. *Benjamin Franklin.* New Haven: Yale University Press, 2002.

Peterson, Merrill D. *Adams and Jefferson: A Revolutionary Dialogue.* Athens: University of Georgia Press, 1976.

———. *Thomas Jefferson and the New Nation: A Biography.* London: Oxford University Press, 1970.

Rhodehamel, John H. *The Great Experiment: George Washington and the American Republic.* New Haven : Yale University Press, 1998.

Wills, Garry. *Cincinnatus: George Washington and the Enlightenment.* Garden City, N.Y.: Doubleday, 1984.

Withey, Lynne. *Dearest Friend: A Life of Abigail Adams.* Simon & Shuster, 2001.

Social and Cultural Changes

Foner, Eric. *Tom Paine and Revolutionary America.* New York: Oxford University Press, 1976.

Gross, Robert A. *In Debt to Shays: The Bicentennial of an Agrarian Rebellion.* Charlottesville: University Press of Virginia, 1993.

———. *The Minutemen and Their World.* New York: Hill and Wang, 1976.

Hoffman, Ronald, and Peter J. Albert, eds. *Religion in a Revolutionary Age.* Charlottesville: University Press of Virginia, 1994.

———. eds. *The Transforming Hand of Revolution: Reconsidering the American Revolution as a Social Movement.* Charlottesville: University Press of Virginia, 1996.

Raphael, Ray. *A People's History of the American Revolution: How Common People Shaped the Fight for Independence.* New York: New Press, 2001.

Rhys, Isaac. *The Transformation of Virginia, 1740–1790.* Chapel Hill: University of North Carolina Press, 1982.

Shalhope, Robert E. *The Roots of Democracy: American Thought and Culture, 1760–1800.* Boston: Twayne, 1990.

Silverman, Kenneth. *A Cultural History of the American Revolution: Painting, Music, Literature, and the Theatre in the Colonies and the United States from the Treaty of Paris to the Inauguration of George Washington, 1763–1789.* New York: Columbia University Press, 1987.

Smith, Barbara Clark. *After the Revolution: The Smithsonian History of Everyday Life in the Eighteenth Century.* New York: Pantheon, 1985.

Young, Alfred F. *The American Revolution: Explorations in the History of American Radicalism.* Dekalb: Northern Illinois University Press, 1976.

Women

Buel, Joy Day, and Richard Buel, Jr. *The Way of Duty: A Woman and Her Family in Revolutionary America.* New York: Norton, 1984.

Kerber, Linda K.. *Women of the Revolution: Intellect and Ideology in Revolutionary America.* Chapel Hill: University of North Carolina Press, 1980.

Norton, Mary Beth. *Liberty's Daughters: The Revolutionary Experience of American Women.* Boston: Little, Brown, 1980.

Salmon, Marylynn. *The Limits of Independence: American Women 1760–1800.* New York: Oxford University Press, 1994.

Zagarri, Rosemarie. *A Woman's Dilemma: Mercy Otis Warren and the American Revolution.* Wheeling, Ill.: Harlan Davidson, 1995.

Text Credits

Main Text

20–21: J. Hector St. John de Crèvecoeur, *Letters from an American Farmer and Sketches of Eighteenth-Century America*, Albert E. Stone, ed. (Garden City, N.Y.: Dolphin, 1981), n.p.

21–23: Merrill Jensen, *English Historical Documents: American Colonial Documents to 1776* (London: Eyre & Spottiswoode, 1955), 650–52.

23–24: Jack P. Greene, *Colonies to Nation, 1763–1789: A Documentary History of the American Revolution* (New York: Norton, 1975), 60–61.

24–27: Greene, *Colonies to Nation*, 61–63.

27–29: John Dickinson, *Letters from a Farmer in Pennsylvania* (Boston: Mein & Fleming, 1768), 13–19, 75–78.

29–31: Jensen, *American Colonial Documents*, 742–44.

31–34: Jensen, *American Colonial Documents*, 750–53.

34–36: Hezekiah Niles, *Chronicles of the American Revolution*, Alden T. Vaughan, ed. (New York: Grosset and Dunlap, 1965), 66–67.

36–38: B. B. Thatcher, *A Retrospect of the Boston Tea-Party, with a Memoir of George R. T. Hewes, a Survivor of the Little Band of Patriots Who Drowned the Tea in Boston Harbour in 1773.* (New York: S. S. Bliss, 1834), 38–41.

39: Peter Force, *American Archives*, 4th series (Washington, D.C.: M. St. Clair Clarke and Peter Force, 1837), IV, 891.

42–43: Alfred F. Young and Terry J. Fife, with Mary E. Janzen, *We the People: Voices and Images of the New Nation* (Philadelphia: Temple University Press, 1993), 44; original pictured, 45.

44: Sheila L. Skemp, *Benjamin and William Franklin: Father and Son, Patriot and Loyalist* (Boston: Bedford, St. Martin's, 1994), 179–80.

45–46: Jack P. Greene, *Colonies to Nation*, 255, 258–59.

46–48: Merrill Jensen, *English Historical Documents: American Colonial Documents to 1776* (London: Eyre and Spottiswoode, 1955), 851–52.

48–51: Michael Foot and Isaac Kramnick, eds., *Thomas Paine Reader* (Harmsworth, Middlesex: Penguin, 1987), 66–67, 72, 75, 76, 81–82, 83, 84–85, 87, 92.

52: Greene, *Colonies to Nation*, 283.

52–53: Hezekiah Niles, *Chronicles of the American Revolution*, Alden T. Vaughan, ed. (New York: Grosset and Dunlap, 1965), 227.

54: Greene, *Colonies to Nation*, 296–97.

55–60: Pauline Maier, *American Scripture: Making the Declaration of Independence* (New York: Knopf, 1997), 236–41.

60: L. H. Butterfield, ed., *Letters of Benjamin Rush*, 2 vols. (Princeton: Princeton University Press, 1951), I, 92.

61–63: John C. Fitzpatrick, ed. *The Writings of George Washington from the Original Manuscript Sources* (Washington: U.S. Government Printing Office, 1931–1944), VI, 107–11.

63: Niles, *Chronicles*, 260.

64: *New York Historical Society Collections*, V, 293–94.

65: Albigence Waldo, "Valley Forge, 1777–1778: Diary of Surgeon Albigence Waldo, of the Connecticut Line," PMHB, XXI (1897), 313.

66–67: Jonathan R. Dull, *A Diplomatic History of the American Revolution* (New Haven: Yale University Press, 1985), 165–68.

68–69: Henry Steele Commager and Richard B. Morris, ed., *The Spirit of 'Seventy-Six: The Story of the American Revolution as Told by Participants* (Indianapolis: Bobbs-Merrill, 1958), 1243–1245.

69: Commager and Morris, *Spirit of 'Seventy-Six*, 1282.

72–74: Benjamin Rush, *The Autobiography of Benjamin Rush: His "Travels Through Life" together with His Commonplace Book for 1789–1813.* George W. Corner, ed. (Princeton,: Princeton University Press, 1948), 117–19

74–75: Catherine S. Crary, *The Price of Loyalty: Tory Writings from the Revolutionary Era* (New York: McGraw-Hill, 1973), 205–06.

75–77: Anne Rowe Cunningham, ed., *Letters and Diary of John Rowe, Boston Merchant, 1759–1762, 1764–1779* (Boston: W. B. Clarke, 1903), 291–307.

78–79: Benjamin Franklin to William Franklin, August 16, 1784, in Albert H. Smyth, ed., *The Writings of Benjamin Franklin* (New York: Macmillan, 1906), IX, 252–54.

79–81: Jonathan Bouchier, ed., *Reminiscences of an American Loyalist, 1738–1789* (Boston: Houghton Mifflin, 1925), 121–23.

81: Michael Foot and Isaac Kramnick, eds., *Thomas Paine Reader* (Harmsworth, Middlesex: Penguin, 1987), 116–17.

82: Hezekiah Niles, *Chronicles of the American Revolution.* Alden T. Vaughan, ed. (New York: Grosset and Dunlap, 1965), 194–95.

83–85: Wayne Franklin, ed., *American Voices, American Lives: A Documentary Reader* (New York: Norton, 1997), 283–87

86–87: James E. Seaver, *A Narrative of the Life of Mrs. Mary Jemison.* June Namias, ed. (Norman: University of Oklahoma Press, 1995), 104–05.

87–88: Frederick Cook, ed., *Journals of the Military Expedition of Major General John Sullivan Against the Six Nations of Indians in 1779* (Auburn, N.Y.: Knapp, Peck & Thomson, 1887), 30, 32.

89–90: Joseph Plumb Martin, *Private Yankee Doodle: Being a Narrative of Some of the Adventures, Dangers and Sufferings of a Revolutionary Soldier.* George F. Scheer, ed. (Boston: Little, Brown, 1962), 99–103.

91–92: Andrew Sherburne, *Memoirs of Andrew Sherburne: A Pensioner of the Navy of the Revolution* (Utica, N.Y.: W. Williams, 1828), 18–20.

93–94: John C. Dann, ed., *The Revolution Remembered: Eyewitness Accounts of the War for Independence* (Chicago: University of Chicago Press, 1980), 241–50.

94–95: Curtis Carroll Davis, "A 'Gallantress' Gets Her Due: The Earliest Published Notice of Deborah Sampson." *American Antiquarian Society Proceedings*, n.s., 91 (1981), 319–23.

95–96: Henry Steele Commager and Richard B. Morris, eds., *The Spirit of 'Seventy-Six: The Story of the American Revolution as Told by Participants* (Indianapolis: Bobbs-Merrill, 1958), 1121–1122.

97–98: "A New Touch on the Times" broadside. reproduced in Laurel Thatcher Ulrich, "'Daughters of Liberty': Religious Women in Revolutionary New England," *Women in the Age of the American Revolution* Edited by Ronald Hoffman and Peter J. Albert, (Charlottesville: University of Virginia Press, 1989), 230.

98–99: *Adams Family Correspondence, The Adams Papers.* Series II. (Cambridge: Belknap Press of Harvard University, 1963), II, 295.

102–04: John C. Fitzpatrick, ed. *The Writings of George Washington from the Original Manuscript Sources* (Washington: U.S. Government Printing Office, 1931–1944), XXVI, 483–86.

104–05: "Extract of a letter from a gentleman in the western country, to his friend in this city, dated Fort-Fenney, near the Miami, Dec. 22d, 1785." *The New-Haven Gazette, and the Connecticut Magazine*, vol. 1, no. 3, (March 2, 1786), 22–23

106–08: Henry Steele Commager and Milton Cantor, ed., *Documents of American History* (Englewood Cliffs, N. J.: Prentice Hall, 1988), I, 128–32.

108–09: Tench Coxe, *A View of the United States of America, in a Series of Papers, Written at Various Times, Between the Years 1787 and 1794* (Philadelphia: W. Hall, 1794), 43–49.

110–11: William Manning, *The Key of Liberty: The Life and Democratic Writings of William Manning, 'A Laborer,' 1747–1814* (Cambridge: Belknap Press of Harvard University, 1993), 164–65.

112–13: Jack P. Greene, *Colonies to Nation* 339–45.

113–16: Charles Francis Adams, *The Works of John Adams* (Boston: Little, Brown, 1850–1856), IV, 193–200.

116–18: Greene, *Colonies to Nation*, 333–34.

119: Michael Kammen, *The Origins of The American Constitution: A Documentary History* (New York: Penguin, 1986), 65–66.

120–23: Kammen, *Origins of the American Constitution*, 126–30.

123–25: Mercy Otis Warren, *Observations on the New Constitution, and on the Federal and State Conventions* (Boston, 1788), 6–12.

129–30: *In the House of Delegates, Friday, the 24th of December, 1784. A Motion . . . Christian Religion,* (Richmond, 1784), 1–2.

130–33: Henry Steele Commager and Richard B. Morris, eds., *The Spirit of 'Seventy-Six: The Story of the American Revolution as Told by Participants* (Indianapolis: Bobbs-Merrill, 1958), 399–401.

134–35: H. Shelton Smith, Robert T. Handy, and Lefferts A. Loetscher, *American Christianity,* vol. 1 (New York: Charles Scribner's Sons, 1960), 367–68.

135–36: Richard Allen, *The Life Experience and Gospel Labors of the Rt. Richard Allen* (Nashville, Tenn.: Abingdon, 1960), 25–26.

136–38: *Testimonies of the life, character, revelations and doctrines of our ever blessed mother Ann Lee* (Hancock, Mass.: J. Tallcott and J. Deming, Junrs., 1816), 15–16, 21–22.

139–40: *The New-Hampshire Gazette,* July 15, 1780.

140–41: Robert A. Gross, *The Minutemen and Their World* (New York: Hill and Wang, 1976), 97–98.

141–42: Henry Steele Commager and Richard B. Morris, ed., *The Spirit of 'Seventy-Six: The Story of the American Revolution as Told by Participants,* 406–07.

142–43: Greene, *Colonies to Nation,* 396–97.

144–45: Jefferson, *Notes on the State of Virginia,* 143, 162–63.

145–46: Dorothy Porter Wesley, ed., *Early Negro Writing, 1760–1837* (Boston: Beacon, 1971), 71, 73–74.

147–48: L. H. Butterfield, Marc Friedlaender , Mary-Jo Kline, eds., *The Book of Abigail and John: Selected Letters of the Adams Family, 1762–1784* (Cambridge: Harvard University Press, 1975), 121, 122–23, 127.

149–51: Judith Sargent Stevens Murray, *The Gleaner,* 3 vols. (Boston: I. Thomas and E. T. Andrews, 1798), III, 188–91.

151: "An Address to the Ladies," *American Magazine,* I (March 1788), 241–46.

152: "On the Supposed Superiority of the Masculine Understanding. [By a Lady]," *The Universal Asylum, and Columbian Magazine,* II (July 1791), 9–11.

152–53: *Women Invited to War. or a friendly Address to the Honourable Women of the United States. By a Daughter of America.* (Boston: Edes and Son, 1787), 3, 11–12

165–66: Ezra Stiles, *The United States Elevated to Glory and Honor. A Sermon . . . May 8th, 1783* (New-Haven, Conn.: Thomas and Samuel Green, 1783), 42–43.

166–68: Mason L. Weems, *The Life of Washington* (Cambridge: Belknap Press of Harvard University Press, 1962), 10–12.

169–70: Roy P. Basler, ed., *The Collected Works of Abraham Lincoln* (New Brunswick, N. J.: Rutgers University Press, 1953–1955), I, 115.

170–72: Henry Wadsworth Longfellow, *Tales of a Wayside Inn* (1863).

172–73: W. D. Howells, "A Sennight of the Centennial," *Atlantic Monthly* (July 1876), 92.

173–74: Rupert Hughes, *George Washington* (New York: Morrow, 1926–1930), II, 664–65; I, 488–89.

175: John Updike, "February 22" in *Telephone Poles and Other Poems* (1963); quoted in Marcus Cunliffe, *George Washington: Man and Monument,* rev. ed. (Boston: Little, Brown, 1982), 3.

175–76: Ann Landers, June 21, 1976, quoted in Kammen, *Season of Youth,* xv–xvi

177: Kammen, *Season of Youth,* 261–63.

178–81: Henry Steele Commager and Milton Cantor, eds., *Documents of American History* (Englewood Cliffs, N.J.: Prentice Hall, 1988), I, 315–17.

181–82: Herbert Apthaker, *A Documentary History of the Negro People in the United States,* 4 vols. (New York: Citadel, 1951), I, 331–34.

183–84: Wayne Franklin, ed., *American Voices, American Lives: A Documentary Reader* (New York: Norton, 1997), 449–54.

185–87: Leo Gershoy, *The Era of the French Revolution, 1789–1799: Ten Years that Shook the World* (Princeton, N. J.: Van Nostrand, 1957), 129–30.

188: Eric Foner, *Tom Paine and Revolutionary America* (New York: Oxford University Press, 1976), 224.

188–89: Vicente Lecuna, comp., *Selected Writings of Bolívar,* 2d ed. (New York: Colonial, 1951), I, 179, 180–81.

190–91: Gareth Porter, *Vietnam: The Definitive Documentation of Human Decisions,* vol. 1 (Stanfordville, N.Y.: Earl M. Coleman, 1979), 64–66.

Sidebars

24: *Boston Gazette,* October 7, 1765.

27: *Pennsylvania Gazette,* January 2, 1766.

34: *Orations Delivered at the Request of the Inhabitants of the Town of Boston to Commemorate the Evening of the Fifth of March, 1770* (Boston: Peter Edes, 1785), 17–24.

36: John C. Fitzpatrick, ed. *The Writings of George Washington from the Original Manuscript Sources* (Washington: U.S. Government Printing Office, 1931–1944), III, 232–33.

37: L. H. Butterfield, ed., *Diary and Autobiography of John Adams* (Cambridge: Harvard University Press, 1961), II, 86.

38: Henry Steele Commager and Richard B. Morris, eds., *The Spirit of 'Seventy-Six: The Story of the American Revolution as Told by Participants* (Indianapolis: Bobbs-Merrill, 1958), 35.

44: Ian R. Christie and Benjamin W. Labaree, *Empire or Independence: A British-American Dialogue on the Coming of the American Revolution* (New York: Norton, 1976), 270.

46: Christie and Labaree, *Empire or Independence,* 248.

51: Alfred F. Young and Terry J. Fife, with Mary E. Janzen, *We the People: Voices and Images of the New Nation* (Philadelphia: Temple University Press, 1993), 51; Henry Steele Commager and Richard B. Morris, eds., *The Spirit of 'Seventy-Six: The Story of the American Revolution as Told by Participants* (Indianapolis: Bobbs-Merrill, 1958), 291–92.

53: Pauline Maier, *American Scripture: Making the Declaration of Independence* (New York: Knopf, 1997), 234.

60: James Thomas Flexner, *Washington: The Indispensable Man* (Boston: Little, Brown, 1974), 61.

63: Commager and Morris, *Spirit of 'Seventy-Six,* 525, 527–29.

72: *The Autobiography of Benjamin Rush,* 117–19.

78: John Jay, *The Correspondence and Public Papers of John Jay,* ed. Henry P. Johnston, 4 vols. (New York: Putnam, 1896) II, 343–345.

81: Michael Foot and Isaac Kramnick, eds., *Thomas Paine Reader* (Harmsworth, Middlesex: Penguin, 1987), 116–17.

85: Sidney Kaplan and Emma Nogrady Kaplan, *The Black Presence in the Era of the American Revolution,* rev. ed. (Amherst: University of Massachusetts Press, 1989).

87: Henry Steele Commager and Richard B. Morris, ed., *The Spirit of 'Seventy-Six: The Story of the American Revolution as Told by Participants* (Indianapolis: Bobbs-Merrill, 1958), 1024–1026.

88: Colin Calloway, *The American Revolution in Indian Country* (Cambridge: Cambridge University Press, 1995), vi.

91: John C. Dann, ed., *The Revolution Remembered: Eyewitness Accounts of the War for Independence* (Chicago: University of Chicago Press, 1980), 298–99.

95: Ester Forbes, *Paul Revere and the World He Lived In* (Boston: Houghton Millflin, 1942), 416.

98: Mary Beth Norton, *Liberty's Daughters,* 199.

107: John Jay, *The Correspondence and Public Papers of John Jay,* ed. Henry P. Johnston. 4 vols. (New York: Putnam, 1890–1893), III, 154.

110: Mary Beth Norton, *Liberty's Daughters,* 199. Quoted in Roger H. Brown, *Redeeming the Republic: Federalists, Taxation, and the Origins of the Constitution* (Baltimore: Johns Hopkins, 1993), 116.

111: Mary Beth Norton, *Liberty's Daughters,* 199.Samuel Eliot Morison, ed., *Sources and Documents Illustrating the American Revolution 1764–1788 and the Formation of the Federal Constitution.* 2d ed. (London: Oxford University Press, 1929), 217–18.

112: Mary Beth Norton, *Liberty's Daughters,* 199.Greene, *Colonies to Nation,* 360–61.

116: Thomas Jefferson, *Notes on the State of Virginia,* William Peden ed., (Chapel Hill: University of North Carolina Press, 1954), 120.

118 *Writings of James Madison* (New York: Putnam, 1900–1910), II, 317–20.

119: W. W. Abbot, ed., *The Papers of George Washington. Confederation Series* (Charlottesville: University of Virginia Press, 1997), V, 331.

122: *Federalist,* No. 85, in *The Federalist* (New York: Modern Library, Random House), 574.

123: Quoted in Jack P. Greene, and J. R. Pole, eds., *The Blackwell Encyclopedia of the American Revolution* (Cambridge, Mass.: Blackwell, 1991), 473.

125: Morison, *Sources and Documents,* 306.

129: William McLoughlin, ed., *Isaac Backus on Church, State, and Calvinism* (Cambridge: Harvard University Press, 1968), 338.

135: Robert Drew Simpson, ed., *American Methodist Pioneer: The Life and Journals of The Rev. Freeborn Garrettson, 1752–1827* (Rutland, Vt.: Academy, 1984), 65.

140: *Some observations on the expediency of the petition of the Africans, living in Boston, &c. lately presented to the General Assembly of this province,* (Boston, 1773), 10.

142: Sidney Kaplan and Emma Nogrady Kaplan, *The Black Presence in the Era of the American Revolution* Rev. ed. (Amherst, Mass.: University of Massachusetts Press, 1989), 11.

143: David Brion Davis and Steven Mintz, *Boisterous Sea of Liberty* (New York: Oxford University Press, 1998), 220.

146: *The Royal American Magazine,* I (1774), 9–10.

151: Thomas Jefferson, *The Papers of Thomas Jefferson,* Julian P. Boyd, ed. (Princeton: Princeton University Press, 1950), XVI, 300.

153: Dagobert D. Runes, *The Selected Writings of Benjamin Rush* (New York: Philosophical Library, 1947), 33–34.

166: Margaret Brown Klapthor and Howard Alexander Morrison, *G. Washington: A Figure Upon the Stage* (Washington, D.C.: Smithsonian Institution Press, 1982), 11.

169: Pauline Maier, *American Scripture: Making the Declaration of Independence* (New York: Knopf, 1997), 185.

169: Lester J. Cappon, ed., *The Adams-Jefferson Letters: The Complete Correspondence Between Thomas Jefferson and Abigail and John Adams* (Chapel Hill: University of North Carolina, 1959), 451.

171: *Paul Revere's Three Accounts of His Famous Ride, A Massachusetts Historical Society Picture Book* (Boston, 1976), n.p.

172: *Paul Revere's Three Accounts of His Famous Ride, A Massachusetts Historical Society Picture Book,* (Boston, 1976), n.p.Michael G. Kammen, *A Season of Youth: the American Revolution and the Historical Imagination* (New York: Knopf, 1978), 59–60.

174: W. E. Woodward, *George Washington; The Image and the Man* (New York: Boni and Liveright, 1926), 453.

175: Klapthor and Morrison, *G. Washington,* 72.

180: Charles M. Wiltse, ed., *David Walker's Appeal, in Four Articles* (New York: Hill and Wang, 1965), 75.

181: Roy P. Basler, ed., *The Collected Works of Abraham Lincoln* (New Brunswick, N. J.: Rutgers University Press, 1953–1955), II, 323.

182: James M. McPherson, *The Negro's Civil War: How American Negroes Felt and Acted During the War for the Union* (New York: Vintage, 1965), 163.

182: Drew Gilpin Faust, *The Creation of Confederate Nationalism: Ideology and Identity in the Civil War South* (Baton Rouge: Louisiana State University Press, 1988), 14

185: Alexander Hamilton, 1784. *A Letter from Phocion to the Considerate Citizens of New-York* (New York, 1784); in Harold C. Syrett, ed., *Papers of Alexander Hamilton,* III, 556–557 (New York: Columbia University Press)

188: *North American Review,* (Sept. 1878).

189: Vicente Lecuna, comp., *Selected Writings of Bolívar,* 2 vols. (New York: Colonial Press, 1951), II, 653–54.

190: *Road to Revolution,* (1927) at www.uwm.edu/People/mbradley/HoChiMinh.html

Picture Credits

Index